Microsoft Word

for

Legal Practitioners

MONICA KORF (B.Comm LLB)

VIRTUAL
LAWYERS

Published by Virtual Online Legal Services (Pty) Ltd
Registration number: 2019/039038/07
office@virtuallawyers.co.za | www.virtuallawyers.co.za

Microsoft® Word for Legal Practitioners
ISBN: 978-0-620-87043-6

Copyright © 2020 Monica Korf

First edition: March 2020

Book designer and typesetter: Ingrid Richards
Editorial advisor: Rachel Bey-Miller
Book production: Quickfox Publishing

CONTENTS

FOREWORD 1

KNOW YOUR WAY 2

TERMS USED 3

CHAPTER 1 OVERVIEW OF FUNCTIONS USED BY LEGAL PRACTITIONERS 5

    1.1   The Ribbon 5

    1.2   Tabs 6

    1.3   The Quick Access Toolbar 13

    1.4   The Mini Toolbar 16

    1.5   Tell me what you want to do 17

    1.6   Many paths to the same function 18

CHAPTER 2 GENERAL DRAFTING 21

    2.1   Font 21

    2.2   Font size 22

    2.3   Margins 23

    2.4   Alignment 24

    2.5   Indents 26

    2.6   Paragraphs versus lines 29

    2.7   Spacing between lines 30

    2.8   Spacing between paragraphs 32

    2.9   Headers 34

    2.10   Footers 38

    2.11   Breaks 40

	2.12	Page numbers	44
	2.13	Numbering	53
	2.14	Bullets	56

CHAPTER 3   EDITING   58

	3.1	Rule Sheet	58
	3.2	Templates	59
	3.3	The customised template	60
	3.4	Professional templates	66
	3.5	Spell check and grammar	69
	3.6	Synonyms	72
	3.7	Thesaurus	73

CHAPTER 4   PROFESSIONAL DRAFTING   74

	4.1	Styles	74
	4.2	Multi-level numbered clauses	85
	4.3	Table of Contents	95
	4.4	Cross-references	103

CHAPTER 5   VIEWING   109

	5.1	View two documents side by side	109
	5.2	View one document in multiple windows	112
	5.3	Other handy page view controls	116
	5.4	The Navigation Pane	117
	5.5	Outline view	119

CHAPTER 6 REVIEWING 120

    6.1   Numbering lines 120

    6.2   Highlight text 121

    6.3   Comments 123

    6.4   Track changes 129

    6.5   Compare and combine documents 140

CHAPTER 7 PROTECTION 147

    7.1   Convert to PDF 147

    7.2   Hide text 152

    7.3   Insert a watermark 155

    7.4   Protect a document 160

    7.5   Restrict editing 169

    7.6   Document inspector 173

CHAPTER 8 TIME SAVERS 176

    8.1   Frequently used text shortcuts – AutoCorrect code 176

    8.2   Frequently used text shortcuts – AutoText 177

    8.3   Quick Parts 179

    8.4   Multiple-paste clipboard 183

    8.5   The Spike 185

    8.6   Control key shortcuts 186

    8.7   Format Painter 189

    8.8   Shrink text to one page 190

    8.9   Email documents directly 190

    8.10 Macros 192

CHAPTER 9   HANDY FUNCTIONS 197

    9.1   Insert a symbol 197

    9.2   Change letter case 197

    9.3   Clear all formatting 198

    9.4   Insert date and time 199

    9.5   Undo and redo anything 201

    9.6   Add a signature line 202

    9.7   Sort data in alphabetical order 203

    9.8   Bookmarks 204

    9.9   Footnotes 207

    9.10   Endnotes 208

    9.11   Tables 208

    9.12   Columns 213

    9.13   Calculate 215

CHAPTER 10   AUTOMATION 216

    10.1   Find and Replace 218

    10.2   Dynamic fields 220

    10.3   Click and type field 230

    10.4   Fillable Forms 233

    10.5   Document Properties 237

    10.6   Content controls (using the Developer tab) 243

    10.7   Summary of features of automation methods 253

CHAPTER 11   TROUBLESHOOTING 254

    11.1   Recover an unsaved document 254

    11.2   Missing scroll bar 257

    11.3   Blank spaces between paragraphs.............................. 258

    11.4   Forgotten file name and file path.............................. 260

    11.5   Pick up where you left off... 261

    11.6   Change the document author.. 262

FINAL WORD 263

FOREWORD

The modern technology-driven fast-moving legal environment demands from Legal Practitioners to draft, edit and review legal documents on the go.

Many frustrations, which **Word** can solve easily, are experienced.

"The client is complaining about spelling errors and poor formatting, while the excellent legal content is overlooked!".

"I am wasting all my time on numbering clauses, checking cross-references and compiling a Table of Contents! I hate Track changes!

This manual contains:

Word   Functions which Legal Practitioners use or will benefit from.

   Step by step visual instructions.

   Important things to understand from **Word**

      Benefits from using the magic **Word** offers

      Time savers

      Solutions to common frustrations

      Handy tools

      Tips to make drafting, editing and reviewing legal documents a pleasure.

Legal Practitioners will, with the use of this manual, be equipped to draft, edit and review legal documents more easily, quickly, correctly, consistently and professionaly.

This manual is based on **Word** 2016, but with a few minor differences can also be used for previous versions of **Word** and on a Mac.

KNOW YOUR WAY

Understanding Word's functions and options

Word consists of different levels of functions and options. The deeper you delve into the application, the more functions and settings you will discover. Here are some of the functions and settings you will encounter as you make your way through this book:

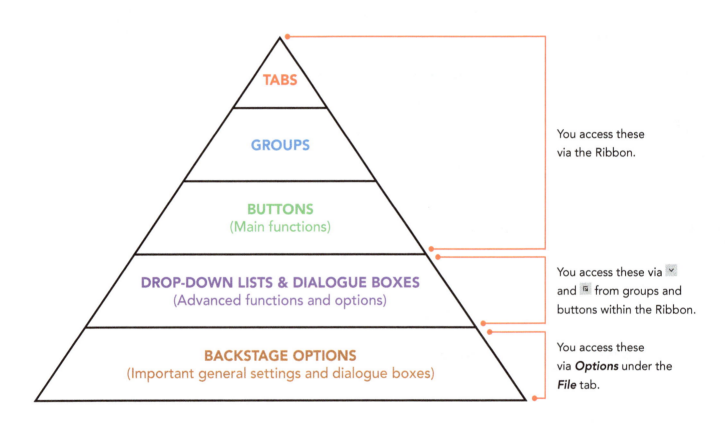

TABS

GROUPS

BUTTONS
(Main functions)

DROP-DOWN LISTS & DIALOGUE BOXES
(Advanced functions and options)

BACKSTAGE OPTIONS
(Important general settings and dialogue boxes)

You access these via the Ribbon.

You access these via ⌄ and ⌐ from groups and buttons within the Ribbon.

You access these via **Options** under the **File** tab.

TERMS USED

In this manual, the terms are used as follows:

TABS   **GROUPS**   **BUTTONS**

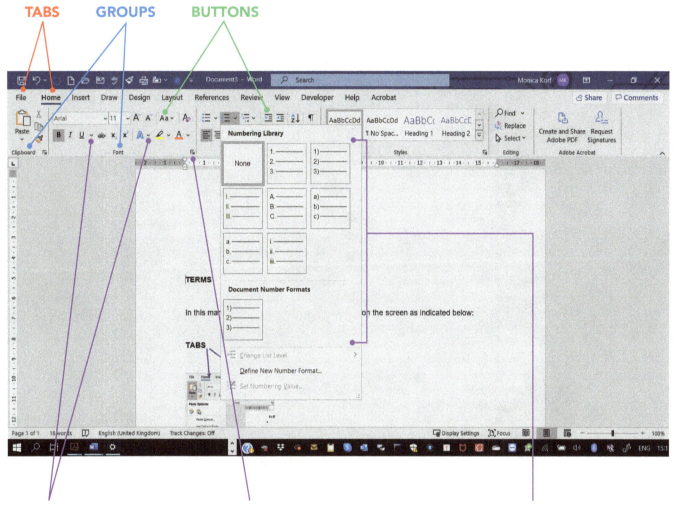

DROPDOWN ARROWS and **DIALOGUE BOX LAUNCHER**

Dropdown arrows and **dialogue box launchers** open up boxes that offer more options.

The extra functions you will find when you click on dropdown arrows and dialogue boxes.

FUNCTIONS: All the nice things Word can do.

KEYS: The squares you hit on your keyboard.

POINTER and **CURSOR**: The ⇧ (pointer) and I (cursor) that you move with the mouse or touchpad. The pointer is used to click on buttons, select objects and options, and move items on a page. The cursor shows the position in your text that will be affected when you type on your keyboard. You use your cursor to insert text and to select text that you want to delete or change.

Legal Practitioners need to know which functions they'll find useful and where to find those functions. Here are the tabs, groups, and functions that you will most often use to find what you're looking for.

1.1 The Ribbon

The toolbar that runs across the top of the **Word** screen is known as the Ribbon.

You use the **tabs** on the Ribbon, such as *File*, *Home*, *Insert*, *Layout*, *References*, *Review*, and *View* to access groups of related functions.

Under the *Home* tab, for instance, you will find the **Font**, **Paragraphs**, **Styles**, and **Editing** groups. Each group has its own set of functions and tools.

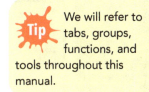

Tip We will refer to tabs, groups, functions, and tools throughout this manual.

Frustration

I can't see the Ribbon!

Click on the up arrow ⬆ button in the upper-right corner of the screen. This displays a dialogue box that you can use to set how the Ribbon displays on the screen. You then choose the option you want.

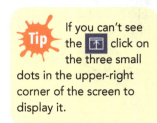

Tip If you can't see the ⬆ click on the three small dots in the upper-right corner of the screen to display it.

Auto-hide Ribbon
Hide the Ribbon. Click at the top of the application to show it.

Show Tabs
Show Ribbon tabs only. Click a tab to show the commands.

Show Tabs and Commands
Show Ribbon tabs and commands all the time.

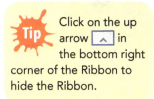

Tip Click on the up arrow ⌃ in the bottom right corner of the Ribbon to hide the Ribbon.

1.2 Tabs

The tabs covered here contain the targeted functions in this manual.

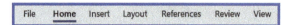

You can use the **Customise Ribbon** option to add other tabs to the Ribbon.

- Click on **File** > **Options** > **Customise Ribbon**.
- Select **Main Tabs** from the drop-down list under **Choose commands from**.
- Select the tabs you want to add to the Ribbon, then click on **Add** and **OK**.
- To remove a tab, select the unwanted tab in the column on the right side of the screen under **Customize the Ribbon**, click on **Remove** and then **OK**.

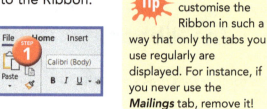

> **Tip** You can customise the Ribbon in such a way that only the tabs you use regularly are displayed. For instance, if you never use the **Mailings** tab, remove it!

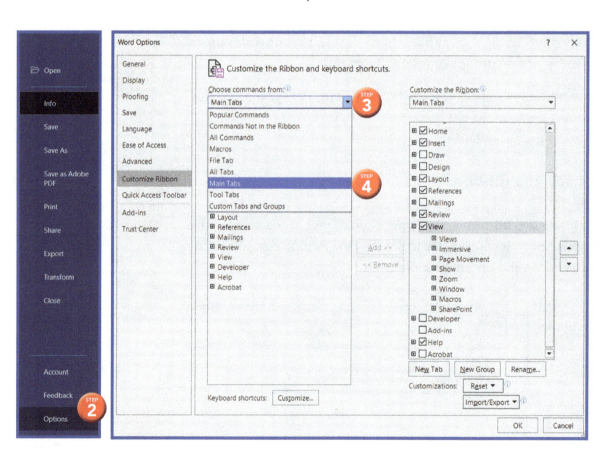

> **Tip** You can find out what a button is used for by hovering your mouse pointer over it. This displays a tooltip that briefly describes its function. For instance, if you hover over the *I* in the **Font** group on the **Home** tab, you will see this tooltip.
>
> Italic (Ctrl+I)
> Italicize your text.

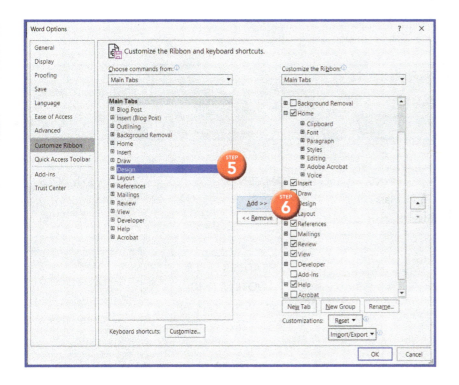

1.2.1 The Home tab

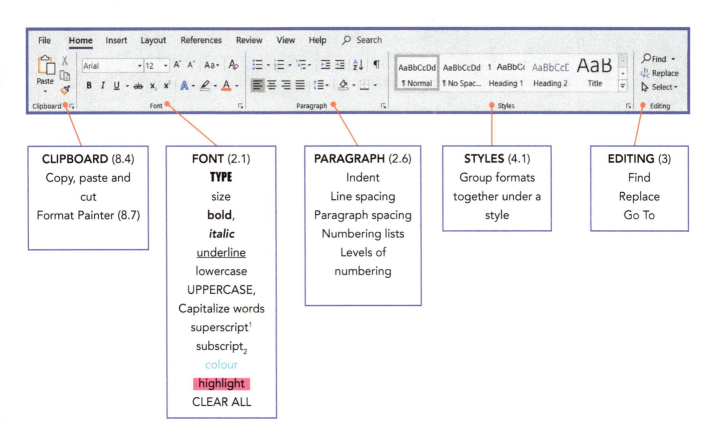

CLIPBOARD (8.4)	FONT (2.1)	PARAGRAPH (2.6)	STYLES (4.1)	EDITING (3)
Copy, paste and cut Format Painter (8.7)	**TYPE** size **bold**, *italic* underline lowercase UPPERCASE, Capitalize words superscript[1] subscript[2] colour highlight CLEAR ALL	Indent Line spacing Paragraph spacing Numbering lists Levels of numbering	Group formats together under a style	Find Replace Go To

1.2.2 The Insert tab

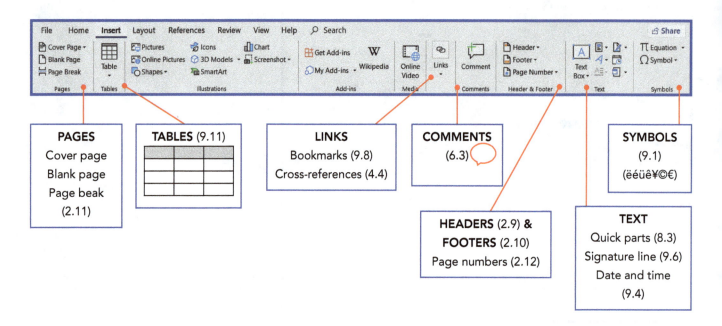

PAGES
Cover page
Blank page
Page beak
(2.11)

TABLES (9.11)

LINKS
Bookmarks (9.8)
Cross-references (4.4)

COMMENTS
(6.3)

SYMBOLS
(9.1)
(ëéüê¥©€)

HEADERS (2.9) **&**
FOOTERS (2.10)
Page numbers (2.12)

TEXT
Quick parts (8.3)
Signature line (9.6)
Date and time
(9.4)

1.2.3 The Layout tab

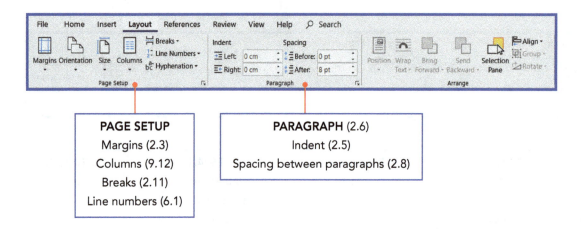

PAGE SETUP
Margins (2.3)
Columns (9.12)
Breaks (2.11)
Line numbers (6.1)

PARAGRAPH (2.6)
Indent (2.5)
Spacing between paragraphs (2.8)

1.2.4 The References tab

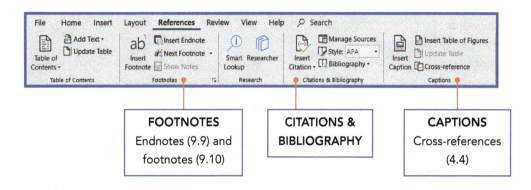

FOOTNOTES
Endnotes (9.9) and
footnotes (9.10)

CITATIONS &
BIBLIOGRAPHY

CAPTIONS
Cross-references
(4.4)

1.2.5 The Review tab

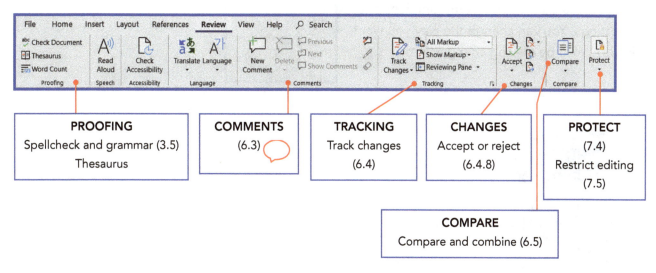

PROOFING
Spellcheck and grammar (3.5)
Thesaurus

COMMENTS
(6.3)

TRACKING
Track changes
(6.4)

CHANGES
Accept or reject
(6.4.8)

PROTECT
(7.4)
Restrict editing
(7.5)

COMPARE
Compare and combine (6.5)

1.2.6 The View tab

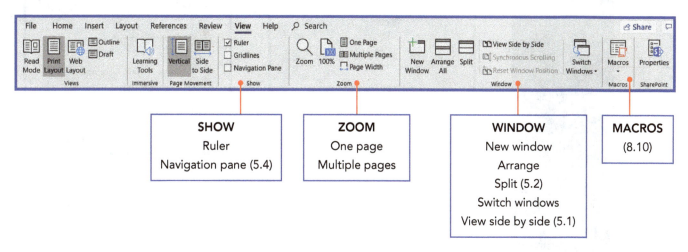

SHOW
Ruler
Navigation pane (5.4)

ZOOM
One page
Multiple pages

WINDOW
New window
Arrange
Split (5.2)
Switch windows
View side by side (5.1)

MACROS
(8.10)

1.2.7 The Design tab: Headers and footers

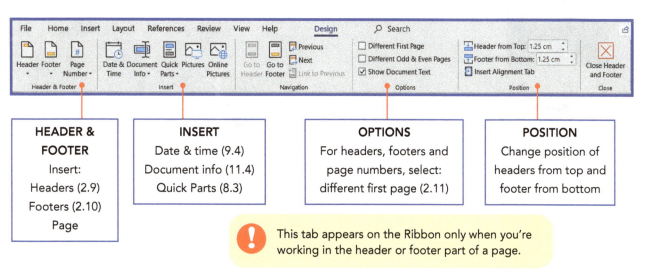

HEADER & FOOTER
Insert:
Headers (2.9)
Footers (2.10)
Page

INSERT
Date & time (9.4)
Document info (11.4)
Quick Parts (8.3)

OPTIONS
For headers, footers and
page numbers, select:
different first page (2.11)

POSITION
Change position of
headers from top and
footer from bottom

! This tab appears on the Ribbon only when you're
working in the header or footer part of a page.

1.2.8 The File tab

The *File* tab is the path to important functions and general settings. You can change the way you want to work with Word by making changes in the settings.

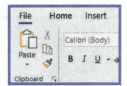

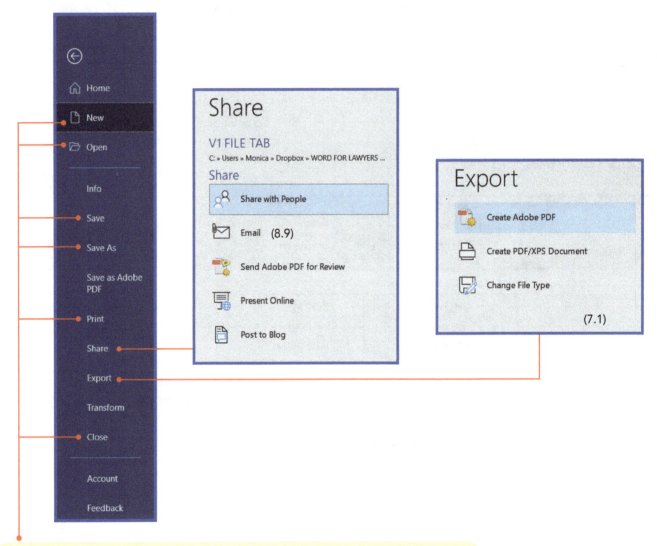

> **Tip** You can make access to the functions you frequently use easier by adding them to the Quick Access Toolbar (1.3). For instance, you might want to add *New*, *Open*, *Save*, *Save As*, *Print* and *Close*.

The *Info* tab gives you access to the following functions:

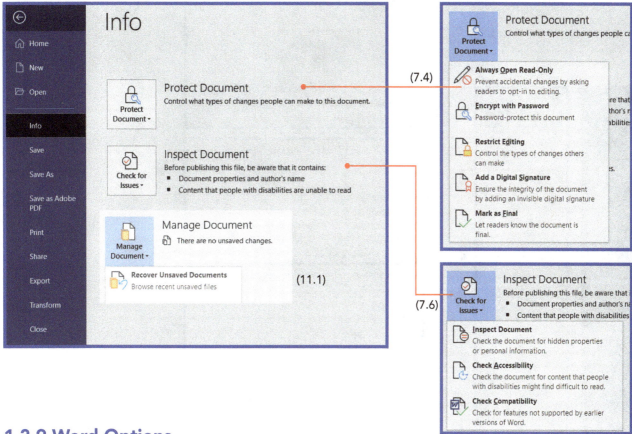

1.2.9 Word Options

Important backstage settings under Word *Options*

Insight

The backstage settings control how **Word** works. When you find yourself fighting with **Word** or **Word** is fighting with you, the problem often stems from a setting that needs to be changed. You can find and change these settings in the *Options* section under the *File* tab.

From the maze of settings available, there are several important settings that relate to the targeted functions in this manual. Check your backstage settings to ensure that these settings are correct.

> ! The settings in the backstage apply to ALL documents, not just the current document you are working on.

- To access the **Word** backstage options, click on *File* > *Options*.

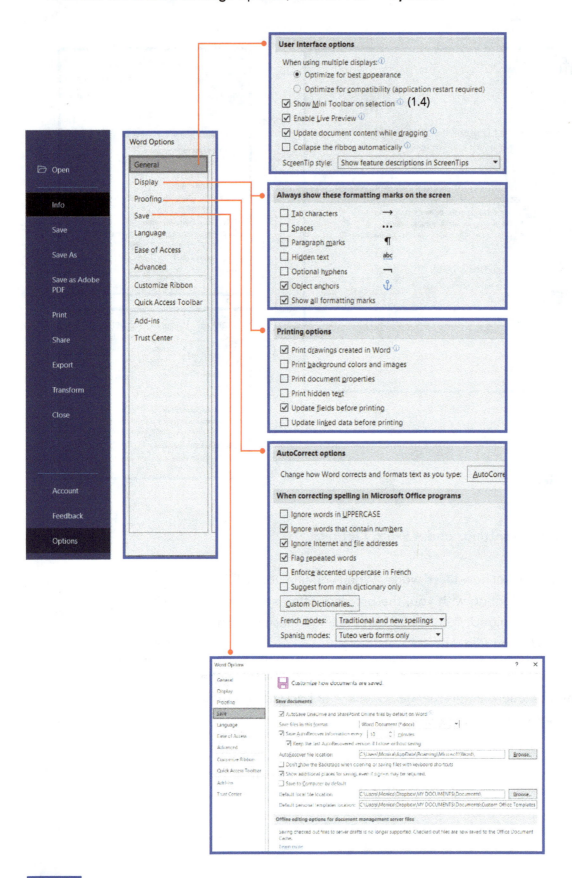

1.3 The Quick Access Toolbar

Work faster and with much less effort by gaining quicker access to the functions you frequently use. You can retain the minimum functions – *Save*, *Undo* and *Redo* – or add as many functions as you like.

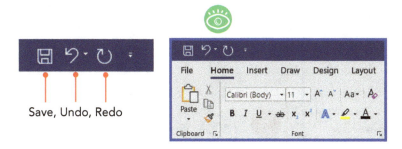

Save, Undo, Redo

The Quick Access Toolbar is at the top left of the **Word** screen, either above or below the Ribbon.

Above Ribbon

Below Ribbon

1.3.1 How to use the function in the Quick Access Toolbar

Simply click once on the function you want to execute. For instance, to e-mail the current document, click on [image]. Microsoft® Outlook will open automatically.

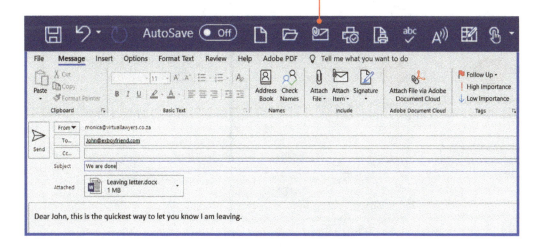

1.3.2 How to add functions to the Quick Access Toolbar

- Click on the down arrow ▾ to the right of the Quick Access Toolbar. A drop-down list of frequently used functions appears.
- Select the functions you want to add.
- If a function you're looking for isn't in the list, click on **More Commands**.

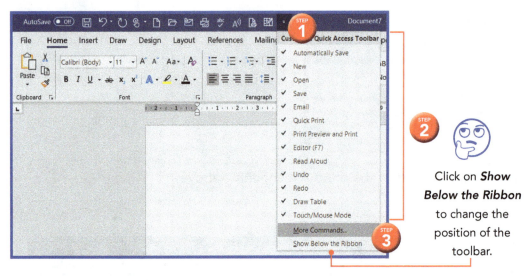

Click on **Show Below the Ribbon** to change the position of the toolbar.

- A dialogue box containing all possible functions displays.
- Scroll down to the function you want to add, select it, click on **Add** and then click **OK**.

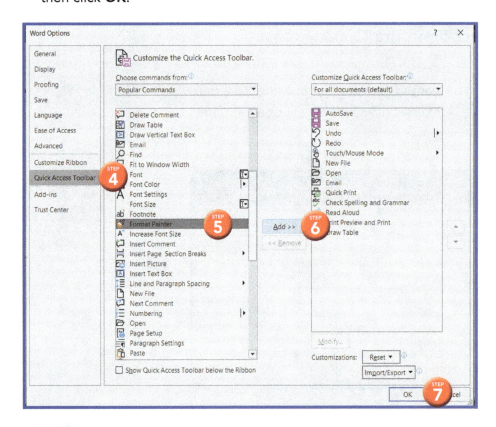

You'll notice that the function you selected appears to the right of the current buttons in the toolbar. This function will be available for all documents.

1.3.3 Suggested functions for the Quick Access Toolbar

There are more functions to choose from under **Choose commands from** such as *All Commands* and *Commands not in Ribbon,* however, shown below are the popular options.

The screenshot on the right shows suggestions specifically for legal documents.

 You can remove functions from the toolbar or reset it to its minimum functions.

Time saver

When you configure a Quick Access Toolbar tailor-made to your needs, you have a useful tool for quick and effortless drafting and editing.

1.4 The Mini Toolbar

You can **right-click** the mouse anywhere in the text or select a word to access the Mini Toolbar. This toolbar contains the most frequently used formatting functions.

Turn the Mini Toolbar on or off:
- Click on the *File* tab
- Click on *Options* > *General*.
- Under **User Interface options**, select or deselect the checkbox called *Show Mini Toolbar on selection.*

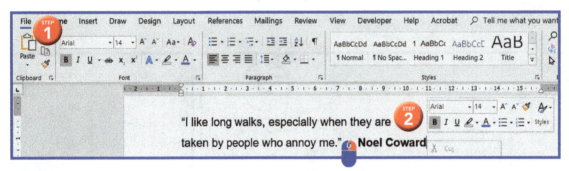

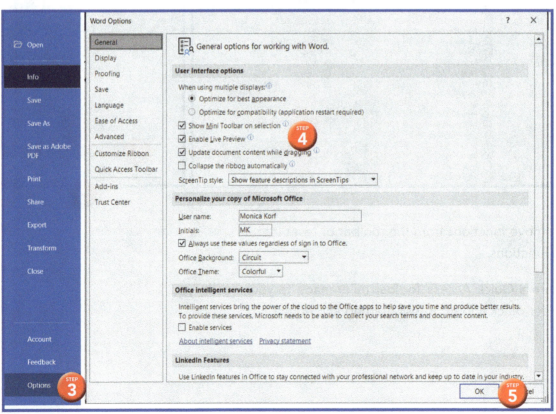

1.5 Tell me what you want to do

This is a new feature in **Word 2016** and the fastest way to find any function.

Frustration

Where is the watermarks function hiding?

Instead of searching frantically through the maze of tabs, groups, functions, and drop-down lists, the **Tell me what you want to do** search box can take you directly to the function you're looking for.

- Click on the *Home* tab.
- Click inside the **Tell me what you want to do** search box.
- Type in what you want to do, for instance "Print". This opens a drop-down list with related functions. When you select a function, **Word** will take you there immediately.

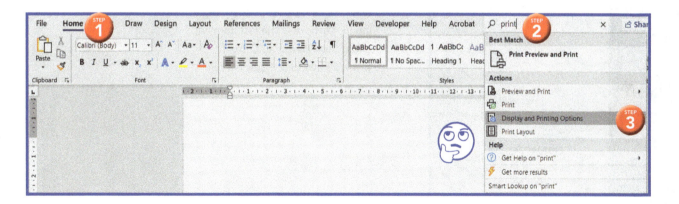

Tip You can access the **Tell me what you want to do** search box very quickly using a keyboard shortcut: Press and hold the *Alt* key, then press **Q**.

Press

Tip **Shortcuts** are written as mini formulas, e.g. *Alt+Q.* Find out more about keyboard shortcuts in *1.6.4 Keyboard shortcuts*

1.6 Many paths to the same function

As you know, all functions can be accessed via the groups of functions in the tabs on the Ribbon. However, there are other quicker paths to the same functions, as listed here.

When you know which paths are available, you can choose the one that works best for you.

1.6.1 Quick Access Toolbar

Using and customising the Quick Access Toolbar is covered in 1.3.

1.6.2 File tab

You click on the *File* tab at the far left of the Ribbon to access a menu of functions that are frequently used, such as *Save*, *Save As*, *New* and *Print*.

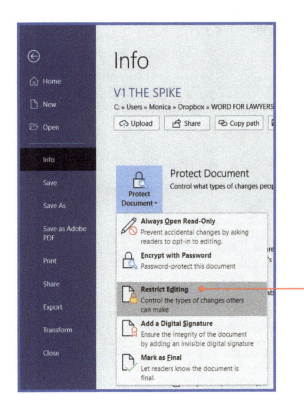

Important backstage settings can only be reached via *Options* in the *File* menu. *Options* is the last item under the *File* menu. Often you will have to scroll down to reach it.

You can also access the *Restrict Editing* options via the *Protect* group in the *Review* tab.

1.6.3 Pop-up (context) menus

You can right-click the mouse anywhere in your text or on a graphic to access the Mini Toolbar as well as a pop-up menu containing functions that are related to what you're doing.

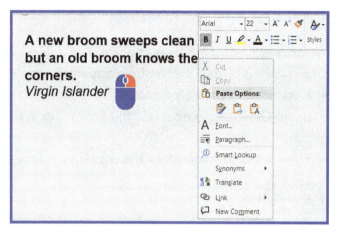

1.6.4 Keyboard shortcuts

As you saw at the end of section 1.5, you can combine keyboard keys that execute frequently used functions. This means that you can execute a function as you type without having to use the mouse to select the function. To use a keyboard shortcut, press the relevant keys down at the same time.

For example, to save your document, press the **Ctrl** button and the **S** button:

Here are the most common keyboard shortcuts:

Task	Shortcut	What it means
Work with files	**Ctrl+S**	Save the current document
	Ctrl+O	Open a document
	Ctrl+N	Open a new, blank document
Style text	**Ctrl+B**	Bold
	Ctrl+I	Italic
	Ctrl+U	Underline
Cut, move, paste	**Ctrl+X**	Remove selected text or image
	Ctrl+C	Copy selected text or image
	Ctrl+P	Paste selected text or image in new location
Find and replace	**Ctrl+F**	Open the Find navigation pane
	Ctrl+H	Open the Find and Replace dialogue box

1.6.5 Screentips (Tooltips)

We covered how to access tooltips in *1.2 Tabs*. But what if you hover your mouse over a button and nothing appears? Here's how to fix that:

- Click on *File*, then *Options.*
- In the **General** screen select the *ScreenTip style* drop-down arrow.
- Then select *Show feature descriptions in ScreenTips.*
- Click on *OK*.

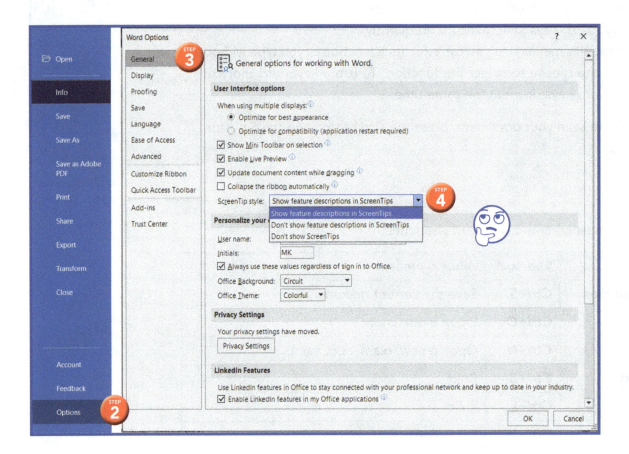

Whenever you open a new **Word** document, it opens with the Normal template. The new document is not like a blank canvas, but is already loaded with a default font, paper and margin sizes, text alignments and other formatting.

The default formats in the Normal template are:

*   Font: Calibri (Body) 11 pt
*   Text alignment: All text is aligned to the left margin
*   Line spacing: Multiple with an 8-pt space after each paragraph
*   Margins: 1 inch (2,54 cm) left, right, top and bottom

These default format settings are not ideal for legal documents. Because legal documents must look professional, the format options can be narrowed down.

2.1 Font

The fonts most commonly used in legal documents are **Arial**, **Calibri** or **Times New Roman**.

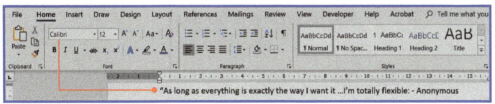

Change the font of an entire paragraph:

- Select the paragraph you want to change and click on the drop-down arrow next to the selected font name in the **Font** group under the **Home** tab.
- As the cursor hovers over a font name in the drop-down list, the text will change to a preview of the text in that font.
- When you find a font you like, click on the font name to choose it.

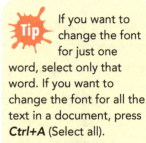

> **Tip** If you want to change the font for just one word, select only that word. If you want to change the font for all the text in a document, press **Ctrl+A** (Select all).

Select all

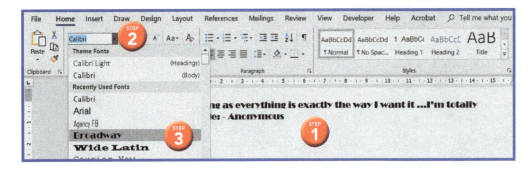

2.2 Font size

Most legal documents contain 10- or 12-point text.

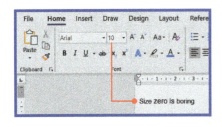

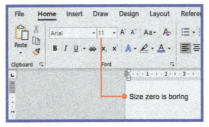

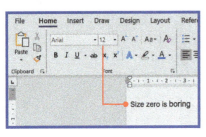

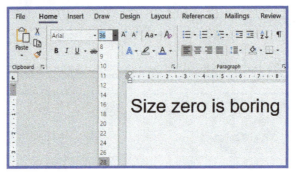

Change the size of your text:

- First, select the text to be enlarged.
- Click on the **Home** tab.
- In the **Font** group, click the drop-down arrow next to the current size.
- As the cursor hovers over a size in the drop-down list, a preview of the size displays.
- Click on the size you want, such as 14 pt for a subheading.

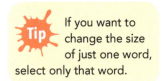

> **Tip** If you want to change the size of just one word, select only that word.

2.3 Margins

The margin is the distance between the edge of the page and the text.

When you open a new document in **Word**, the margins are automatically set to 2,54 cm (one inch) at all four edges of a page. This is due to the preset Normal Template in **Word**.

My normal template does not have these margins!

At some time, the default margins were changed (see 🔴 below).

The left and right margins in a legal document are usually narrower than the Normal template default, as shown here.

Top: 2,54 cm (1 inch)
Bottom: 2,54 cm (1 inch)
Left: 2,25 cm
Right: 2 cm

To make sure that the text fits well on the page, you can choose one of the predefined margin settings in **Word** or customise the margins yourself.

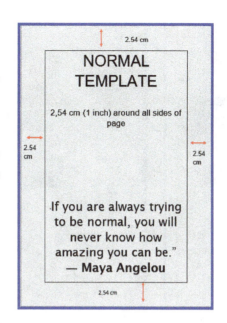

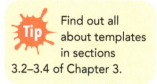

Tip: Find out all about templates in sections 3.2–3.4 of Chapter 3.

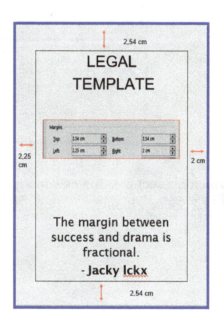

2.3.1 Create a custom margins

To customise the margins:
- Click on the *Layout* tab.
- In the **Page Setup** group, click on *Margins*.
- Click on the *Custom Margins* option. The **Page Setup** dialogue box opens.
- Use the up and down arrows next to the *Margins* fields to enter the values you want.
- Click *OK* when done.

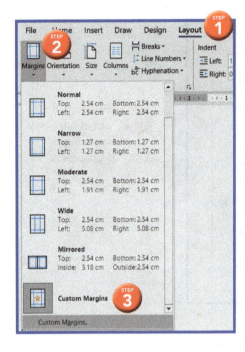

> ⚠️ Only click on **Set As Default** if you are sure you want to change the Normal template. When clicking this option, you will be prompted to confirm your choice.

If the document contains multiple sections, the new margins apply only to the selected sections. (See *2.11.2 Section breaks.*)

2.4 Alignment

Neat legal documents are 'blocked', meaning that the text is aligned on both sides of the page. This alignment is called **justified**.

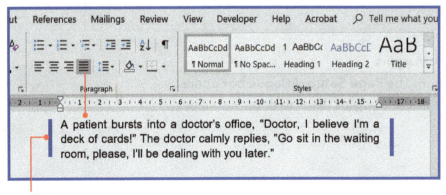

Justified text

CHAPTER 2: GENERAL DRAFTING

Text can also be aligned to the **left**, as it is in most business documents or to the **right**, as it is for contact details in a letterhead, for instance. It can also be **centred**. You might use this for the title of a document.

To change the text alignment:
- Place the cursor anywhere in a paragraph.
- Click the *Home* tab.
- Select an alignment from the **Paragraph** group.

Right-aligned text

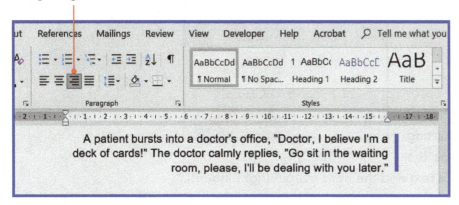

Centered text

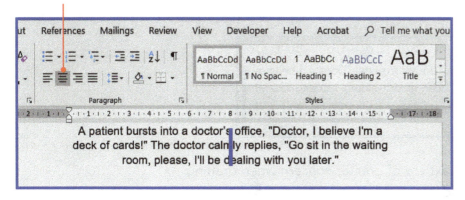

Left-aligned text

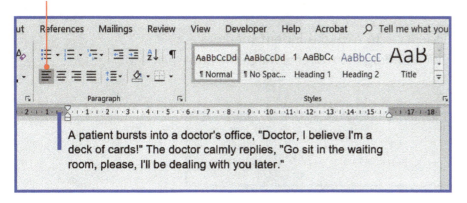

Text alignment can also be set in the Paragraph dialogue box.

- To open the Paragraph dialogue box, click on the dialogue launcher in the bottom right of the **Paragraph** group.
- In the Paragraph dialogue box, click on the *Alignment* setting in the **General** section and choose your preferred alignment option.
- Click *OK*.

2.5 Indents

An indent is the distance between the left margin of a document and the starting position of the text (left indent), or the distance between the end position of text and the right margin (right indent).

For legal documents, **justified alignment** (discussed in *2.4 Alignment*) is advised. The right indent is therefore zero.

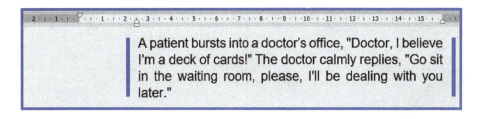

A patient bursts into a doctor's office, "Doctor, I believe I'm a deck of cards!" The doctor calmly replies, "Go sit in the waiting room, please, I'll be dealing with you later."

The indents on the left side of the text are of greater concern when drafting legal documents, because if these indents are neatly structured and consistent throughout the document, the document will look more professional and will be easier to read and navigate.

Insight

The easiest way to adjust the indents is to click the **indent markers** located on the left side of the ruler and drag them over towards the right side of the ruler.

Each marker marks the indent of a specific line of text in a paragraph.

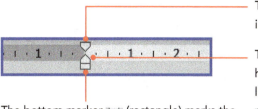

The top marker (down arrow) marks the indent for the first line of text in a paragraph.

The middle marker (up arrow) marks the hanging indent. In a hanging indent, the first line in a paragraph is not indented while the rest of the paragraph is indented. This is not generally applied in legal documents.

The bottom marker (rectangle) marks the left indent of an entire paragraph.

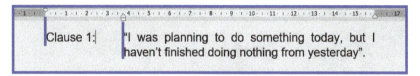

Clause 1: "I was planning to do something today, but I haven't finished doing nothing from yesterday".

Frustration

I don't have a ruler bar with indent markers!

- Click on the *View* tab.
- In the **Show** group click on the *Ruler* check box to show the horizontal and vertical rulers.

"Whatever you do in life give 100%.... unless you're giving blood"

2.5.1 Indenting for legal documents

Here is an indenting scheme that can be used for legal documents. Paragraphs and lines have specific indents according to their level of numbering in the multilevel structure. The Heading styles have been updated to include the correct indents for each paragraph. (See *4.2 Multilevel numbered clauses.*)

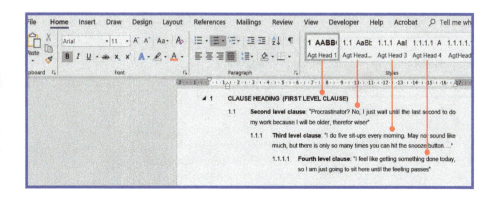

In each paragraph, the indents are determined by the level of the paragraph in the numbering scheme:

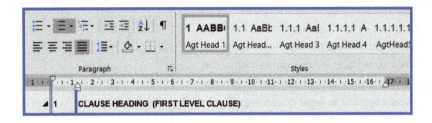

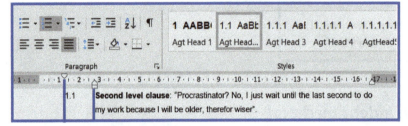

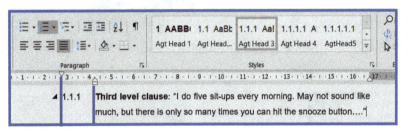

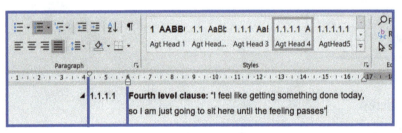

The top marker is dragged to mark the indent for the first line of text in the paragraph.

The middle marker is dragged to mark the indent for the second line of text in the paragraph.

The marker at the bottom is dragged to mark the left indent of the rest of the lines in the paragraph.

2.5.2 Setting exact indentation measurements

The indents can also be adjusted in the Paragraph dialogue box to fit exact measurements.

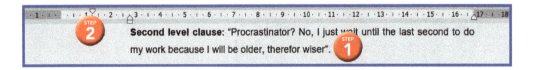

- To open the Paragraph dialogue box, place the cursor anywhere in the paragraph you want to adjust and then double-click on the markers in the ruler.
- When the dialogue box opens, click on the **Indents and Spacing** tab.
- Adjust your left, right and hanging indents in the Indentation section.

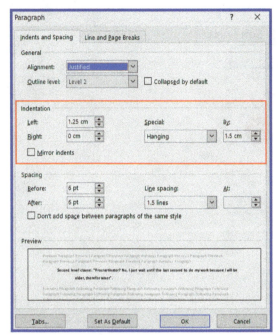
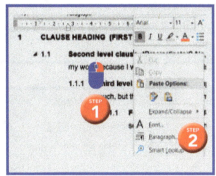

 You can also right-click your mouse and select **Paragraph** from the pop-up list to open the Paragraph dialogue box.

2.6 Paragraphs versus lines

The text in legal documents is usually arranged in paragraphs. Each paragraph may consist of many lines.

To start a new paragraph, you press **Enter** on the keyboard. This creates what is known as a **hard paragraph break ¶**, which means that there will be a line space between the current and next paragraph.

When you are typing a line and reach the end of that line, **Word** will automatically move the cursor to a new line for you, so never press **Enter** at the end of a line unless you want to start a new paragraph.

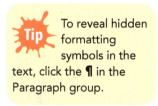 To reveal hidden formatting symbols in the text, click the ¶ in the Paragraph group.

MICROSOFT WORD FOR LEGAL PRACTITIONERS

If you want to break a line to continue the text on the next line without creating a new paragraph, you can insert a **soft line break** using the **Shift+Enter** keyboard shortcut.

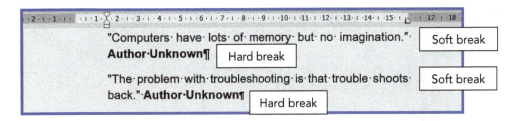

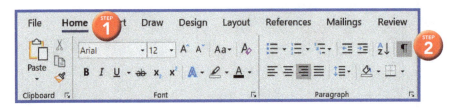

 The line ended mid-way! What is the white space between the lines?

Frustration

> "Man·is·a·slow,·sloppy·and·brilliant·thinker;·the·¶
>
> machine·is·fast,·accurate·and·stupid."·**William·M.·Kelly**¶

A new paragraph was started, because 'someone' pressed **Enter** in the middle of a line. To solve this problem simply delete the ¶.

2.7 Spacing between lines

The spaces between lines in a legal document can be set at 1,5 or even at 2 to make the text more readable.

Set the line spacing:
- Place the cursor anywhere in the text.
- Click on the **Home** tab.
- Then click on the **Line and Paragraph Spacing** down arrow in the **Paragraph** group.
- Choose the spacing you want, such as single, double, or triple.

30

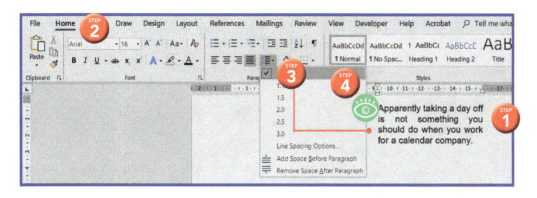

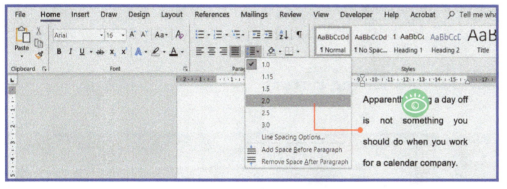

You can also set the line spacing in the Paragraph dialogue box. The default spacing in the Line spacing section is Multiple. To change this, do the following:

- Place the cursor anywhere in the text.
- Click on the **Home** tab.
- Click on the dialogue box launcher in the **Paragraph** group.
- Under **Line spacing**, choose from single line spacing, one and a half, double, or even specify a minimum or exact line spacing.

 When you want to adjust the line spacing for an entire document, you need to select all the text (*Ctrl+A*) before accessing the line spacing options.

Insight

2.8 Spacing between paragraphs

Spaces before and after paragraphs in legal documents can be set at 6 pt, or even at 12 pt to make the text more readable.

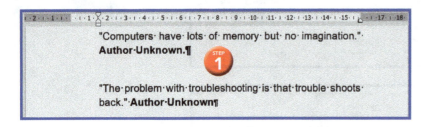

2.8.1 Set the paragraph spacing for the current paragraph

- Place the cursor anywhere in the text.
- Click on the *Home* tab.
- Click on the dialogue box launcher in the **Paragraph** group.
- Under **Spacing**, click the up and down arrows next to Before and/or After to set the paragraph spacing you want.

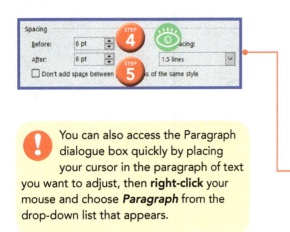

> ! You can also access the Paragraph dialogue box quickly by placing your cursor in the paragraph of text you want to adjust, then **right-click** your mouse and choose *Paragraph* from the drop-down list that appears.

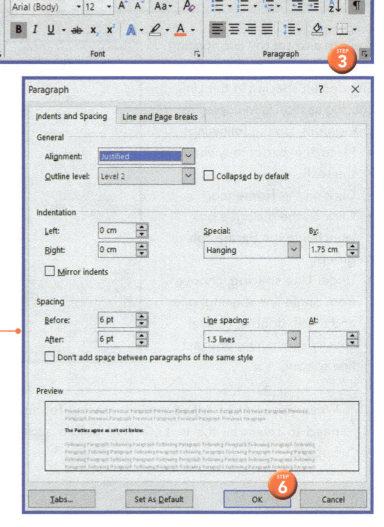

2.8.2 Set the paragraph spacing for the entire document

- Click on the *Design* tab.
- Choose *Paragraph Spacing* in the Document Formatting group.
- Choose an option from the drop-down menu, such as **Compact**, **Tight**, **Open** or **Relaxed**.

> ! If the *Design* tab is not in the Ribbon, you can add it using the guidelines in *1.2 Tabs*.

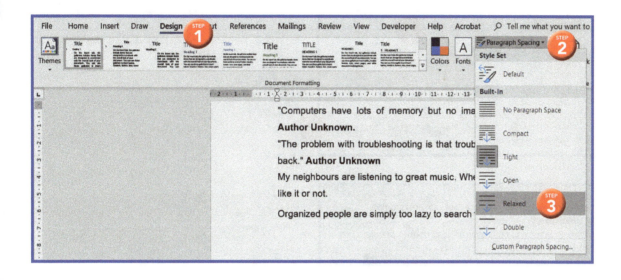

 Frustration

I don't want wide white spaces between the paragraphs!

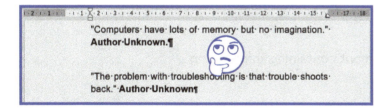

First check to see if there are hidden break symbols in the text, such as section breaks. Delete the hidden breaks. If this does not solve the problem, the spacing before or after the paragraph is most likely set too wide.

Quickly remove extra paragraph spacing:

- Click the *Home* tab.
- Click on *Line and Paragraph Spacing*.
- Select *Remove Space Before Paragraph*.

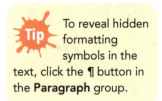

> **Tip** To reveal hidden formatting symbols in the text, click the ¶ button in the **Paragraph** group.

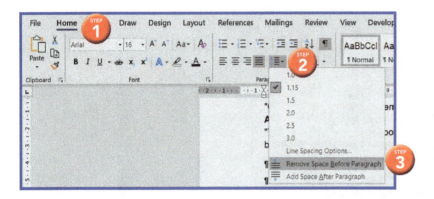

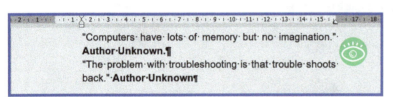

Should you not want to remove the spaces totally, the spaces can be set in the Paragraph dialogue box, as explained in 2.8.1 above.

2.9 Headers

A header is a static section at the top of a document containing information that automatically repeats on each page.

2.9.1 How to insert a header

- Click on the *Insert* tab.
- Look for the **Header & Footer** group and click *Header*.
- In the drop-down list, click on the type of header you want.
- The body of the document is faded out to indicate that you are now working in the Header part of the document.

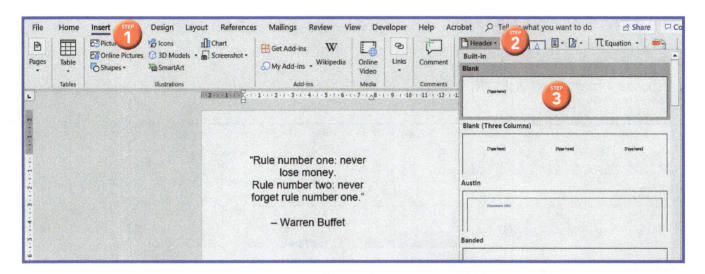

- Type the text for the header.
- Double-click in the body of the document to resume working in the document.

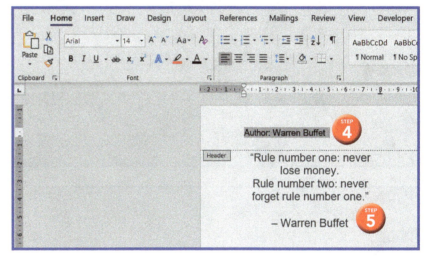

 Tip The quickest way to access the header part is to double-click on it. You can also right-click on it and select **Edit Header** from the drop-down list that appears.

☆ **Benefit** When you access the header part, the **Design** tab will open with a range of useful functions.

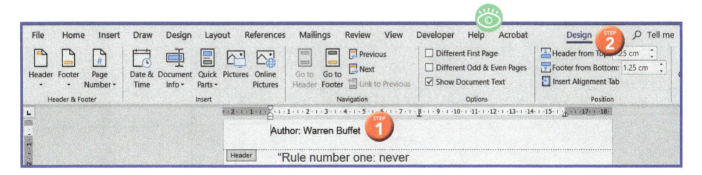

Insert a date and time in the header:

- Click on the **Design** tab.
- Click on **Date & Time**.
- Choose a format and click **OK**.

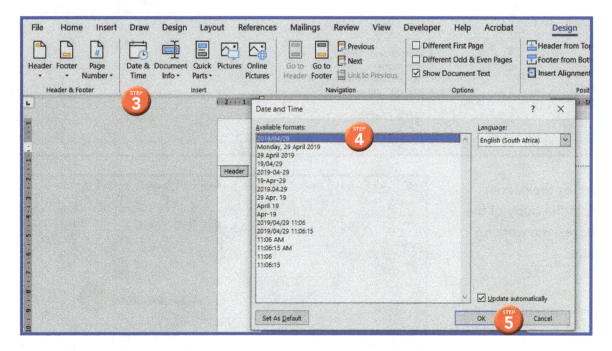

In a similar way, you can insert Author, File Name, File Path and Document Title in the Header part by clicking on **Document Info**.

Use a different header on the first page:

- Click on the *Design* tab.
- In the **Options** group, select *Different First Page* to automatically delete the text in the Header of the first page.
- Then type in different header text.

Tip Page numbers can also be inserted from the *Insert* tab, under Headers & Footers.

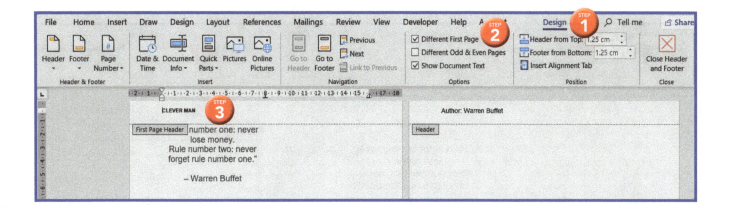

If you want to use a different header in another part of the document, you will first have to insert a section break in that part of the document (see 2.11.2 Section breaks).

Note

The text in the header disappeared when I inserted page numbers!

Frustration

To solve this, first insert the page numbers and then type the text for the header in the header part. This way both the header and page numbers will be displayed (see *2.12 Page numbers*).

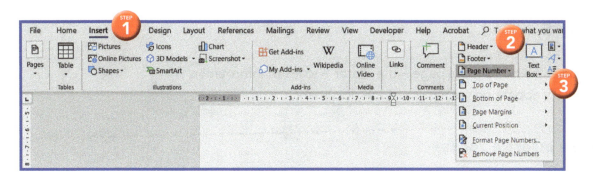

2.9.2 How to delete a header

A header can be deleted as follows:

- Click on the *Insert* tab.
- Look for the **Header & Footer** group and click *Header*.
- From the drop-down list, select *Remove Header*.

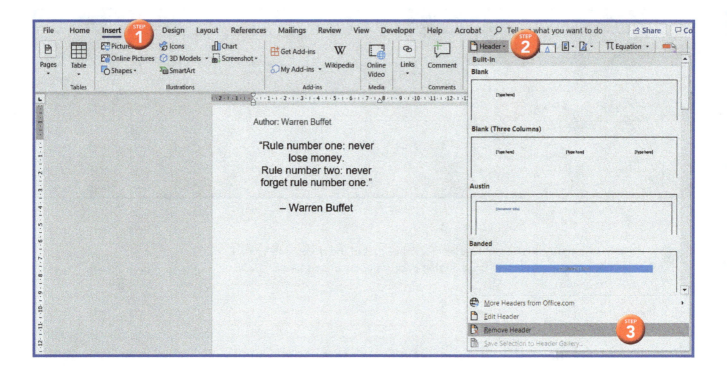

 Double-click in the header part to gain quick access to header and edit the header text. You can also delete the text by selecting the text and pressing the *Delete* key on the keyboard.

Time saver

2.10 Footers

You use the section at the bottom of a page – the footer – to insert information that will automatically appear on each page of the document.

2.10.1 How to insert a footer

- Click on the *Insert* tab.
- Look for the **Header & Footer** group and click *Footer*.
- From the drop-down list, click on the type of footer you want.

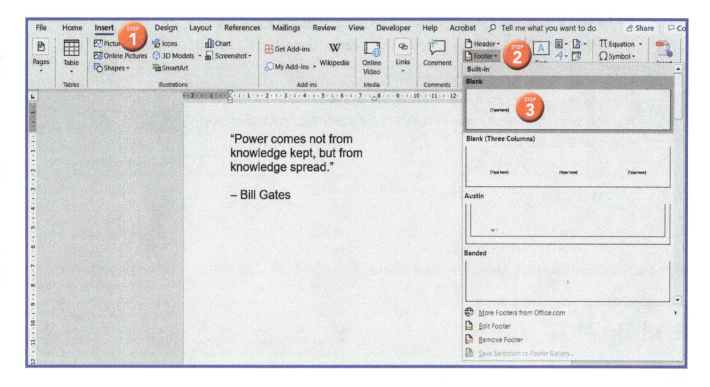

- The body of the document is faded out to indicate that you are now working in the footer section of the document.
- Type the text for the footer, as you did for the header.
- To resume working in the body of the document, double-click in the body of the document or click on the *Close Header and Footer* button.

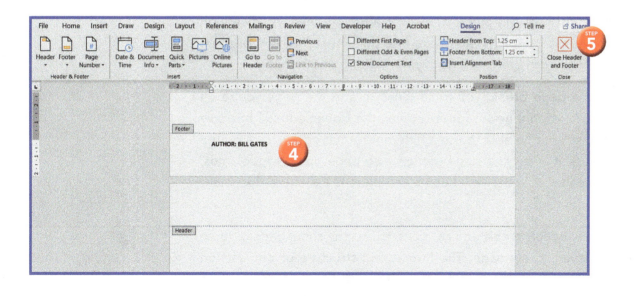

Benefit

When you access the footer section, the *Design* tab will open with a range of useful functions, as it does with headers (see *2.9.1 How to insert a header*)

Time saver

The quickest way to access the footer section is to double-click in it. You can also right-click on it and select *Edit Footer* from the drop-down list that appears.

Note

If you want to use a different footer in another part of the document, you will first have to insert a section break in that part of the document (see *2.11.2 Section breaks*).

2.10.2 How to delete a footer

- Click on the *Insert* tab.
- Look for the **Header & Footer** group and click *Footer*.
- From the drop-down list, select *Remove Footer*.

Tip

You can delete text in the footer by double-clicking in the footer section, selecting the text and pressing the *Delete* key on the keyboard.

2.11 Breaks

Using breaks in legal documents ensures that documents look professional and neat. A cover page or a table of contents can be separated from the rest of the document with different or no page numbers, headings, footers, and fonts.

Word has two types of breaks: **page breaks** and **section breaks**.

To understand the difference between the two, you need to know that Word does not 'see' pages. Word only sees sections. When you open a new document in Word, it consists of only one section, even after you have typed enough text to cover several pages. You can divide one document into two or more sections. Each section can then have its own formatting and layout.

When you insert a **page break**, you force Word to end the page you're on and continue the text on a new page. However, the document still has only one section. You will not be able to use a different format or structure on the next page because it is still the same section – so page numbers, columns, margin sizes, a header, or footer will appear throughout the entire document (section).

When you insert a **section break**, you can continue on the same page or force Word to continue on a new page. The format and structure of one section can differ from the other sections, even though the sections are in the same document. For instance, if you want to restart the page numbers somewhere in the middle of the document or want to have a different header in different chapters or annexures, you can insert a section break to tell Word that you want to change the formatting.

2.11.1 How to insert page breaks

- Place the cursor at the end of the paragraph where you want the text to end, so that the text that comes after can start again on a new page.
- Click on the Insert tab.
- In the **Pages** group, click the **Page Break** option.
- The text in the rest of the document will start on the next page.

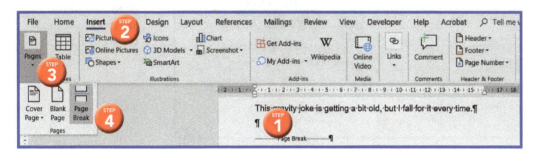

2.11.2 How to insert section breaks

- Place the cursor where you want to insert the section break in your document.
- Click on the **Layout** tab.
- In the **Page Setup** group, click the **Breaks** option.
- Under **Section Breaks**, select an option.

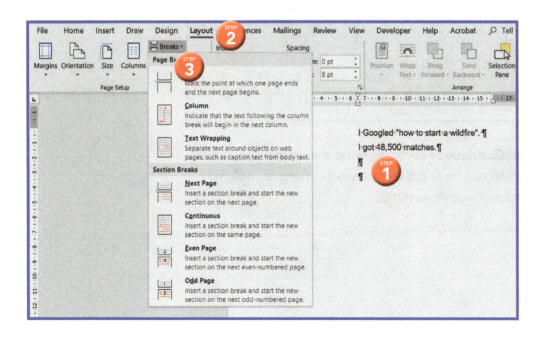

There are various section break options to choose from:

Next Page – a new section starts on a new page, so the text in the rest of the document will start on the next page.

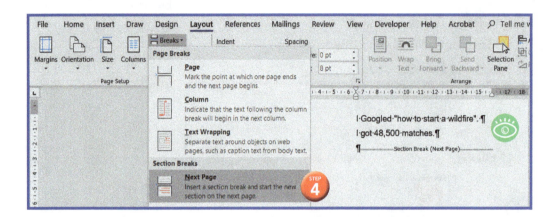

Tip You cannot restart page numbering in the middle of a document or have different headers and footers in the same document without inserting a section break.

Continuous – this type of section break starts a new section without starting a new page.

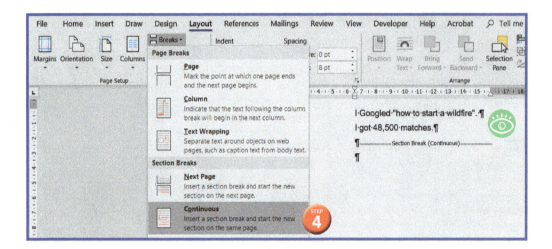

Both the **Next Page** and the **Continuous** section breaks divide the document into two sections. Each section can have different layouts, margins, columns, tables, headers, footers, and many other settings.

Why can't I type here?

Frustration

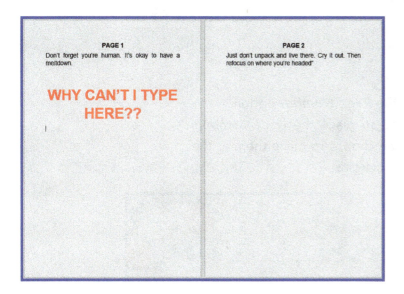

Start by looking for hidden formatting.

> **Tip** To reveal hidden formatting symbols in the text, click the **¶** button in the **Paragraph** group under the *Home* tab.

A page break has been inserted. To delete the page break, select **Page Break** and press the *Delete* key on your keyboard.

I don't want page numbers on the cover page and Table of Contents page!

Frustration

Insert a **Next Page** section break at the bottom of the cover page and another one just beneath the Table of Contents. The document will then consist of three sections. Insert page numbers only in the section containing the body of the document (see *2.12 Page numbers*).

2.12 Page numbers

Every legal document should have page numbers.

2.12.1 How to insert page numbers

- Click on the **Insert** tab.
- In the **Header and Footer** group, click on the *Page Number* option.
- Choose an option in the drop-down menu to place the page numbers exactly where you want them to be. You can choose to place them at the top or bottom of the page, as well as in the margins.

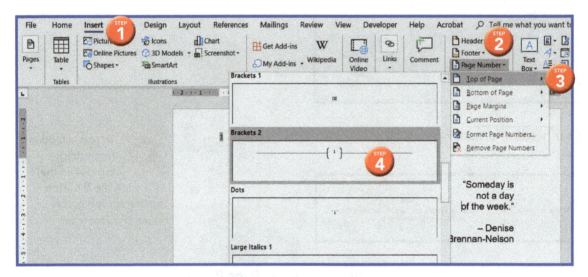

- The body of the document becomes greyed out when you work in the header or footer of the document.
- Double-click in the body of the document to resume working there or click on the **Close Header and Footer** option at the far right side of the Ribbon.

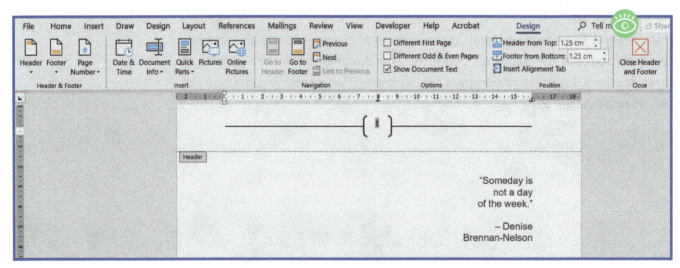

Continuous page numbers will automatically be inserted on every page of the document.

2.12.2 How to change the formatting of page numbers

- While working in the header or footer part of the page, click on the *Design* tab.
- Click on *Page Number* > *Format Page Numbers*. The Page Number Format dialogue box opens.

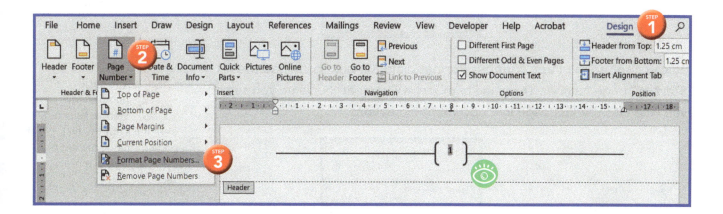

When you are working in the body of the document, the *Design* tab for headers and footers will not be open. You can access page numbers from the *Insert* tab instead by doing the following:

- Click on the *Insert* tab.
- Click on *Page Number* > *Format Page Number*s. The Page Number Format dialogue box opens.

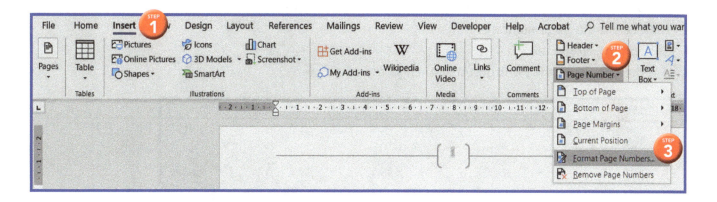

- Change the format of the numbers in the **Number format** drop-down menu.

In the **Page Number Format** screen, the format of the numbers can be changed:

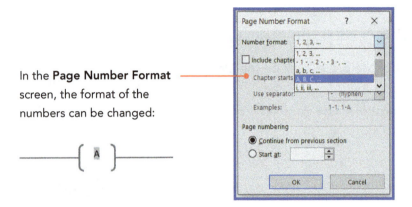

You can also use the **Page Number Format** dialogue box to change the "***Start at***" page number. The page numbers will start at the value you select, even when it's the first page in a document or section.

In the **Page Number Format** screen, the format of the numbers can be changed:

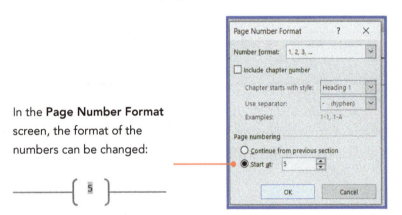

Tip The page numbers will start as selected, even if it's not the first page of the document or the first page of a new section.

The text style of the page numbers – such as font, colour, weight, and so on – can be changed.

- Double-click in the header part on any page in the document.
- Then select the page number.
- Click on the *Home* tab.
- Use the options in the **Font** group to change the text style.

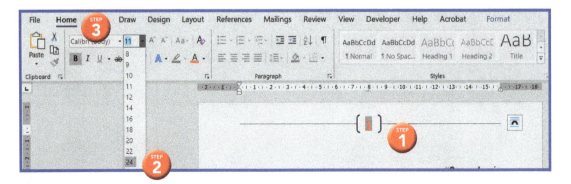

2.12.3 How to delete all the page numbers

- Double-click in the header part of the document.
- Select the page number and press the **Delete** key. The page number will be deleted on all the pages.

If you're already working in the header part:

When you work in the header part of a document, the **Design** tab is automatically open and the text in the body is greyed out.

- Click on **Page number.**
- **Select Remove Page Numbers** in the drop-down menu.

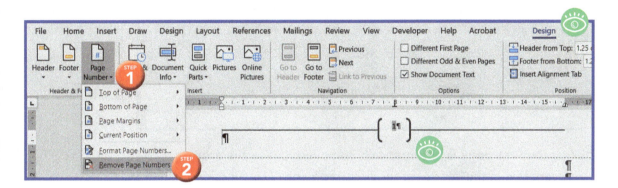

If you are working in the body of the document:

When working in the body of a document, the **Design** tab will not be open, so you should do the following:

- Click on the **Insert** tab.
- Click on **Page Number** and select **Format Page Number**.
- You can then select **Remove Page Numbers** in the drop-down menu.

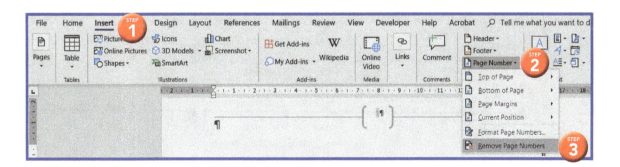

Frustration

I don't want a page number on the cover page!

Word has a built-in function that allows you to specify a different page number or no page number on the **first page** of a document.

- Double-click in the header part of the document to activate the *Design* tab.
- In the **Options** group, select the *Different First Page* checkbox.

The page number on the **first page** is automatically removed. Leave the area blank or type in different text in the header of the **first page** only. This function can't be used for any other pages in the document.

Frustration

I want to restart the page numbering in the next chapter!

This new chapter must start on page 1.

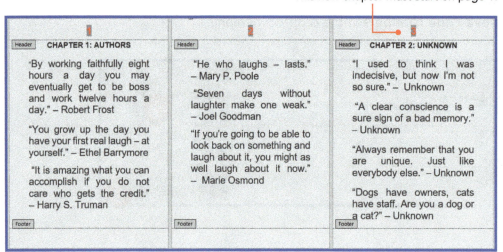

Inserting **section breaks** is the only way to restart page numbering partway through a document, to exclude certain pages from having page numbers, or to have different types of numbering (numerical and alphabetical) in the same document.

Section breaks divide one document in two or more separate sections. Each section can have its own set of page numbers or no page numbers at all (see *2.11.2 Section breaks*).

A **page break** forces the text to end on the current page and resume on the next page. In this case, the page numbers continue uninterrupted.

2.12.5 How to insert a section break to restart page numbers

Insert a section break:
- Place the cursor where you want the first section to end. If you already have a page break there, delete the page break.
- On the *Layout* tab, click on *Breaks.*
- Then click *Next Page* in the **Section Breaks** part of the drop-down menu.

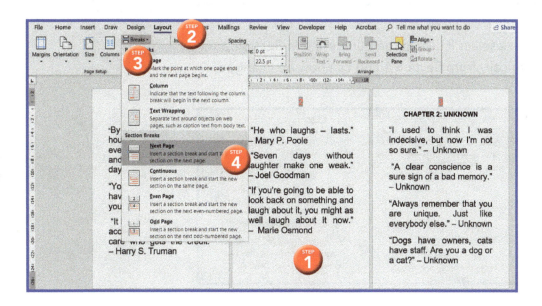

The document is now divided into two sections.

Double-click in the header part of the second section. The **Design** tab for **Headers & Footers** will open. You will be able to identify each section by the tag attached to it. By default, Section 2 is linked to Section 1 because 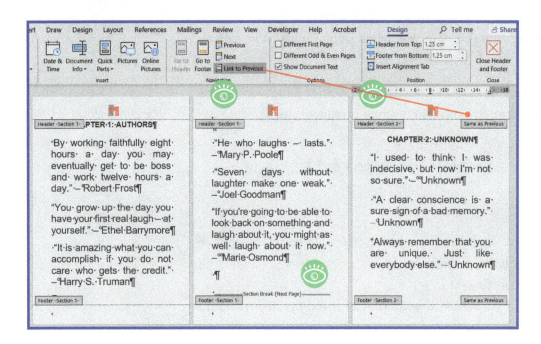 is selected.

Click on 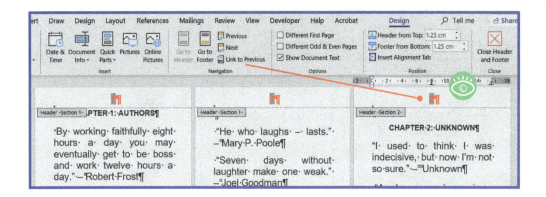 to deselect it. The page numbering in Section 2 will no longer continue automatically from Section 1 and can now be changed.

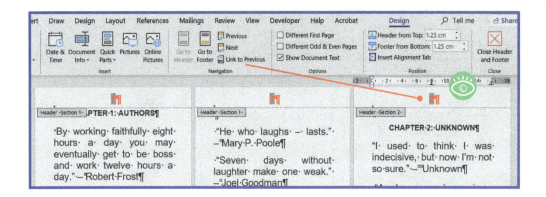

Change the page numbers in the new section:

- Double-click in the header of Section 2. The **Design** tab for **Headers & Footers** will open.
- Click **Page Number** and select **Format Page Number** from the drop-down menu. The **Page Number Format** dialogue box opens.

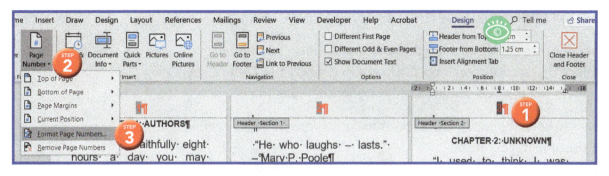

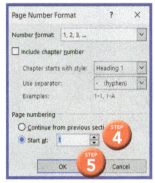

- Select a "Start at" number and click **OK**.

The same can be done with Chapter 3 of the document, if needed.

- Insert a section break where Section 2 must end. While in the header part of Section 3, click 🔲 Link to Previous to deselect the option so that Section 3 is not linked to Section 2, and then format the page numbers for Section 3.

There can be as many sections as needed in a document, with each section starting at page number 1.

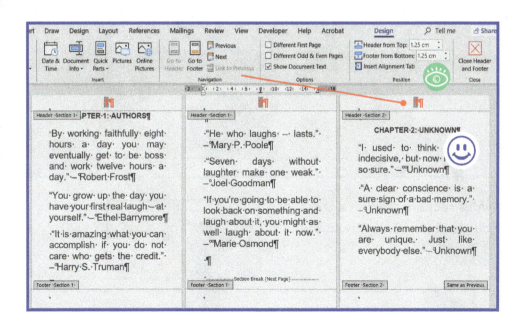

2.12.6 How to revert to continuous page numbering

Delete the section breaks to change the document back to one section. To do this, select the section break on the page and press the **Delete** key. The page numbers will then be continuous throughout the document.

Should you want to keep the sections but revert to continuous page numbering for the entire document, you must:

- Double-click in the header part of Section 2. The **Design** tab will open.
- Select **Link to Previous**, then click **Yes**. This action will delete the header and/or footer and connect this section to the previous section.

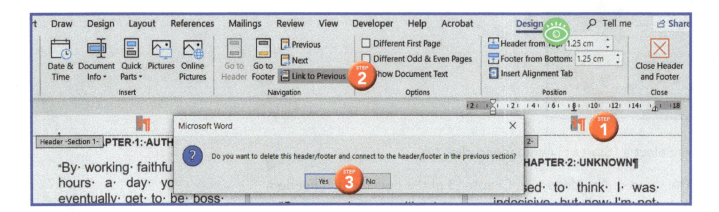

The page numbers in Section 2 can now be changed.

- Double-click in the header part of Section 2. The **Design** tab will open.
- Click **Page Number** and select **Format Page Numbers** from the drop-down menu. The Page Number Format dialogue box opens.

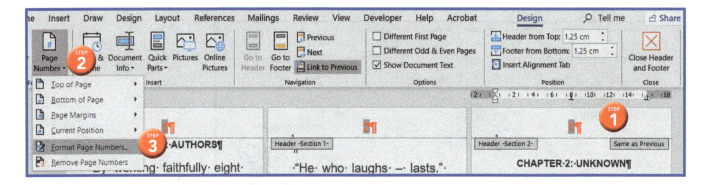

- Click on **Continue from previous section**, then click **OK**. The page numbers will now be continuous throughout the document.

2.13 Numbering

To start a numbered list, type 1 and press the **Tab** key. Then type the text of the first item in the list and press **Enter**.

Word will automatically start a numbered list and insert the next number, 2.

This process can be repeated as many times as required. Each time you press **Enter**, **Word** automatically inserts the next number in the list.

To finish the list, press **Enter** twice or press the **Backspace** key to delete the last number in the list.

> 1.→Stay·low¶
> 2.→¶

> 1.→Stay·low·¶
> 2.→Stay·quiet¶
> 3.→Keep·it·simple¶
> 4.→Don't·expect·too·much¶
> 5.→Enjoy·what·you·have¶
> ¶
> Dean·Koontz¶

> **Tip** Another way to create a numbered list is to enter the text of the list without numbers. Then select all the text items and click the **Numbering** button in the Paragraph group on the **Home** tab. You can also choose a number style from the drop-down list.

2.13.1 Instantly change to a different number style

- Position the cursor inside the text of the numbered list.
- Click on the **Home** tab.
- In the **Paragraph** group, click the arrow next to the **Numbering** button .
- Navigate through the gallery of number styles until you find the style you want.

> **Early to bed and early to rise, makes a man:**
> 1. healthy,
> 2. wealthy and **STEP 1**
> 3. wise.
> *Ben Franklin (1706-1790)*

> **!** Don't try to change the numbers in a list manually. When you use numbering options to make changes, **Word** keeps track. Other list changes can be done easily later.

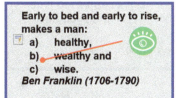

> **Early to bed and early to rise, makes a man:**
> a) healthy,
> b) wealthy and
> c) wise.
> *Ben Franklin (1706-1790)*

2.13.2 Change the numbering in a numbered list

Restart numbering at 1:

- Double-click on any number in the list. All the numbers will be selected automatically, however, the text items will not appear selected.
- To restart a new list at 1, right-click the number you want to change to 1 and click **Restart at 1**.

Continuous numbering:

- To revert to continuous numbering, double-click any number in the list.
- Then right-click the number you want to continue the numbering with and select **Continue Numbering**.

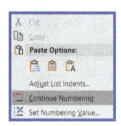

Set numbering value:

- Double-click any number in the list.
- Right-click the number for which you want to set the number value and select **Set Numbering Value**.
- In the Set Numbering Value dialogue box, use the arrows to change the value to the number you want.

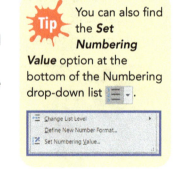

You can also find the **Set Numbering Value** option at the bottom of the Numbering drop-down list.

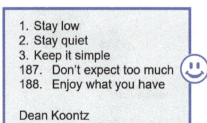

The numbering does not start automatically!

When this happens, the backstage settings need to be set to start numbering automatically.

- Click on **File** > **Options** > **Proofing**.
- Click the **AutoCorrect Options** button to open the AutoCorrect dialogue box.

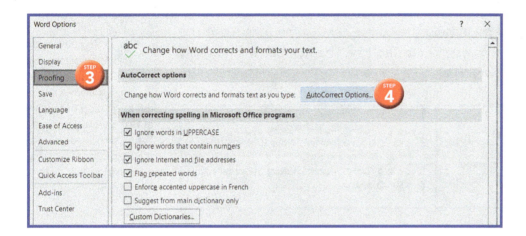

- In the AutoCorrect dialogue box, click the **AutoFormat As You Type** tab.
- In the **Apply as you type** section, select the **Automatic numbered lists** checkbox.

Stop numbering my lists!
Frustration

You can turn off the automatic list recognition feature by deselecting the **Automatic numbered lists** checkbox (see above).

2.13.5 Multi-level numbers

A numbered list can have sub-levels.

You can create a sub-level by placing the cursor next to the number at the beginning of a text item and pressing the **Tab** key. The number will move to the right and change to a lower level.

> 1. Yesterday's the past,
> 2. tomorrow's the future, but
> 3. today is a gift.
> 4. That's why it's called the present.
> Bil Keane

> 1. Yesterday's the past,
>   a. tomorrow's the future, but
> 2. today is a gift.
> 3. That's why it's called the present.
> Bil Keane

To move the item back to a higher level, hold down the **Shift** key and press the **Tab** key.

2.14 Bullets

Text items in an unnumbered list are usually indicated by **bullets**.

To start a bulleted list, you type an asterisk (*) followed by a tab. Then enter the text for the first item and press enter.

As with numbered lists, **Word** recognises this so that each time you press **Enter**, a new line starting with the same bullet appears. The default bullet is a solid black circle.

(!) When you turn off the list recognition feature and create your list manually, you will no longer be able to change the numbering in a numbered list or instantly change to a different number style.

Note Remember that the cursor must be next to the number and at the beginning of the line of text before pressing **Tab**. If the cursor is inside the text item, the text will move instead.

Tip To find out more about multi-level numbering, view *Chapter 4: Professional Drafting, 4.2 Multi-level numbered clauses in legal documents.*

As with numbers, bullets can instantly be changed to a different bullet style:

- Position the cursor inside the text of the bulleted list.
- Click on the **Home** tab.
- In the **Paragraph** group, click the drop-down arrow next to the **Bullet Library** button.
- Choose your preferred style from a gallery of bullet styles.

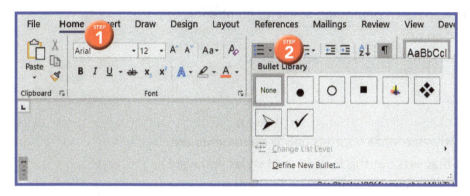

For even more bullet options:

- Select **Define New Bullet** from within the **Bullet Library**.
- Click on the **Symbol** tab.
- Choose a suitable bullet for your list, and click **OK**.

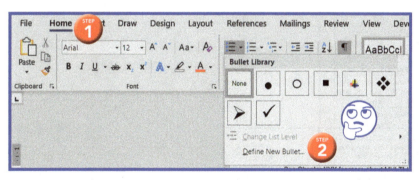

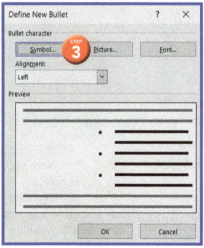

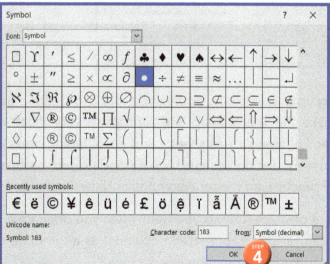

Legal practitioners don't have time to waste on editing and formatting. Setting up a document before drafting according to your preferred format ensures consistency and will lighten the load of final proofreading.

Editing is all about consistency throughout the document: consistent font, font size, alignment, margins, line spacing, paragraph spacing, numbering of clauses, numbering of pages, and so on.

3.1 Rule Sheet

It would be useful to decide in advance what your editing requirements are. So, compile your own rule sheet that sets out the formats and styles you want for your documents going forward. You can then give the rule sheet to anyone else working with you.

Here is a sample rule sheet, which includes good practices when sharing a document with others.

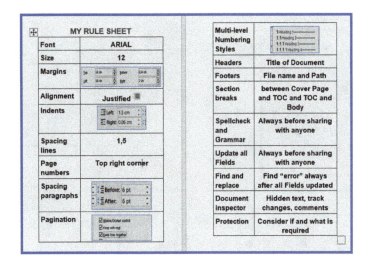

Setting up and following a rule sheet prior to drafting a document will make the final editing and formatting very much easier and quicker. Following a rule sheet – and encouraging others to do the same – will also ensure that documents have a standardised, professional look within your legal practice, no matter who edits or draws them up.

Once you are sure of which formats you want when you open up a new blank document, you can save your formatted document as a template or you can update the default *Normal.dotm* template.

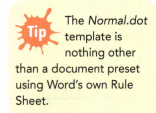

Tip The *Normal.dot* template is nothing other than a document preset using Word's own Rule Sheet.

3.2 Templates

Templates are sample documents that contain pre-applied settings such as page size and layout, formatting, tabs, text styles, colour, boilerplate text, and so on. When you open a template, these pre-applied settings are immediately available to you to use.

You can create and save new documents as templates, modify existing templates to better suit your needs, or use one of **Word's** templates as is. As a Legal Practitioner, you will most likely create your own templates or modify existing ones to suit your day-to-day drafting needs. When using templates, you will enjoy the enormous time-saving benefits of having all the settings and styles you need already in your documents.

Tip Templates are especially useful for frequently used documents. Templates reduce or prevent errors, save time and effort, and ensure consistency and accuracy.

3.2.1 The Normal template (*.dotm)

The Normal template opens whenever you open a new blank document in **Word**. It is **Word's** default Template.

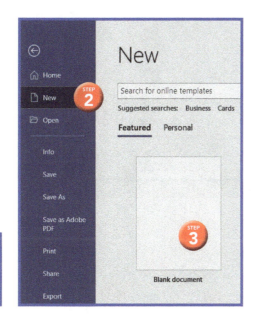

The Normal template includes default styles and formatting that determine the overall look and feel of a document (see the introduction to Chapter 2 for a list of the defaults).

It is possible to change the default styles and formatting of the *Normal.dotm* template. Any changes you make to the Normal template will be applied to all future documents created while **Word** is open. However, when you close **Word** and reopen it again, none of your customisations will reflect on the Normal template. Modifying and saving the Normal template can sometimes be tricky, so we recommend that you use the simpler method of creating your own document templates or customise existing templates, and work from those.

3.3 The customised template

You can create as many customised templates as you like to accommodate the types of documents you require in your practice.

3.3.1 Create a new blank template

Step 1: Open a new blank document (it will still have the default Normal template font, paragraph, and style settings).

Step 2: Set your page margins
To find out more about setting page margins, see *2.3.1 Create a custom margin*.

Step 3: Change the font settings
- Click on the *Home* tab.
- Click the dialogue box launcher next to the **Font** group.
- Change the font style and size in the dialogue box that pops up.
- Click *Set As Default*, then select the button for *This document only?*
- Click *OK.*

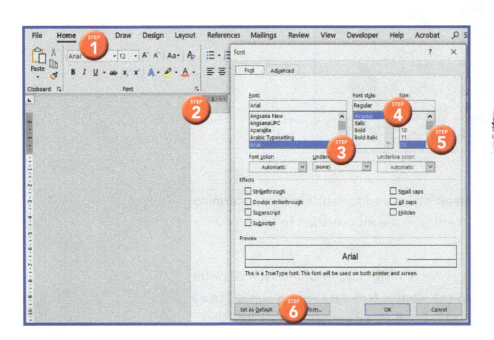

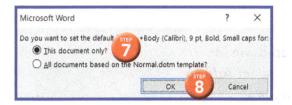

Step 4: Change the paragraph settings

- Click on the *Home* tab.
- Click the dialogue box launcher next to the **Paragraph** group.
- Click the *Indents and Spacing* tab to make your paragraph changes.
- Click *Set As Default*, then select the button for *This document only?*
- Click *OK.*

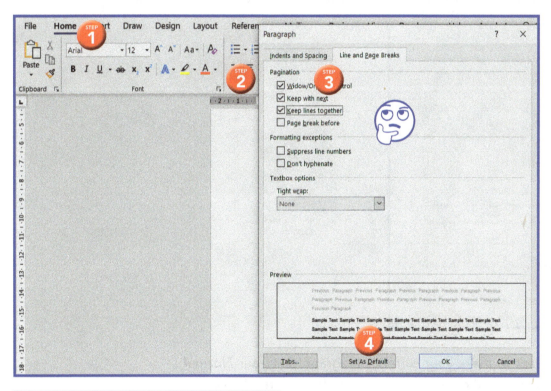

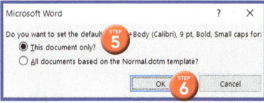

- Click on the *Line and Page Breaks* tab to set your line and page break options.
- Click *Set As Default*, then select the button for *This document only?*
- Click *OK.*

Step 5: Change the style settings

- Click on the *Home* tab.
- **Right-click** on *Normal* style and select *Modify* from the drop-down list.
- Make your changes in the dialogue box that pops up, then select *Add to the Styles gallery* and *New documents based on this template*.
- Click *OK* when you're done.

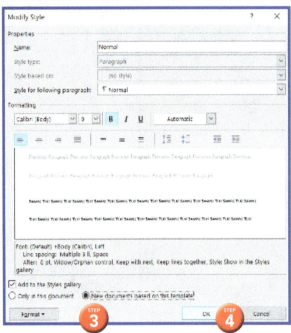

Alternatively, if you want to make your current paragraph text your *Normal* text style, place your cursor in the paragraph, **right-click** on *Normal* style and select *Update normal to match selection*. Your modification will not be saved as a default when using this method.

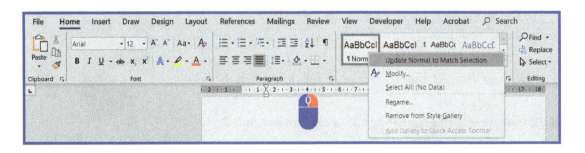

Step 6: Save your document as a template

To save your document as a template file with all your style settings:

- Click on *File*
- Choose *Save as Template*.
- Select where you want your template saved.
- Next to **File Format** at the bottom of the dialogue box, click the drop-down menu to choose your preferred format.
- Choose *Microsoft Word Template (.dotx)* for a normal document or *Microsoft Word Macro-enabled template (.dotm)* to create a template document capable of containing macros.
- Click *Save*.

> **Tip** When saving your Template, select a place on your hard drive that is quick and easy to find, and name your document in a way that makes it easy to identify.

What are *.docx, *.docm, *.dotx and *.dotm?

They are all file extensions under which **Word** documents are saved. The extension depends on what kind of document it is. M stands for Macro and T for Template.

*.docx: This is the default extension for most **Word** documents. Documents with this extension are not templates and don't contain macros.

*.docm: Documents with this extension contain macros or are macro-enabled. These documents are not templates.

*.dotx: Documents with this extension are templates saved under a designated folder in **Word** to be used at various times. These documents do not contain macros.

*.dotm: Documents with this extension are templates and contain macros.

> **Tip** Macros are shortcuts that automate formatting tasks. Macros can be accessed under the *View* tab in the Ribbon. Documents and Templates must be saved as *.docm* or *.dotm* to use them.

> **Tip** You can find out more about the magic of macros and how to create and use them in Chapter 8 – *8.10 Macros*.

3.3.2 Save your existing document as a Template

Make sure that the contents and formatting of your document are correct. Delete all references to specific clients, names, addresses, amounts, and so on. and other information which you know you will have to change every time you use the document in the future.

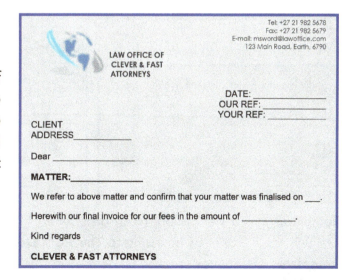

Option 1: To save in Word's default location

- Click on *File > Save as*.
- In the drop-down menu, scroll down and click on **Word Template (*dotx)**.
- Give your Template a name that easily identifies the type of document it is.
- Click on **Save**.
- Word automatically saves all Templates in a special folder under **This PC > Documents > Custom Office Templates**.

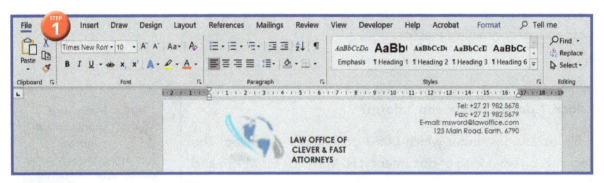

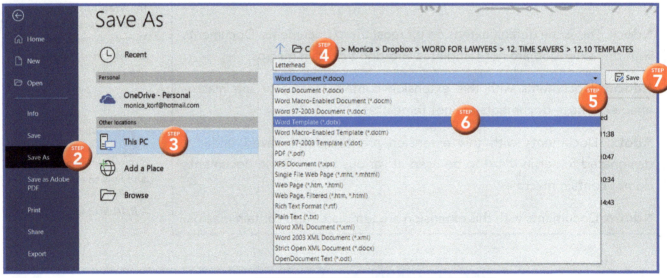

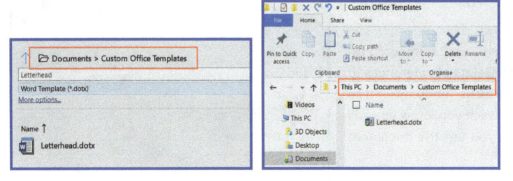

Templates saved via Option 1 can be opened from the Personal Template Gallery (see 3.3.3) or by browsing to **This PC > Documents > Custom Office Templates**. (Templates can also be deleted at this last location.)

Option 2: To save in your own location

- Click on *File > Save as*.
- Click on the drop-down arrow in the box below the file name (next to the *Save* button) to open a drop-down menu; scroll down and click on *Word Template (*dotx)*.
- Give your Template a name that easily identifies the type of document it is.
- Click on *More options* and choose a special place on your PC where you want to save your Template.
- Click on *Save*.

> **Tip** When saving your Template, select a place on your hard drive that is quick and easy to find, and name your document in a way that makes it easy to identify.

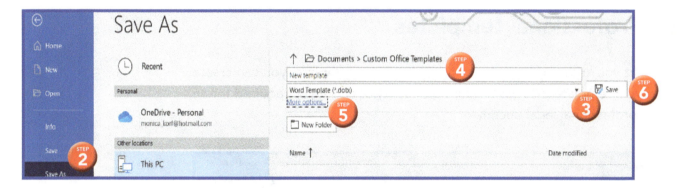

3.3.3 How to open a Template to be used again

Option 1: Open from the Personal Templates Gallery

All Templates that Word saves in its default location (*This PC > Documents > Custom Office Templates*, see *3.2.2 Option 1*) can be found in this **Gallery**.

- Click on *File > New > Personal*.
- A gallery of all your saved templates will be shown.
- Click on your preferred template to open it.
- A new, unnamed document will open up. Changes made in this document will not change or affect the original **Word** template.
- When you've finished working in the document, remember to save it under a new name.

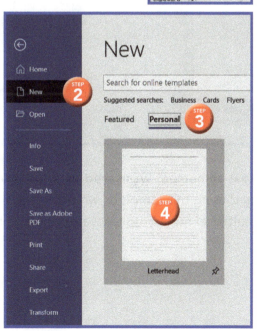

Option 2: Open a Template saved in your own location

- Open the template by browsing to the special place on your PC where you saved it (see *3.3.2 Option 2*).
- Click on your preferred template to open it.
- A new, unnamed document will open up. Changes made in this document will not change or affect the original **Word** template
- When you've finished working in the document, remember to save it under a new name.

3.4 Professional templates

Now that you know how to create and save a **Word** template, you can create and save a template that has the formatting, styles and fields required for an instant professional legal document.

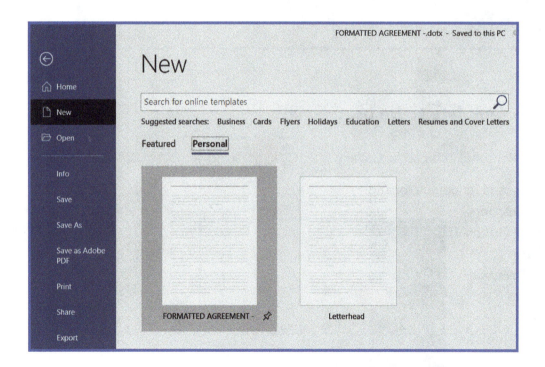

In the example below, a legal agreement was saved as a **Word** template. A new document can be opened using this template, which already includes the correct heading styles for multilevel numbered clauses, page numbers, and a Table of Contents.

New unnamed document.

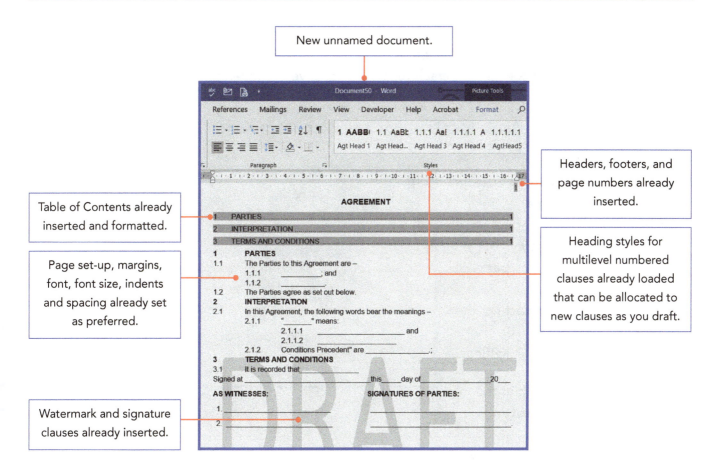

Table of Contents already inserted and formatted.

Page set-up, margins, font, font size, indents and spacing already set as preferred.

Watermark and signature clauses already inserted.

Headers, footers, and page numbers already inserted.

Heading styles for multilevel numbered clauses already loaded that can be allocated to new clauses as you draft.

You will learn more about creating Heading styles, multi-level numbered clauses, and a Table of Contents in **Chapter 4: Professional Drafting**. You will also learn how to insert a watermark in **Chapter 7: Protection**.

Frustration

My template is not in the personal template gallery!

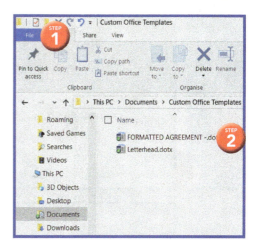

Tip The location is normally part of the standard settings, but sometimes when files and folders are moved the location settings are lost.

Your **Word** template can also be opened directly from the **Custom Office Templates** directory. Remember that **Word** automatically saves all templates in a special folder under **This P**C > **Documents** > **Custom Office Templates**.

To open your personal **Word** template, browse to the **Custom Office Templates** folder in the **Documents** folder and open a new document by clicking the name of the template you're looking for.

This is a short-term solution, however. It will be faster and easier to insert the location of your personal **Word** templates in the **Word** backstage settings as shown below so that it becomes the default repository for saved templates.

3.4.1 Change the default location for saving customised templates

Step 1: Copy the file path to *Custom Office Templates*

- Browse to the location of the **Word** templates in the directory.
- Click on the *File* tab. The path will become highlighted.
- Copy the path by selecting the entire path. This path will be inserted in the **Word** backstage settings.

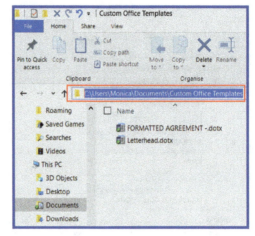

Tip Copy the correct path and paste it into the **Default personal templates location** field.

Step 2: Insert the file path in the Word backstage settings

- Click on the *File* tab.
- Click on *Options* and select *Save*.
- Under the **Save documents** section, insert the correct path in the **Default personal templates location** field.
- Click *OK*.

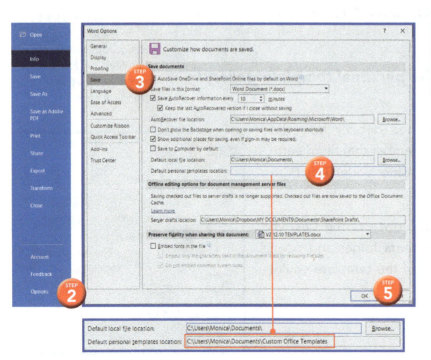

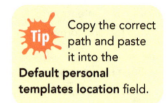

3.5 Spell check and grammar

Word has an in-built spelling and grammar checker and will show spelling and grammar errors as you type.

3.5.1 How are spelling and grammar errors indicated?

Spelling errors are shown by **red** squiggly underlines. Grammar or formatting errors are shown by **blue** double underlines.

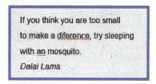

If you think you are too small to make a diference, try sleeping with an mosquito.
Dalai Lama

3.5.2 How to correct spelling and grammar errors

Right-click on the word that is underlined with the red squiggle or blue lines. Suggestions on how to rectify the error will display in a dialogue box.

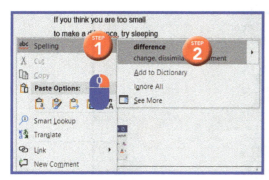
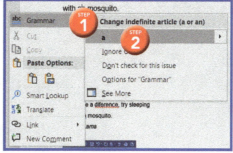

You will notice that the suggestions offered differ depending on whether it is a spelling error or a grammar error.

Click the small right arrow to the right of the options to view even more options. **Word** will provide the correct spelling, give an explanation of the word, provide synonyms, and offer grammar fixes. You can even click on **Read Aloud** to have words read back to you.

3.5.3 How to check the entire document for errors

- Click on the **Review** tab.
- Click on **Check Document** (in some versions of **Word** it is called **Spelling & Grammar**). The results will appear in the **Editor** pane.
- Click the **Results** button and then click the suggested correction if you agree. **Word** will make the correction in the text for you.

Tip **Word** highlights the incorrect word in the text.

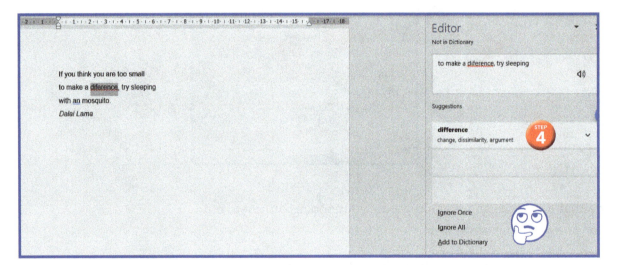

If you do not agree with **Word's** suggested correction, you can do the following:

- Click **Ignore Once** if you want to skip only that instance but display all other instances of the word;
- Click **Ignore All** if you want to ignore all other instances of the word in your document;
- Click **Add to Dictionary** to prevent the word from ever coming up as an error in any of your documents. If this feature is not available, you need to install a dictionary from the list that displays when you click the option.

If no suggestions are given for the incorrect word, type the correct spelling directly in the text.

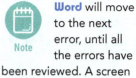 **Word** will move to the next error, until all the errors have been reviewed. A screen will appear confirming that the spelling and grammar check is complete.

 Time saver You can add the **Check Document** button 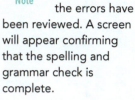 to your Quick Access Toolbar. See *1.3.2 How to add functions to the Quick Access Toolbar*.

 Frustration ***I don't want Word to check spelling and grammar as I type!***

You can disable the spelling and grammar function by changing the backstage settings in **Word**.

- Click on the **File** tab.
- Click on **Options** and select **Proofing** to pull up the proofing options.
- Under **When correcting spelling and grammar in Word**, deselect the checkboxes next to **Check spelling as you type** and **Mark grammar errors as you type**.
- Click **OK**.

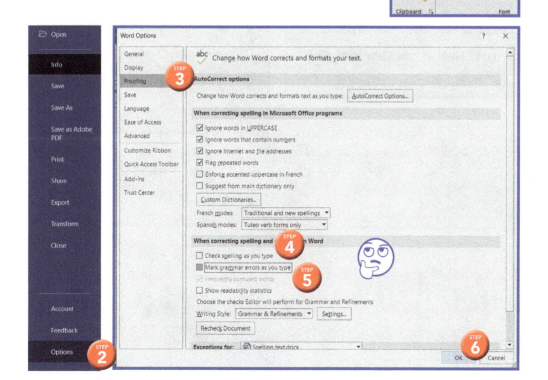

You can also access the backstage settings by clicking on **Settings** ⚙ Settings while you are in **Check Document** abc Check Document mode in a document. The same proofing screen as above will open. Select and deselect the options you prefer.

3.6 Synonyms

Frustration

I need another word with the same meaning!

- **Right-click** 🖱 on the word you want to change
- Click on **Synonyms** in the drop-down list and then click on the synonym you want to accept. Word replaces the word automatically.

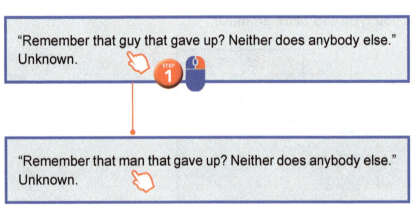

"Remember that guy that gave up? Neither does anybody else." Unknown.

STEP 1

"Remember that man that gave up? Neither does anybody else." Unknown.

Cut
Copy
Paste Options:

A Font...
Paragraph...
Smart Lookup
Synonyms   STEP 2 ▶   man   STEP 3
Translate   dude
Link   ▶   fellow
New Comment   type
                         fella
Thesaurus...

3.7 Thesaurus

Frustration

I need another suitable word!

Thesaurus is a built-in dictionary in **Word** that can help you draft your documents using the correct expression, words, and spelling, giving your document a professional touch.

To use Thesaurus:

*   Select the word you want to replace.
*   Click on the **Review** tab.
*   Click on **Thesaurus** – a drop-down box will appear on the right side of the window.
*   **Right-click** on a suitable word, then click **Insert**. The word in your document will automatically be replaced with the selected new word.

When you **left-click** on a word, more alternatives for the word will display.

The key to drafting a legal document that looks professional is to use **Styles**. If Styles are not used in a document, it will be difficult to maintain consistent formatting and you will not be able to benefit from other excellent features available in Word.

This chapter starts with a basic explanation of what Styles are. The use of Styles as the "magic wand" to draft multi-level numbered clauses, a table of contents, cross-references, and other important components of legal documents, is also explained.

4.1 Styles

Styles are vital to ensuring consistent, well-formatted text. They also help to save a lot of time and prevent frustration. Styles can be applied to paragraphs of text and to one or more words within a paragraph of text.

A **paragraph** is any amount of text that ends with a carriage return (Enter). This can be a single sentence, a sentence without a full stop, a heading or subheading, or indeed a group of many sentences.

When working with paragraphs, we use Paragraph styles to format the text. When formatting just one or a few words within a paragraph of text, we use Character styles. For now, we will be learning about paragraph styles.

> IF·YOU'RE·GOING·TO·DO·SOMETHING,·DO·IT·WITH·STYLE!·
> –·JASON·STATHAM¶

Insight

- A style is a group of formats (i.e. font, size, indent, case, numbering, spacing, etc.) saved together as a unit to be used several times in a document to format different paragraphs to the same style.
- All paragraphs of the text in a document are allocated to a specific style.
- If one or more of the formats in a style is changed, the change automatically appears in all the paragraphs allocated to that style. This means that there will be no need to manually apply the style change to each paragraph in the document.

Word has built-in Styles. These styles are saved as "blocks" under the **Home** tab in the **Styles** group.

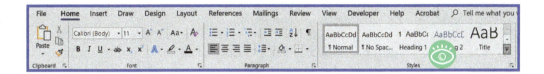

When a new document is opened, these built-in Styles are available. Click on the drop-down arrow to see all the built-in Styles.

To take a closer look at the different formats that have been grouped together under each built-in Style, click on the dialogue box launcher in the **Styles** group.

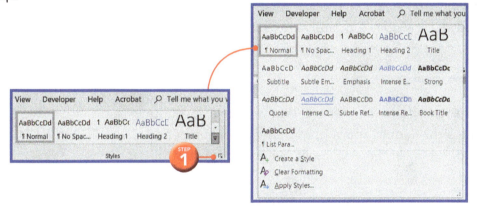

Click on the **Style Inspector** to **Reveal Formats** to see which formats Word thinks you might want to use.

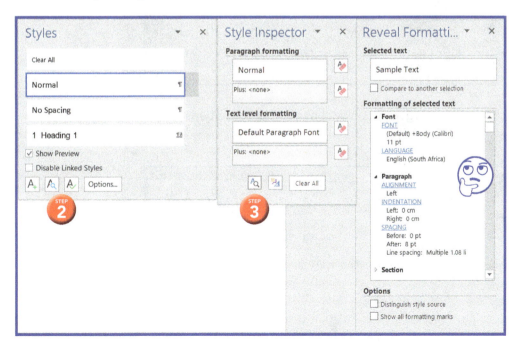

Frustration

I don't like these styles! I don't have time to look at all these formats!

If you don't like any of the built-in styles, you can create your own styles.

Custom-made styles are not an overall setting in Word but are part of the document in which they are created and used. If you want to use your favourite styles in other documents, a template must be created with the styles in it. New documents based on the template will then contain the styles you have created (see *3.3 The customised template* and *4.1.5 Save styles as templates*).

There are two ways to create your own styles. You can either create a new style from scratch (*4.1.1 Create your own style*), or you can modify the settings of one of Word's existing styles (*4.1.2 Modify (update) an existing style*).

4.1.1 Create your own style

To create your own style, manually format a piece of text with your favourite settings. Make sure the font, size, indents, spacing, alignment and numbering are set as you want them to display in the document. Select any part of the text you have just formatted.

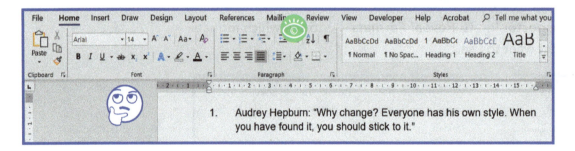

- Under the **Home** tab, click on the dialogue box launcher to open the Styles gallery.

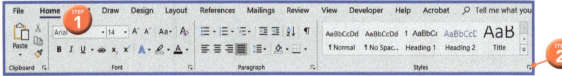

- Click on **Create a Style** and type in a name for the new style.
- Click **OK**.

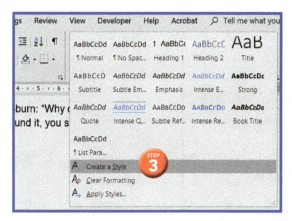

A screen will appear offering a final opportunity to review your style settings. If you are happy with your style settings, click **OK**.

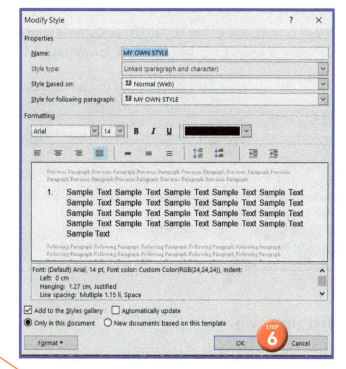

The style you created will now appear in the **Styles** gallery.

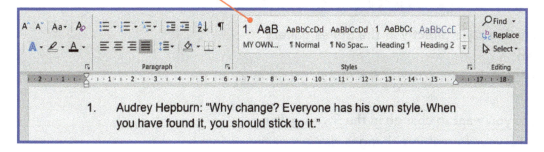

Repeat this process for each new style you want to create.

You can now format other text in your document using your favourite styles. To do this, simply place your cursor anywhere in the text you want to format and click on your new style in the Styles gallery. Your text will immediately format to the new style.

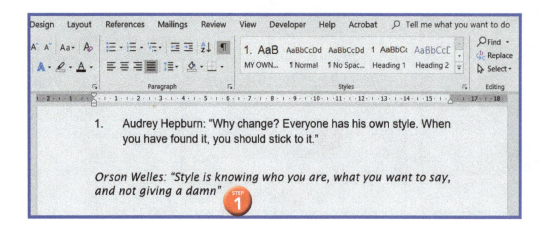

If at a later time you edit any of your styles, all the text in the document allocated to those styles will automatically change to reflect the new formatting.

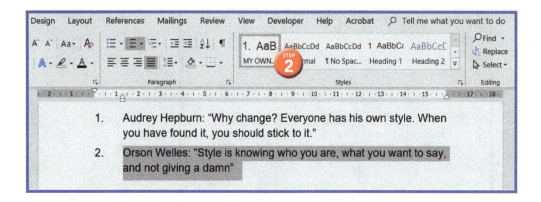

4.1.2 Modify an existing style

You can **modify an existing style** directly in the Styles gallery, or you can **update** your Styles gallery using formatted text in your document.

Option 1: Modify an existing style directly in the Styles gallery

- Click on the *Home* tab.
- Then click on the dialogue box launcher in the **Styles** group to open the Styles gallery.
- **Right-click** on the style you want to change in the Styles gallery.
- Click *Modify* and make your formatting changes directly in the dialogue box.
- Click *OK* when you're done.

All text in your document allocated to this style will immediately change to reflect your new settings

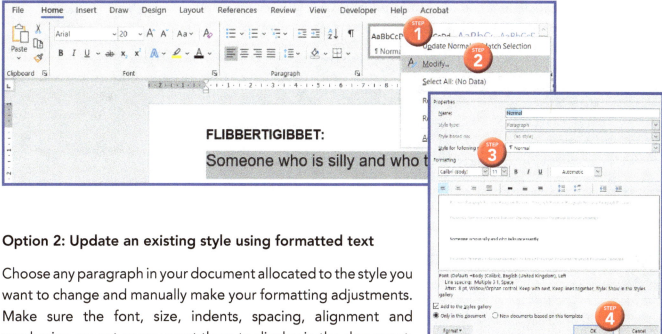

Option 2: Update an existing style using formatted text

Choose any paragraph in your document allocated to the style you want to change and manually make your formatting adjustments. Make sure the font, size, indents, spacing, alignment and numbering are set as you want them to display in the document.

- Select the text you have just formatted.
- Under the **Home** tab, click on the dialogue box launcher in the **Styles** group to open the Styles gallery.
- **Right-click** on the style in the Styles gallery that you want to update with your new formatting.
- Select **Update [style name] to Match Selection**. This will update the style in the gallery with your new settings.

> **Tip** It is important to right-click on the style. If you left-click, Word will use the current formats saved under that style. If you accidentally left-clicked, just click on the **Undo** button in the Quick Access Toolbar and try again.

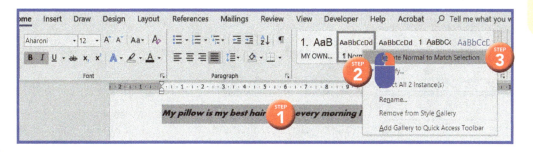

The preview of the relevant style will change to reflect your new format.

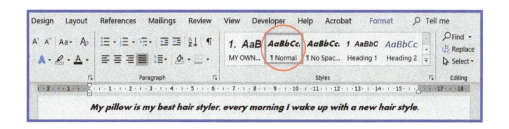

Other text in the document can be formatted with your favourite formats by placing your cursor anywhere in the text and clicking on the new style.

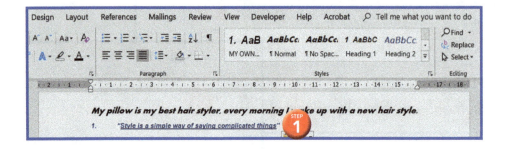

The other text is now also allocated to the updated style.

Should you want to change the style again, select any of the text allocated to the style, change the formatting, then right-click on the relevant style in the Styles gallery and select *Update [style name] to Match Selection*.

This will not only update the style in the Styles gallery, but it will instantly update the formatting of all text in the document to which that style had been applied.

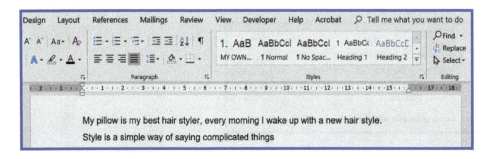

4.1.3 Rename a style

Sometimes you may need to rename your styles, particularly those you have modified, so that you can easily identify them and the formatting settings that you have applied to them.

- To rename a style, **right-click** on the relevant style in the Styles gallery and select **Rename**.

- Type in a different name and click **OK**.

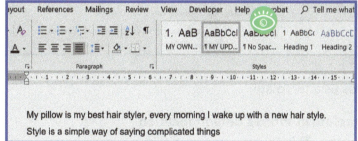

4.1.4 Remove a style

You can remove a style from the Styles gallery if you don't intend using it in that document. This streamlines your Styles gallery, making it quicker and easier to find the styles you are using.

- **Right-click** on the style you would like to delete in the Styles gallery.
- Click **Remove from Style Gallery**.

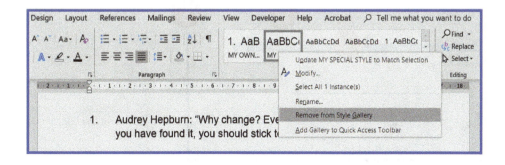

4.1.5 Save your styles as a template

Frustration

I don't want to reinvent the styles wheel in every document!

Save yourself tons of time and frustration by saving your favourite styles as a template. When the template is reopened, the styles will be ready and available to use.

Draft a document with your favourite **formatting settings** (you will only need to do this once).

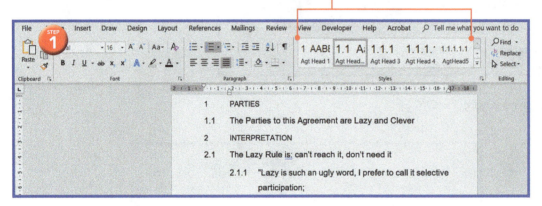

Now save your styles as a template.

Option 1: Save template in Word's default location

- Click *File* > *Save As* > *This PC*.
- Type in an appropriate file name.
- Under *File Format* at the bottom of the dialogue box select *Word Template (*.dotx)*.
- Click *OK* to save the document as a template. Word automatically saves the template in this default location: *This PC* > *Documents* > *Custom Office Templates*.

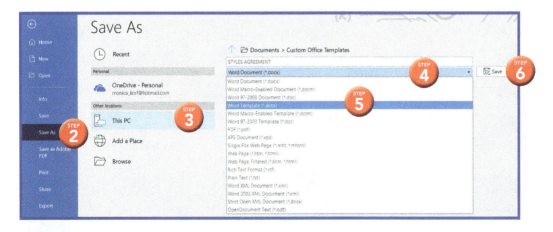

Option 2: Save your template in a location of your choice
- Click on **More options** and choose where you want to save the file.
- Then click on **Save**.

Apply your styles template

To apply your template you need to create a new document and choose the template you want. To do this click on **File** > **New** > **Personal** > **the name of the template** or browse to the location where you saved your styles template.

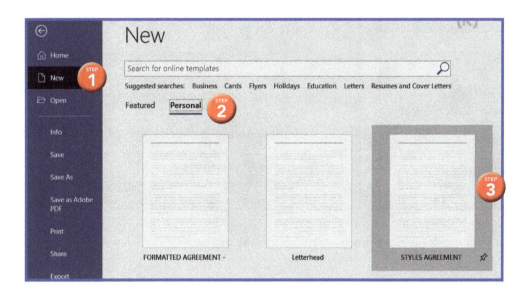

A new, unsaved document will open with the styles intact. Save the document. The template will not be affected.

As you draft, apply a style to each new clause according to its level of numbering.

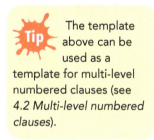

Tip The template above can be used as a template for multi-level numbered clauses (see *4.2 Multi-level numbered clauses*).

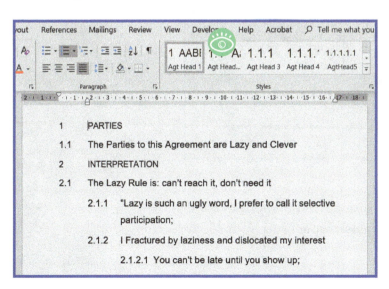

4.1.6 "Borrow" styles from another document

Frustration

I want the styles quickly – I don't want to create a template!

Open a document that has styles you like and copy the styled text. Paste this styled text into the document you are working on.

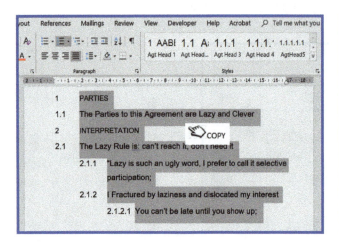
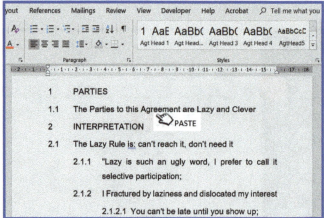

Now update each text style in your working document with the format of the corresponding copied clause:

- Select the copied clause.
- **Right-click** on the style you want to update in the Styles gallery (this will be the style you are currently using in your working document).

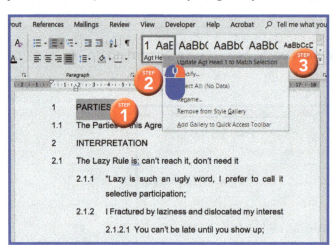

- Select *Update [style name] to Match Selection*. Your current style will be updated to match the style of your copied text.

Multi-level numbered clauses and templates are discussed in more detail in *4.2 Multi-level numbered clauses* and *3.2 Templates*, respectively.

4.2 Multi-level numbered clauses

4.2.1 What are multi-level numbered clauses?

Clauses and sub-clauses in legal documents are numbered according to different levels.

In the text on the right, the levels are:

1 (one digit)
1.1 (two digits)
    1.1.1 (three digits)
        1.1.1.1 (four digits)

1	**DEFINITIONS**
1.1	In this agreement the following meanings shall apply:
	1.1.1 Authorised Representative: in respect of
	1.1.1.1 The First Party: TRUSTEE GH
	1.1.1.2 The Second Party: TRUSTEE MN
	1.1.2 Equity: a deceased / permanently disabled Party's:
	1.1.2.1 shares in the Company including any
	1.1.2.2 claim against the Company
2	**OBLIGATION TO PURCHASE EQUITY OF SECOND PARTY**
2.1	The First Party shall be obliged to buy the Equity of the Second Party:
	2.1.1 for the purchase price; and
	2.1.2 on any further conditions herein pertained.
3	**PURCHASE PRICE**
3.1	The Purchase Price for the Equity is R
3.2	Upon the death or Permanent Disability of the First Party (the Affected Party herein), the Parties agree as follows:

4.2.2 Why use multi-level numbered clauses?

Benefit

- Word keeps track of the numbering levels and applies the same numbering system throughout the document. When adding and deleting clauses in the document, you won't have to manually renumber the clauses.
- Changes to the format of clauses and numbering levels can be done easily and implemented instantly.
- Other useful features of Word are available once a document is formatted using multi-level numbered clauses, such as inserting a table of contents, and creating Quick Parts and templates.

4.2.3 Understanding multi-level numbered clauses

The magic behind multi-level numbered clauses lies in Styles.

Different-level styles are required for multi-level numbered clauses. The different-level styles are created and saved in the **Styles** group under the *Home* tab.

> **Tip** A style is a group of formatting settings (i.e. font, font size, indent, case, numbering and spacing, etc.) saved together. When you apply a style to text, that text immediately takes on all of the formatting characteristics associated with that style.

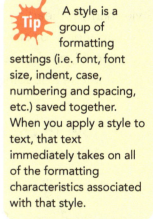

Each clause in the document is then linked to a different-level style according to its level of numbering.

Think of the word "Level" instead of "Heading" to make more sense of this.

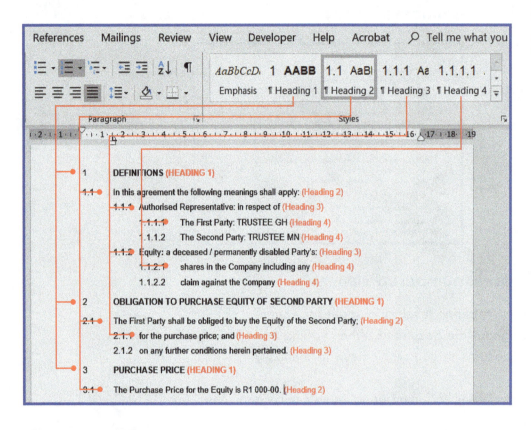

Styles named "heading" must be used to create multi-level numbered clauses. The numbering for all clauses with 1 digit (1, 2, 3, etc.) will always be named "Heading 1", all clauses with 2 digits will be "Heading 2", and all clauses with 3 digits will be "Heading 3", and so forth.

4.2.4 How to create styles for multi-level numbered clauses

In Step 1, you will learn to create text numbered in the different levels.

In Step 2, the different "heading" styles are loaded and updated in accordance with the different levels of numbering in the text.

Insight

Each clause in a document can be linked to a style according to its numbering level. Word keeps track of the numbering in the document and will know that all clauses linked to a specific heading style must be numbered according to the numbering level and the formatting settings saved to that style.

Step 1: Create text numbered in levels

Open the document you want to format with multi-level numbered clauses. At the top of page one of your document, type in the text shown below.

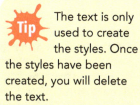

Tip The text is only used to create the styles. Once the styles have been created, you will delete the text.

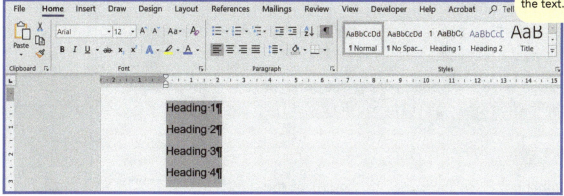

- Select all the text.
- Click the *Home* tab.
- Then click the *Multi-level List* button in the **Paragraph** group.
- Select the option in the drop-down list that shows multi-level numbered text.

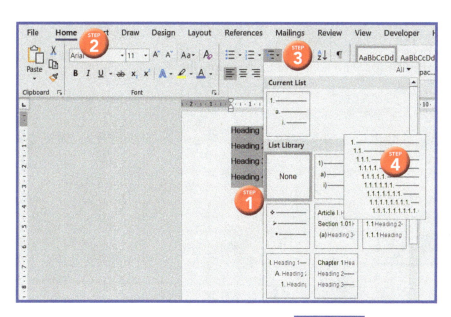

The text will now be numbered like this:

1. Heading 1
2. Heading 2
3. Heading 3
4. Heading 4

Tabs are used to create different numbered levels:

1. Heading 1
   1.1. Heading 2
      1.1.1. Heading 3
         1.1.1.1. Heading 4

1. Heading 1

The **1st level of numbering** is already numbered correctly (one digit).

1.1 Heading 2

2nd level of numbering: Place the cursor to the left of the "H" of the text **2. Heading 2**.

Click the Tab button on the keyboard **once**. The level of numbering will change from one digit (1.) to two digits (1.1.)

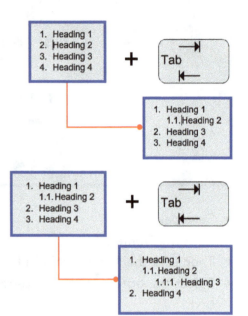

1.1.1 Heading 3

3rd level of numbering: Place the cursor to the left of the "H" of the text **2. Heading 3**.

Click the *Tab* button on the keyboard **twice**. The level of numbering will change from digit (2.) to three digits (1.1.1.).

1.1.1.1 Heading4

4th level of numbering: Place the cursor to the left of the "H" of the text **2. Heading 4**.

Click the Tab button on the keyboard **three times**. The level of numbering will change from digit (2.) to four digits (1.1.1.1.).

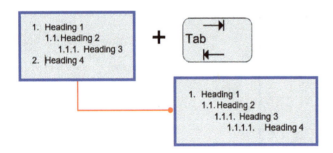

Step 2: Load the heading styles with the levels of numbering

Now that you have created numbered levels of text in your document, the next step is to link your numbered text to its corresponding "Heading"-style level in the **Styles** group. In this way, the formatting of the numbered text is loaded to the relevant style. You can then save the style for future use in your document.

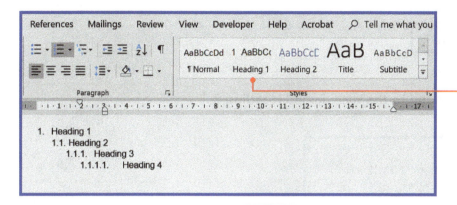

The Heading 1 style is in the **Styles** gallery but still has the default Word formats loaded. The Heading 1 style must be updated.

Changing the Heading 1 style

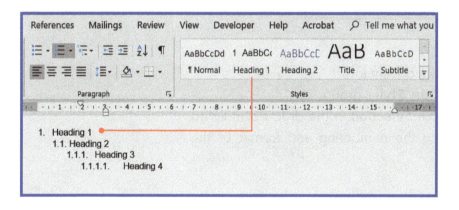

The formatting of the first level of numbered text (one digit) must be loaded to the style named Heading 1

To do this:

- Click on the text *1. Heading 1* in your document.
- Right-click on the *Heading 1* style in your *Styles* group.
- Click on *Update Heading 1 to match Selection* in the drop-down list to change the default Word formats to the numbering and format of the first level of numbered text.

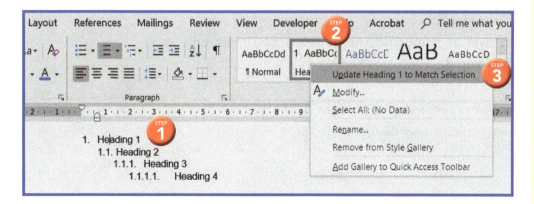

 Tip It is important to **right-click** on the **Heading 1** style in the **Styles** group. If you left-click, Word will use its own default formats saved under the Heading 1 style.

Note: As your cursor hovers over the **Heading 1** style, the formatting of the text in your document may "try" to change. This is Word attempting to revert to its default formats. Don't worry, your formatting will only change if you left-click the style.

If you accidently left-clicked, just click on the *Undo* button in the Quick Access Toolbar (top left corner of your window) and try again.

Changing the Heading 2 style

The formatting of the second level of
numbered text (two digits) must be loaded to the style named **Heading 2**.

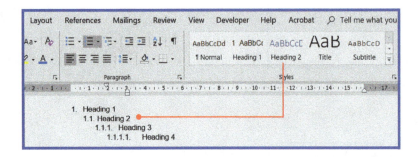

To do this:

- Click on the text **1.1. Heading 2** in the document.
- Right-click on the **Heading 2** style in the **Styles** group.
- Click on **Update Heading 2 to match Selection** in the drop-down list to change the default Word formats to the numbering and format of the second level of numbered text.

Changing the Heading 3 style

The formatting of the third level of numbered text (three digits) must be loaded to the style named **Heading 3.**

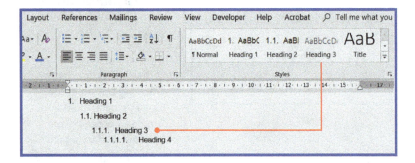

To do this:

- Click on the text *1.1.1. Heading 3* in the document.
- Right-click on the **Heading 3** style in the **Styles** group.
- Click on **Update Heading 3 to match Selection** in the drop-down list to change the default Word formats to the numbering and format of the third level of numbered text.

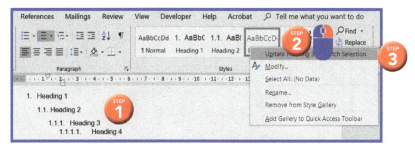

Changing the Heading 4 style

The formatting of the fourth level of numbered text (four digits) must be loaded to the style named **Heading 4.**

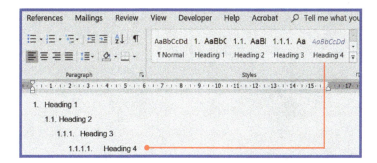

To do this:

- Click on the text *1.1.1.1. Heading 4* in the document.
- Right-click on the **Heading 4** style in the **Styles** group.
- Click on **Update Heading 4 to match Selection** in the drop-down list to change the default Word formats to the numbering and format of the fourth level of numbered text.

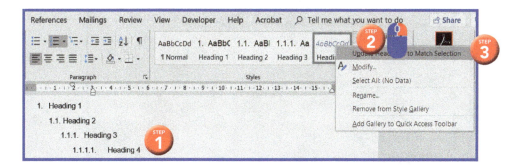

The Heading styles are now updated with the correct levels of numbering. The styles can be used to number other clauses in the document with corresponding levels of numbering.

 Word keeps track and will know that all clauses linked to a Heading style will have the formatting and level of numbering loaded for that style.

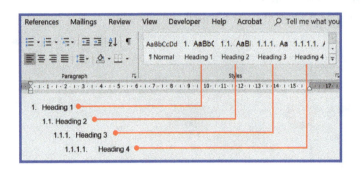

Once all the styles for multi-level numbered clauses have been loaded and updated, the initial Heading 1, Heading 2, Heading 3, and Heading 4 text typed in at the beginning of your document on page one (Step 1) can be deleted. The required styles are now part of the document.

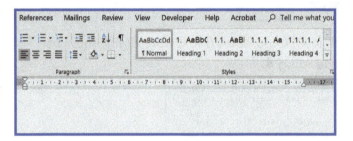

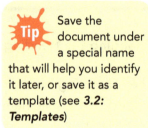 Save the document under a special name that will help you identify it later, or save it as a template (see *3.2: Templates*)

4.2.5 How to use the styles for multi-level numbered clauses

THE FUN STARTS HERE!

Link each clause in the document only once to its relevant Heading style.

Start typing your document. Place the cursor anywhere in the clause to apply your first level of numbering (one digit). Click on the **Heading 1** style. The text will be numbered accordingly.

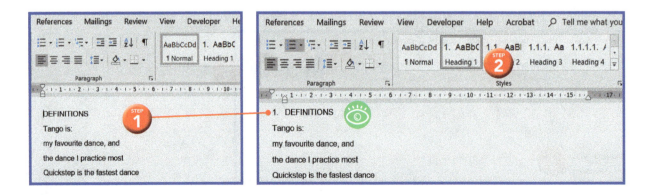

The same can be done for all the clauses that require the second level of numbering (two digits). Place the cursor anywhere in the clause and click on the *Heading 2* style. The text will be numbered accordingly.

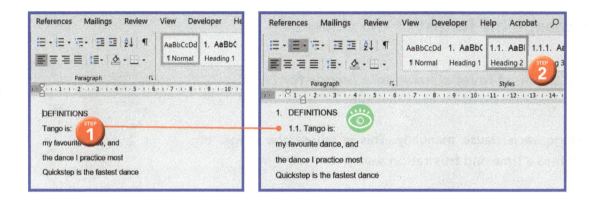

Do the same with all the clauses for which you want the third level of numbering (three digits). Click on the *Heading 3* style.

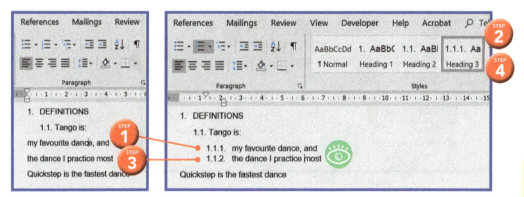

The same style is linked to all the clauses with the same level of numbering.

Here the second level of numbering (two digits) is again used. Click on the *Heading 2* Style.

> **Tip** You only need to **left-click** on the applicable style since the formatting and level of numbering have already been updated in the style (Step 1).

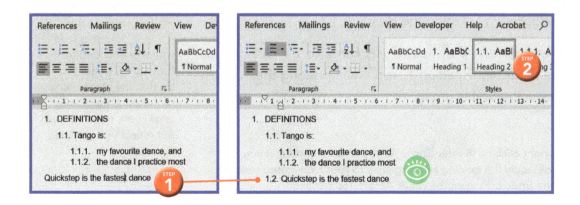

Word keeps track of the sequence and level of numbering throughout the document and will automatically adjust the numbering as you add and delete clauses.

4.2.6 How to change the format of the clauses

I want all the first-level clauses in a larger font!

Don't change each clause manually. This is where the magic of styles becomes a time and frustration saver!

First, select the text you want to change and adjust the formatting as required. For instance, to change the formatting to Arial, 16, bold and uppercase, click on the buttons indicated below.

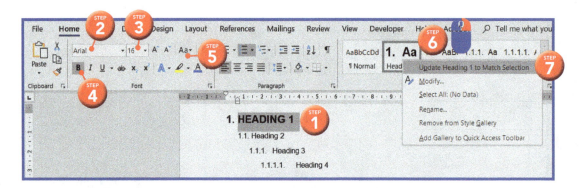

Now, the amended formatting settings must be loaded to the corresponding Heading style and updated. **Right-click** on *Heading 1*, then click on *Update Heading 1 to match Selection* in the drop-down list. The Heading 1 style is now updated.

The amended formatting is automatically and instantly applied to all clauses in the document linked to the Heading 1 style.

The formatting for the other levels of numbering can also be changed by formatting their text as we did for Heading 1, and then updating their corresponding Heading styles in the **Styles** group.

Tip Remember to update the Heading style with the amended text formatting. If you don't do this, the other clauses of the same numbering level in the document will not reflect your updated formatting.

Tip It's important to **right-click** on the Heading style you want to update. If you left-click, Word will apply the existing Heading style to your highlighted text. To undo this, click the *Undo* button on the Quick Access Toolbar and try again.

Benefit

Re-using the multi-level numbered text and styles

Once all the Heading styles have been created:

- The multi-level numbered and formatted document can be saved as a **template** (see *3.2 Templates*); or
- The multi-level numbered and formatted text can be saved as a **Quick Part** (see *8.3 Quick Parts*); or
- The multi-level numbered and formatted text can be copied and pasted into another document. The multi-level numbered and formatted styles are part of the text and will be inserted with the text in the other document.
- The steps and commands to create the multi-level numbered and formatted text and heading styles can be saved as a **macro** (See 8.10: Macros).

4.3 Table of Contents

Surprise your clients and colleagues with a neat and correct Table of Contents for their ease of reference.

TABLE OF CONTENTS	
1 INTRODUCTION	1
2 DEFINITION OF QUOTABLE QUOTATIONS	1
3 QUESTION AND ANSWER SAYINGS	1
4 FUNNY QUOTES BY FAMOUS PERSONS	1
5 TRUE QUOTES	1
6 ITALIAN PROVERBS	1

Frustration

I don't have time to do a Table of Contents!

Don't waste precious time and energy manually keeping track of clauses and page numbers in your document. Word can keep track of them all and compile a Table of Contents instantly, complete with correct page numbers. Better still, when clauses are added, deleted, edited, or change their position within the document, Word can update the Table of Contents to reflect all the changes.

! **Word will not be able to compile a Table of Contents if Heading styles are not used in the document.** This is because Heading styles convey the hierarchy of information in the document – they tell Word what's important to include, and the order of importance of that information. A Table of Contents uses this information to create a quick navigational reference to important topics in the document. It cannot do this if you haven't used any Heading styles, or if you have used Heading styles randomly and without clear purpose. Your resulting Table of Contents will end up being a mess and won't be at all useful.

4.3.1 Understanding the Table of Contents

The magic behind a Table of Contents is Heading styles.

Heading styles can be found in the **Styles** group under the *Home* tab.

> **Tip**
> A **Heading style** is a group of formatting settings (i.e. font, font size, indent, case, level of numbering, and spacing, etc.) saved together to be used more than once. When you apply a style to text, that text immediately takes on all of the formatting characteristics associated with that style.

To find out how to create and use **Heading styles** and **Multi-level numbered clauses** in your document, refer to *4.1 Styles* and *4.2 Multi-level numbered clauses*.

Insight Each clause in the document must be allocated a Heading style according to its level of numbering. Word keeps track of the clauses and clause numbers in the document. A Table of Contents can be inserted by indicating to Word which of the Heading levels must be included in the Table of Contents.

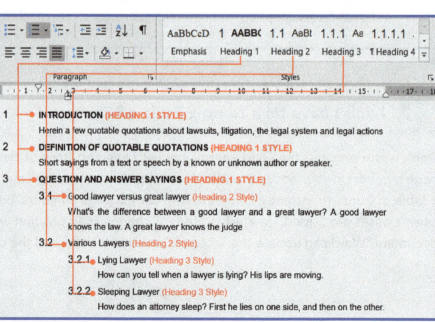

Allocating heading levels to your clauses

Clauses with 1 digit (i.e. 1, 2, 3, etc.) must be allocated to the Style named "Heading 1"; all clauses with 2 digits (i.e. 1.1, 1.2, etc.) must be allocated to the Style named "Heading 2"; and all clauses with 3 digits (i.e. 1.1.1, 1.1.2, etc.) must be allocated to the Style named "Heading 3", and so forth.

The **Automatic Table of Contents** includes Headings down to three levels. This means that it will contain all "Heading 1" to "Heading 3" clauses. The sub-clauses (clauses with 2 or 3 digits) in your document are therefore included by default.

You can customise the Table of Contents to include only the clauses allocated to "Heading 1" (clauses with 1 digit) or the clauses allocated to "Heading 1" and "Heading 2" (clauses with 2 digits).

4.3.2 How to insert a Table of Contents

Step 1: Create Heading styles.

Step 2: Allocate a Heading style to each clause in the document in accordance with its level of numbering.

(Steps 1 and 2 are discussed in detail in *4.2. Multi-level numbered clauses*.)

Step 3: Insert the Table of Contents, which is quite easy once Step 1 and Step 2 have been completed.
- Place the cursor at the beginning of the document where you want the Table of Contents inserted.
- Click on References > *Table of Contents* .
- Click on either *Automatic Table 1* or *Automatic Table 2* (it is only the heading that is different, that is: "Contents" and "Table of Contents". Both include text formatted with the Heading 1 to Heading 3 styles).
- Word will compile and insert a Table of Contents instantly.

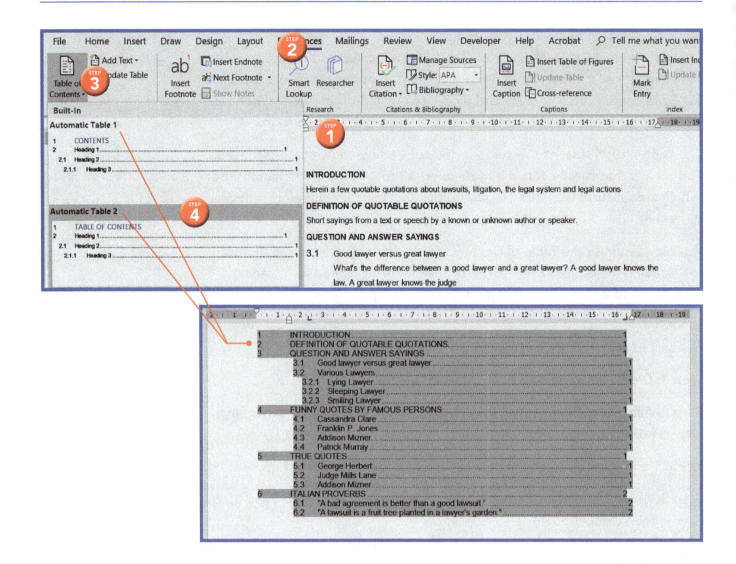

If **Automatic Table 1** or **Automatic Table 2** are clicked, **three levels of numbering** will be included in the Table of Contents automatically. To include fewer levels of numbering, select "Custom Table of Contents" (see below).

To include only the first level of numbering:

- Click on the **References** tab.
- Click on **Table of Contents**, and then on **Custom Table of Contents**. A new screen will appear.
- At **Show Levels**, change the level to 1.
- Click **OK**.

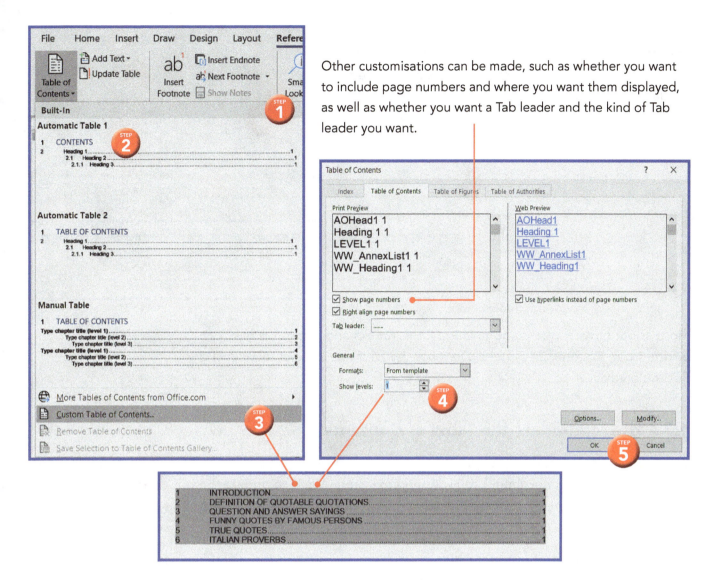

Other customisations can be made, such as whether you want to include page numbers and where you want them displayed, as well as whether you want a Tab leader and the kind of Tab leader you want.

4.3.3 How to set the Table of Contents on its own page

To separate the Table of Contents from the rest of the document simply insert a **Page Break** or **Section Break** just below the Table of Contents.

Insert a Page Break:
- Place your cursor underneath the Table of Contents, or after the last letter of the last line of text
- Click *Insert* > *Pages* > *Page Break*

Insert a Section Break:
- Place your cursor underneath the Table of Contents, or after the last letter of the last line of text.
- Click the *Layout* tab, and then click on *Breaks.*
- Under *Section Breaks* select *Next Page*.

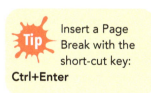

Tip Insert a Page Break with the short-cut key: **Ctrl+Enter**

The text in the rest of the document will start on the next page. The document is divided into two sections. Each section can have different formats, page numbers, headers, and footers.

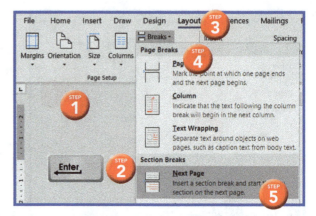

More about how to create and manage Page Breaks and Section Breaks can be found in *Chapter 2: General Drafting, 2.11.1 Page Breaks*, and *2.11.2 Section breaks.*

4.3.4 How to update the Table of Contents

Word does not automatically update the Table of Contents as you add or delete clauses in your document. You will need to instruct Word to update the Table of Contents when you have finished editing your text and have applied your Heading styles to new clauses.

To update your Table of Contents:

- **Right-click** anywhere in the Table of Contents.
- Click on *Update Field* and then select *Update entire table*.
- Click *OK*.

> **Tip** If you add a new clause that must also be listed in the Table of Contents, remember to allocate a Heading style to the clause otherwise Word will not know that the clause should be included.

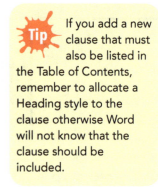

 Insight The Table of Contents can also be updated by clicking on the *References* tab and then *Update Table*.

4.3.5 How to jump to pages and headings from the Table of Contents

Position the cursor on a heading in the Table of Contents and hold down the **Ctrl** key on the Keyboard – the cursor will change to a hand symbol – then **Left-click** on the heading to jump to that heading in the document.

4.3.6 Troubleshooting

Frustration

I forgot to update!

The client received a document with errors in the Table of Contents!

While Word will not remind you to update a Table of Contents when you close the document or email it to a client or colleague, fortunately you can set it to always update a Table of Contents **before printing** your document.

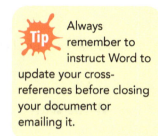
Tip Always remember to instruct Word to update your cross-references before closing your document or emailing it.

Here's how:
- Click on the **File** tab.
- Click on **Options**, and then on **Display**.
- Under **Printing options**, select **Update Fields before printing**.
- Word will prompt you to update your Table of Contents before printing the document. Click on **Update entire table**.
- Click **OK**.

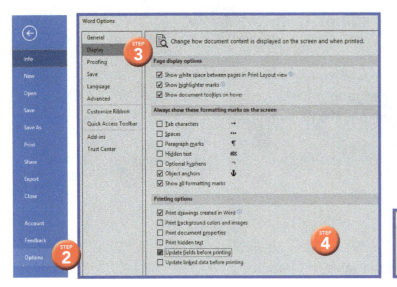

You only need to do this once, since this is a setting in the backstage of Word and will remain set until changed.

 Frustration

What weird codes are these?!

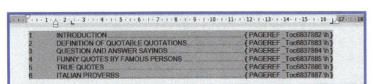

To see the page numbers, press

Alt + **F9**

Sometimes your Table of Contents may display field codes instead of page numbers. To solve this problem permanently, make sure that the backstage of Word is set to show the values and not the field codes.

Here's how:

- Click on the **File** tab.
- Click on **Options**, and then on **Advanced**.
- Scroll down to **Show document content**. The block next to **Show field codes instead or their values** should NOT be ticked.
- Click **OK**.

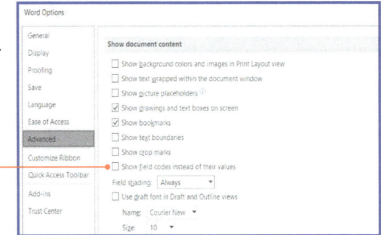

Frustration

The Table of Contents is not updating!

The Table of Contents does not automatically update. You need to instruct Word to update it.

To update your Table of Contents:
- **Right-click** anywhere in the Table of Contents.
- Select *Update Field*.
- Select *Update entire table*.
- Click *OK.*

Frustration

I'm getting error messages in my Table of Contents!

Use the Find and Replace function to locate update errors

Once you have updated your Table of Contents, search for the word "Error" in the document to easily find the instances where the Table of Contents did not update correctly.

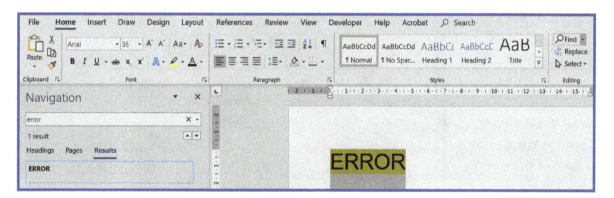

Check that the clauses in the document causing the error messages have been allocated the correct Heading Style. (Refer to *10.1 Find and Replace* for how to find a word in a document.)

4.4 Cross-references

A **cross-reference** is when reference is made in one clause to another clause in the same document.

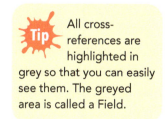
Tip All cross-references are highlighted in grey so that you can easily see them. The greyed area is called a Field.

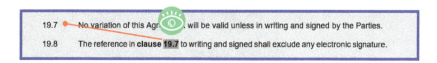

I hate cross-references!

Frustration

| 19.7 | No variation of this Agreement will be valid unless in writing and signed by the Parties. |
| 19.8 | The reference in **clause** Error! Reference source not found. to writing and signed shall exclude any electronic signature. |

19.7	No reference is made to writing in this clause. A clause was added!! What a disaster!!.
19.8	No variation of this Agreement will be valid unless in writing and signed by the Parties
19.9	The reference in **clause 19.7** to writing and signed shall exclude any electronic signature.

Don't waste time and energy manually keeping track of the clauses referred to. Word can keep track of all references as clauses are added and deleted in the document.

4.4.1 How to insert a cross-reference

- Place the cursor where the cross-reference must be inserted.
- Click on the **References** tab.
- Look for the **Captions** group, then click on **Cross-reference**.

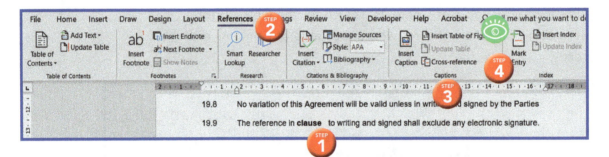

On the left side of the dialogue box under **Reference type**, click on **Numbered item** (if this option is not visible, click the drop-down arrow to display more list options).

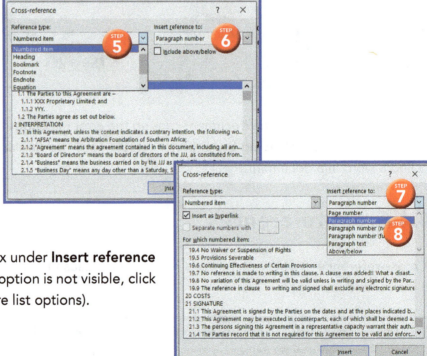

On the right side of the dialogue box under **Insert reference to** select **Paragraph number** (if this option is not visible, click the drop-down arrow to display more list options).

All the numbered clauses in the document are listed under **For which numbered item**. Scroll down and click on the numbered clause you want to refer to. Click *Insert*.

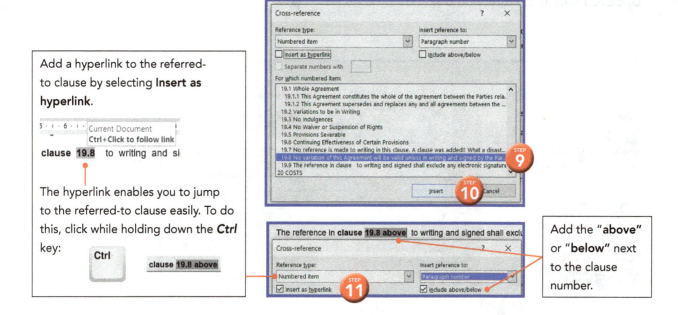

Add a hyperlink to the referred-to clause by selecting **Insert as hyperlink**.

The hyperlink enables you to jump to the referred-to clause easily. To do this, click while holding down the *Ctrl* key:

Add the "**above**" or "**below**" next to the clause number.

4.4.2 How to update cross-references

Although Word keeps track of the cross-references between clauses, changes in the cross-references are not automatically updated. You still need to instruct Word to update the cross-reference numbers. When you do this, the cross-reference numbers in the text will update automatically and instantly.

To update only one cross-reference:
- **Right-click** on the cross-reference.
- Click on *Update Field*.

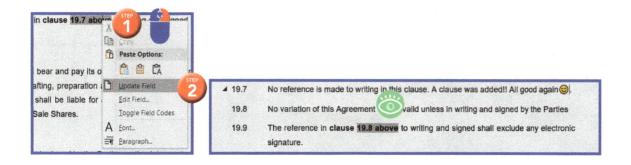

To update all the cross-references in the document simultaneously:

- Select all the text in the document.
- Right-click anywhere in the document.
- Click **Update Field** in the dialogue box.

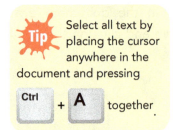

Tip Select all text by placing the cursor anywhere in the document and pressing

Ctrl + **A** together.

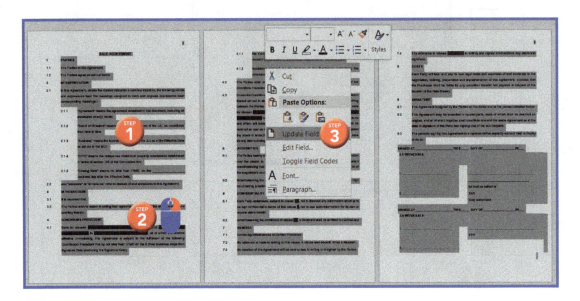

Frustration

I'm getting cross-referencing update errors!

Using the Find and Replace function to locate update errors

Once you have updated your cross-references, search for the word "Error" in the document to easily find the instances where the cross-references did not update correctly. Check that the reference to the referred to clause is correct. It often happens that the referred-to clause has been deleted or replaced.

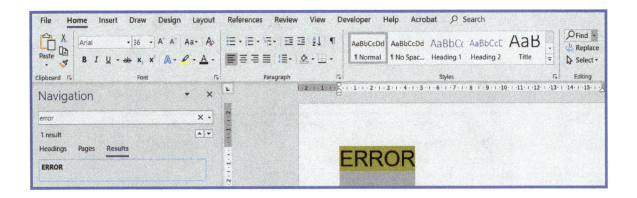

(Refer to *10.1 Find and Replace* for how to find a word in a document.)

Frustration

I want to update the Table of Contents AND Cross-References together!

Fortunately, the Table of Contents and Cross-References can be updated **simultanously** by selecting all the text in the document.

- Press `Ctrl` + `A` to select all text instantly.

- **Right-click** anywhere in the selected text and click on **Update Field** > **Update entire table** > **OK.**

4.4.3 Troubleshooting

Frustration

What weird code is this?!

The field code instead of the referred to clause number are displayed.
- **Right-click** on the weird code.
- Click on **Toggle Field Codes** to see the referred to clause number.

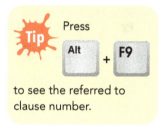

Tip — Press `Alt` + `F9` to see the referred to clause number.

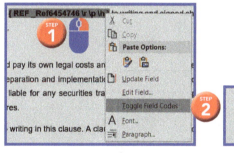

See the permanent solution for this problem in the Table of Contents section, *4.3.6 Troubleshooting*.

Frustration

The clause numbers in my cross-references are not updating!

Cross-references are not automatically updated. You need to instruct Word to update them. Find out how in *4.4.2 How to update cross-references*.

Also note that the cross-reference will be shaded in grey to indicate that it is a Field that can be updated. (If the area is not highlighted, no cross-reference has been inserted and the numbers were merely typed in or the backstage of **Word** is set not to shade the fields.)

Make sure that fields are always shaded so that you are warned of their existance and can prevent errors.

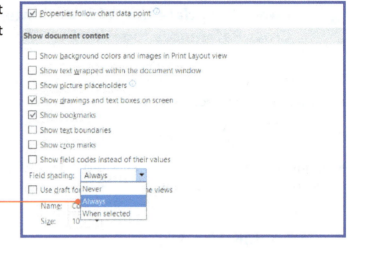

Here's how:

- Click on the *File* tab.
- Click on *Options*, and then on *Advanced*.
- Scroll down to *Show document content*.
- The option *Always* should be selected.
- Click *OK*.

Frustration

I forgot to update!

The client received a document with cross-referencing errors in it!

4.1   Save for clauses Error! Reference source not found. to 4 and Error! Reference source not found. to Error! Reference source not found., all of which will become

Tip Always remember to instruct Word to update your cross-references before closing your document or emailing it.

While Word will not remind you to update cross-references when you close the document or email it to a client or colleague, fortunately you can set it to always update cross-references **before printing** your document.

Here's how:

- Click on the *File* tab.
- Click on *Options*, and then on *Display*.
- Select *Update Fields before printing*.

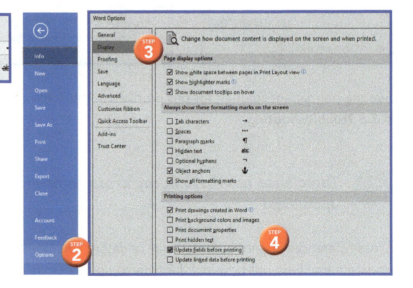

You only need to do this once, since this is a setting in the backstage of Word and will remain set until changed.

Tip Once your cross-references have been updated, search for the word "Error" to easily find instances in the document where the cross-references did not update correctly (refer to *10.1 Find and Replace* for how to Find a word in a document).

Drafting is so much easier when you can view your documents properly. In this chapter we will look at the different viewing options available to help you work more efficiently and save time.

5.1 View two documents side by side

Looking at one document, while working on another, is very convenient. It is also useful when you want to copy text from the one and paste it into the other.

There are two ways to go about this. You can choose the method that is the easiest and most comfortable for you. The first option requires a skilled "click, drag and release" action to set two documents side by side in your window, while the second works using the click of a few buttons.

5.1.1 Option 1: "Click, drag and release"

The first document:

- Open the first document and place the cursor over the document name at the top of the screen.
- Hold the left-click button down and drag the entire document to the left until the cursor touches the left side of the screen and then release.
- Word will automatically adjust the document to fill only the left half of the screen.

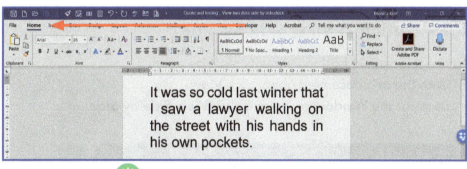

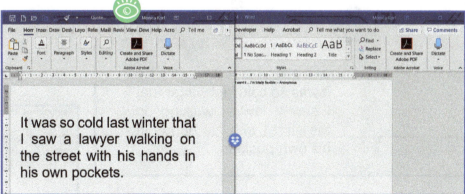

The second document:

- Open the second document and place the cursor over the document name at the top of the screen.
- Hold the left-click button down and drag the entire document to the right until the cursor touches the right side of the screen and then release.
- Word will automatically adjust the document to fill only the right half of the screen.

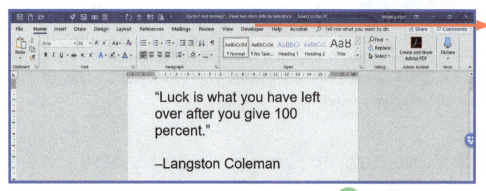

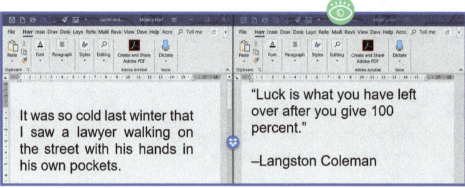

5.1.2 Option 2: View Side by Side

To use this option, both documents must be open.
- With the one document open, click **View**.
- Look for the **Window** group and click **View Side by Side**.

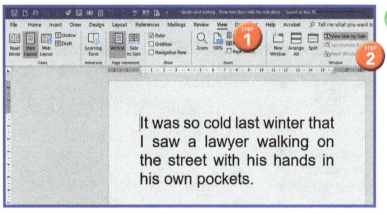

- A list of all the documents currently open will pop up.
- Select the name of the other document you want to view simultaneously, then click **OK**.

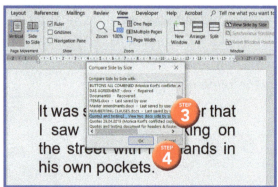

Either method will produce the same result: Both documents can be viewed side by side.

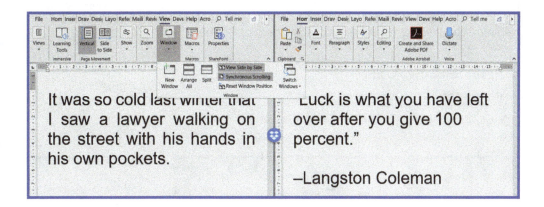

5.1.3 Synchronous Scrolling of both documents

When both documents are open in Side by Side View, Word allows you to scroll through them simultaneously so that you can compare their contents. This option is called **Synchronous Scrolling**.

Activate Synchronous Scrolling:

- Click **View** > **Window** > **Synchronous Scrolling**.

You will now be able to scroll up and down both documents simultaneously.

De-activate Synchronous Scrolling:

Deselect **Synchronous Scrolling** to scroll the two windows separately again.

- Go to **View** > **Window** > **Synchronous Scrolling**.

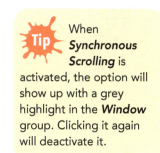

Tip When **Synchronous Scrolling** is activated, the option will show up with a grey highlight in the **Window** group. Clicking it again will deactivate it.

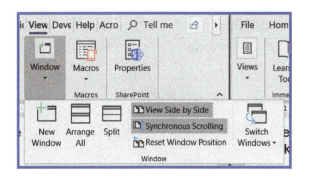

5.1.4 Return to a single document view

To exit the side by side viewing mode and return to a single document view, you can do any one of the following:

1. Close one window to get back to viewing the other document in only one window again
2. Click **View** > **Window** > **Reset Window Position**
3. Click on □ in the top right corner of the document screen.

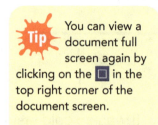

Tip You can view a document full screen again by clicking on the □ in the top right corner of the document screen.

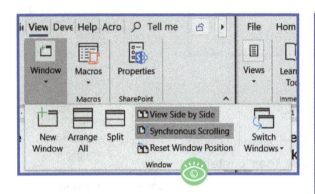

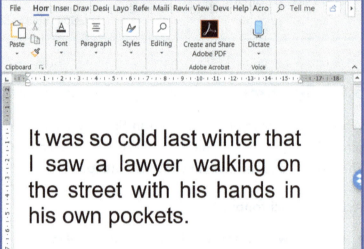

5.2 View one document in multiple windows

Draft and review a document efficiently by seeing different parts of the document simultaneously in multiple windows.

You will be able to view, zoom and scroll separately in each window. Changes made in the one window will simultaneously appear in the other windows because it is still one document.

The same document can be viewed in two horizontal windows, one above the other (called a Split view), it can be viewed side by side, or it can be open in two or more separate windows that can be freely moved around.

5.2.1 View one document using the Split option

With the Split option, only one Ribbon will appear at the top of the screen and you will not be able to synchronise scrolling.

To split a document and view the two parts simultaneously:
- Click on the *View* tab.
- Look for the **Window** group and click on *Split*.

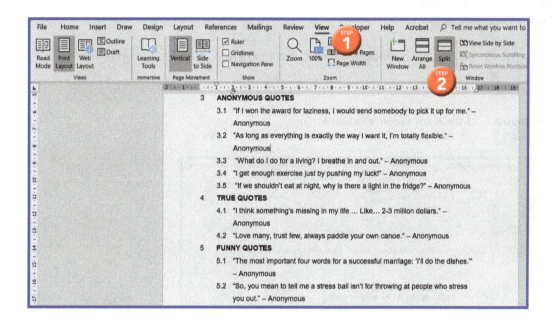

You will be able to scroll up and down in each document separately.

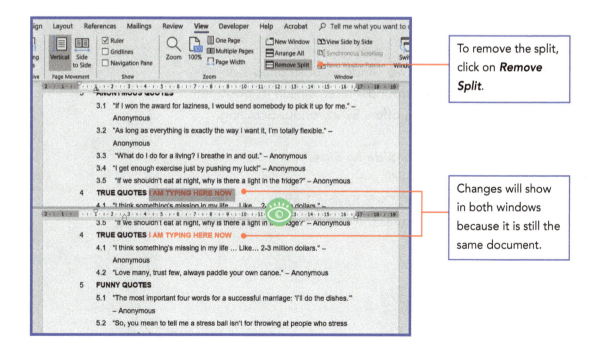

To remove the split, click on *Remove Split*.

Changes will show in both windows because it is still the same document.

5.2.2 View one document in separate windows or side by side

View in separate windows

When you view one document in two separate windows, the same document will open up in a new window in front of the first window. The name of the document in the new window contains a 2, indicating this is window 2. (Note that a second version of the document was not created. The 2 only indicates the second window of the same document.)

With this option, you can move the second window around and position it where you want it.

- Click on the *View* tab.
- Look for the **Window** group and click on *New Window*.

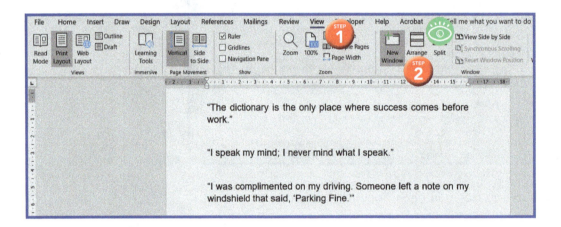

View Side by Side

With this option, one document is open in two windows positioned side by side. The second document does not move around – it remains in its position to the right of the first document. This option offers Synchronous Scrolling.

- With the one document open, click *View*.
- Look for the **Window** group and click *View Side by Side*.
- A list of all the documents currently open will pop up.
- Select the document with the same name (it will have a 1 after the name, which indicates that it is the same document as the one in the first window).
- Click *OK*.

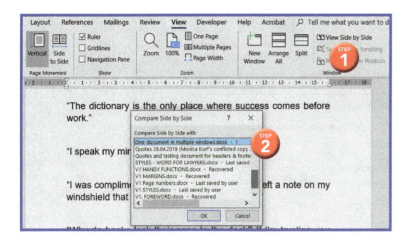

5.2.3 Synchronous scrolling

To use Synchronous Scrolling, you must be using the **View Side by Side** option (see *5.2.2 View one document in separate windows or side by side*).

Activate Synchronous Scrolling:

Click **View** > **Window** > **Synchronous Scrolling**

You will now be able to scroll up and down both windows simultaneously. Changes will show in both windows, because it is still the same document.

De-activate Synchronous Scrolling:

Deselect **Synchronous Scrolling** to scroll the two windows separately again.

• Go to **View** > **Window** > **Synchronous Scrolling**.

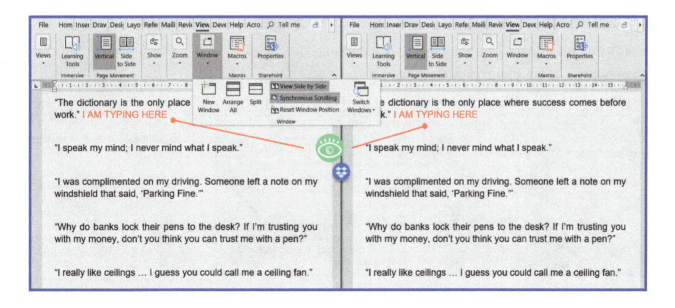

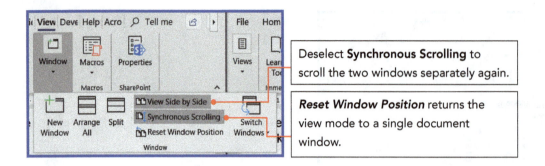

Deselect **Synchronous Scrolling** to scroll the two windows separately again.

Reset Window Position returns the view mode to a single document window.

5.2.4 Return to a single document view

To view the document in a single window again:

• Close the second window or click *View* > *Window* > *Reset Window Position*.

5.3 Other handy page view controls

Multiple pages: Open the document and click on the *View* tab. Look for the **Zoom** group and click *Multiple Pages*.

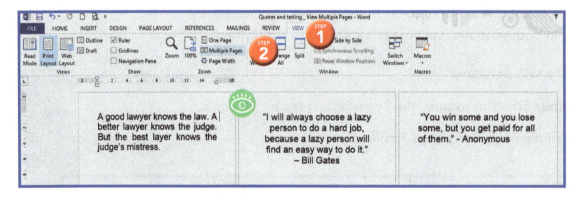

One page: To go back to viewing only one page at a time, click on the *View* tab, then under the **Zoom** group click *One Page*.

One page at 100% zoom: To view one page at 100% zoom level, click on the *View* tab, go to the **Zoom** group, and click on the button.

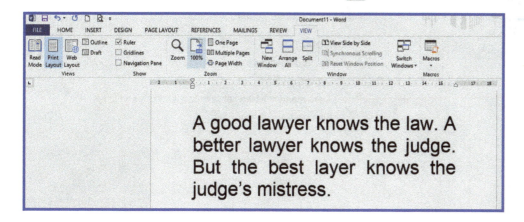

5.4 The Navigation Pane

The Navigation Pane is like a map of the document. The headings are listed like a Table of Contents, making it easy for you to see the structure of the document and browse through the clauses.

- Click on the *View* tab.
- Under the **Show** group, click on *Navigation Pane*.

> **Tip** Use the Navigation Pane to reorganise the document. Grab a heading and drag it up or down to reorder your text.

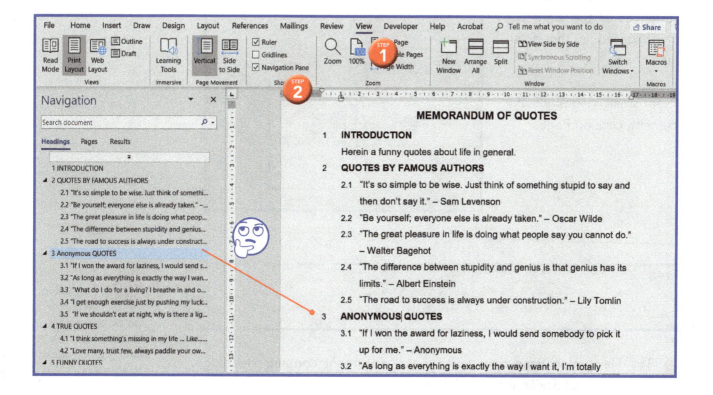

- Click on a heading to be taken to that part of the document.
- The part of the document that you are currently in will show up highlighted in the Navigation Pane.

Benefit

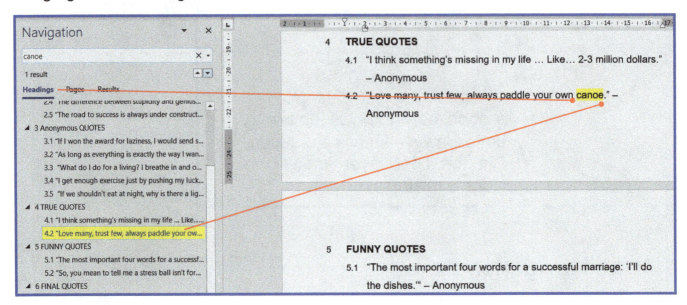

Use the **Search** function to search for a word or text in the document. Type in the word and click on **Results**. All occurrences of the word will be highlighted in the document.

To see small pages of the document, click on Pages.

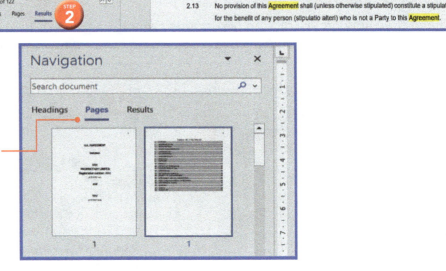

The Navigation Pane only works if the document contains Heading styles (see *4.1 Styles* and *4.2 Multi-level numbered clauses*).

Tip
The Navigation Pane can also be opened by clicking **Find** in the **Editing** group under the **Home** tab

5.4.1 Search for a word or text

Use the Search function to search for a word or text in your document.

- In the Navigation Pane, type in the word you want to search for.
- Click the ENTER key on your keyboard, then click on **Results**.
- All occurances of the word searched for will he highlighted in the body of the document.

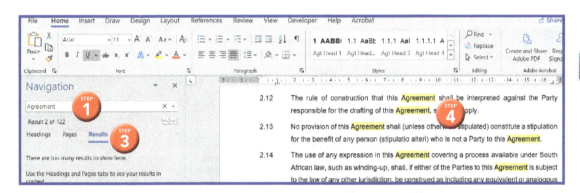

5.5 Outline view

Sometimes you may want to grasp the structure and contents of a large document by seeing all of the headings. This is where **Outline** view comes in handy.

To access it click **View** > **Outline**.

The view of the document will change to show only the headings.

Expanding and collapsing
Click on the plus or minus symbols next to any heading listed in outline view to see more or fewer headings and text.

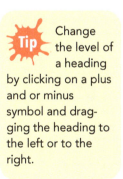
Tip Change the level of a heading by clicking on a plus and or minus symbol and dragging the heading to the left or to the right.

Select **Print Layout** to close Outline view.

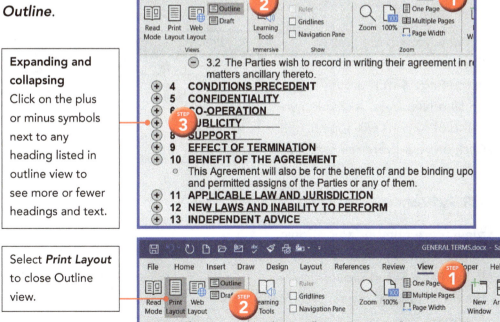

Outline view only works if the documents has heading styles (see *4.1 Styles* and *4.2 Multi-level numbered clauses*).

Legal practitioners need to be able to review legal documents efficiently because this is what their work mainly consists of. Reviewing your own work, and that of a client or colleague, will be easier if you know what options are available in Word, and how to use them.

6.1 Numbering lines

Frustration

The fifth word in the tenth line from the end of the paragraph is wrong!

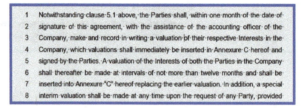

It's quicker and easier to refer to a numbered line when documents are discussed.

Word numbers lines in the left margin of the document.

Benefit

When referring to a particular word in a line when discussing the document with someone else, the task will be much easier if each printed copy included line numbers to which the other person could refer.

Tip You can choose to number only part of a document, and you can also set how far from the text the numbering must be.

This is how you do it:
- Click on the **Layout** tab.
- In the **Page Setup** group, click on **Line Numbers**. A drop-down menu of options will appear. Click on your preferred option.

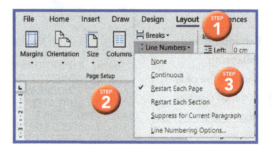

6.1.1 Advanced options

To view more numbering options:
- Click on the **Layout** tab.
- In the **Page Setup** group, click on the drop-down arrow next to **Line Numbers**.
- Select **Line Numbering Options**.

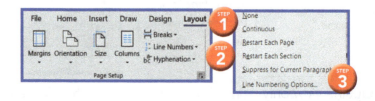

A dialogue box with options will open.

- Under the **Layout** tab, click on the **Line Numbers** button.
- Select **Add line numbering** and set your other options.
- Click **OK**.

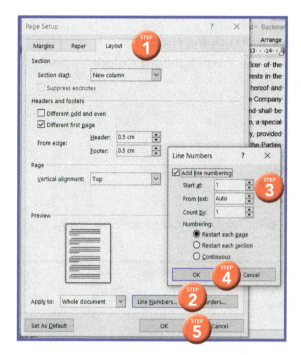

Tip When the document is printed, the numbered lines will also print. To print the document without the numbered lines, line numbers must be turned off.

Turn off line numbering:

Select **Layout > Line Numbers > None**.

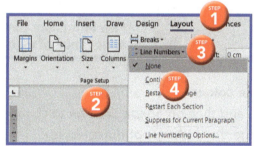

6.2 Highlight text

Perhaps the easiest way to review a document is by using the highlight functions in Word. For this you will use the **Text Highlight Colour** button 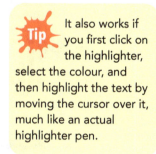.

To highlight the text:
- Select the text you want to highlight and click the **Home** tab.
- In the **Font** group, click the **Text Highlight Colour** button.
- Click on any colour in the gallery to apply the colour.

Tip It also works if you first click on the highlighter, select the colour, and then highlight the text by moving the cursor over it, much like an actual highlighter pen.

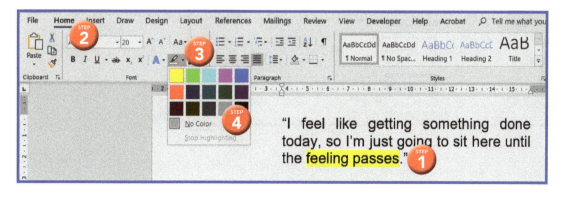

To remove the highlight:
- Select the highlighted text and click the *Home* tab.
- Under the *Font* group, click the *Text Highlight Colour* button.
- Click *No Color* in the gallery.

Tip It also works if you first click on the highlighter, select the colour, and then highlight the text by moving the cursor over it, much like an actual highlighter pen.

6.2.1 Freeform scribble

Scribble directly in a document.
- Click on *Insert* > *Shapes* > ⟨scribble icon⟩.

The cursor will change to a "plus" sign for you to scribble away.

Change the weight and line colour
- Click on the *Format* tab, and then on *Shape Outline* to change the colour.
- Click on *Weight* to change the thickness of the scribbles.

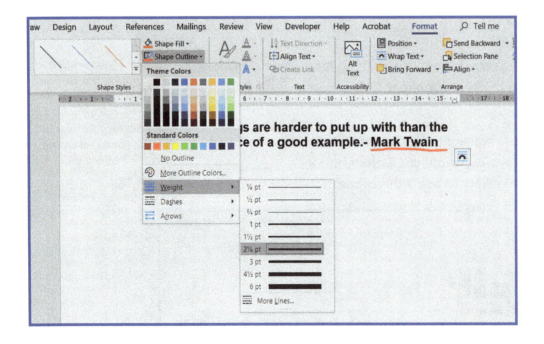

6.2.2 Draw highlighter

Write, mark, or draw on the text using a digital highlighter.

Activate the highlighter: Click on *Draw*, then click a writing instrument to enable the highlighter. The cursor will be replaced by a small "dot" (the point of the writing instrument) to use on the text.

Draw with Touch will be shaded when the highlighter is active.

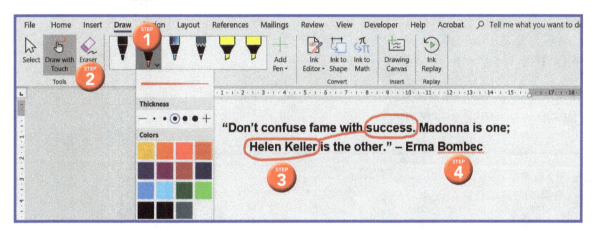

Deactivate the highlighter: Click on *Draw with Touch* again so that it's no longer shaded.

Click on *Eraser* to erase markings.

I don't see Draw *in the ribbon!*

Frustration

See *1.2 Tabs* for how to customise the Ribbon to include a tab. Since this is the only time an option on the *Draw* tab is likely to be used by Legal Practitioners, it is probably not worth the trouble. Rather use one of the other options above.

6.3 Comments

Comments are a useful tool for reviewing documents and are normally used where a matter requires further discussion. The old way of reviewing documents by printing them and writing comments on the pages with a red pen is inefficient and impractical.

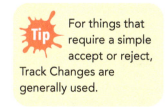

Tip For things that require a simple accept or reject, Track Changes are generally used.

6.3.1 How are comments shown in Word?

By default, Word shows comments in boxes in a panel on the right side of the text. A dotted line indicates to which part of the text the comment applies.

> "My grandfather once told me that there were two kinds of people: those who do the work and those who take the credit. He told me to try to be in the first group; there was much less competition." –
>
> **Indira Gandhi**
>
> **A** **Author**
> This refers to the people doing the work

6.3.2 Where is the Comments function?

Anything to do with making, viewing, and deleting comments can be found in the **Comments** group under the *Review* tab.

6.3.3 How to add a comment

- Place the cursor in the text where the comment has relevance.
- Click *Review* and look for the **Comments** group.
- Now click on *New Comment*. A comment box will open on the right side of the document, type your comment in the box.

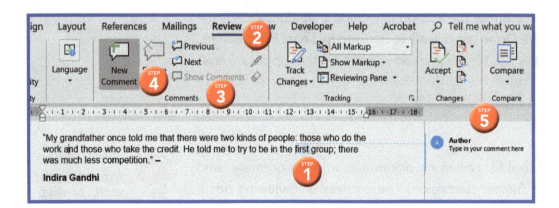

- When done, close the comment box by pressing the *Esc* key on the keyboard, or by clicking anywhere outside the comment box in the body of the text.

6.3.4 How to reply to a comment

- Hover the cursor over the comment box, then click on **Reply** 💬 Reply . Type in your reply.

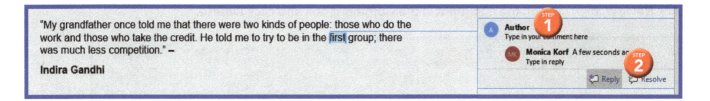

- When done, close the comment box by pressing the **Esc** key on the keyboard, or by clicking anywhere outside the comment box in the body of the text.

6.3.5 How to mark a comment as resolved

- Hover the cursor over the comment box, then click on **Resolve** 💬 Resolve (in Word 2013, right-click on the comment and click on **Mark Comment Done**)

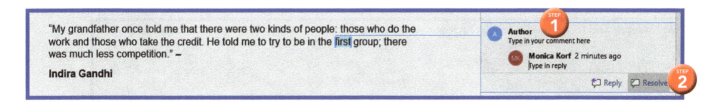

The comment box will be greyed out, but not deleted. The comment box can be reopened or replied in (even without reopening it).

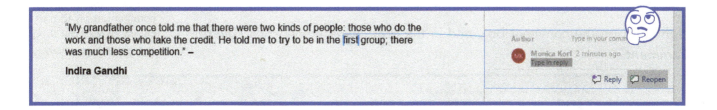

6.3.6 How to delete a comment

Word offers two ways of deleting a comment.

Option 1:

Click *Review*, then click on the comment in the Comment box and click *Delete*.

You can also click on the drop-down arrow under 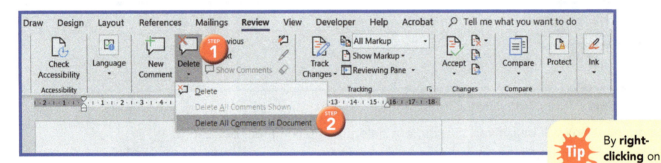 and choose *Delete* to delete one comment or *Delete All Comments in Document*.

Option 2:

Right-click on the comment box, and in the drop-down menu, click *Delete Comment.*

> **Tip** By **right-clicking** on the comment you can delete the comment, reply to the comment, or mark the comment as resolved.

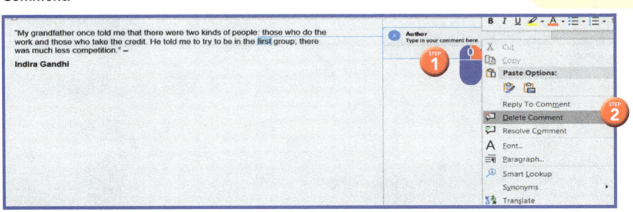

I don't want everybody to know I made the comments!

Frustration

The Author can be changed in the backstage settings of Word.

- Click on the **File** tab.
- Click on **Options** and then on **General**.
- Under **Personalise your copy of Microsoft Office** change the **User name** or leave it blank.

6.3.7 How to view comments

I can't see the comments!

Frustration

Tip The Author must be changed before the comments are made in the document.

To see all comments, click **Review** and in the **Tracking** group, select **All Markup**.

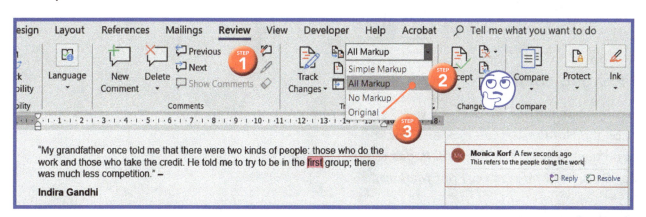

If **Simple Markup** is selected, only a comment symbol ☐ will show on the right side of the document to indicate that there is a comment. If you hover over the ☐, the related text will be highlighted. Click on the comment symbol to see the comment in the comments box.

If one of these options are selected: **Original** **No Markup**, nothing will be shown in the document to indicate that there is a comment.

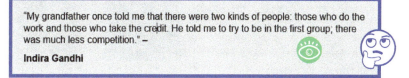

6.3.8 Can I prevent someone from reading the comments by restricting editing?

X NO. Even if editing is restricted, the ☐ can still be seen when **Simple Markup** is selected. Anybody can click on the ☐ to read the comment.

If **Original** or **No Markup** are selected, the viewer will not be able to see that there is a comment. Although the **New Comment** function is greyed out, the comment can still be read by clicking on **Previous**, **Next** or **All Markup**.

The function to inspect the document for comments will however not be available if editing is restricted.

To learn how to restrict a document from being edited, see *7.5 Restrict Editing*. To learn how to inspect a document for comments, see *7.6 Document Inspector*.

Insight

6.3.9 Printing comments

How to print **showing comments**:
- Click on the **Home** tab, then click on **Print**.
- Click on the arrow next to **Print All Pages** to open a gallery with options.
- Under **Document Info**, select **Print Markup.**

How to print **without showing comments**:

• Click on the *Home* tab.

• Click on *Print*, and then under *Document Info*, deselect *Print Markup*.

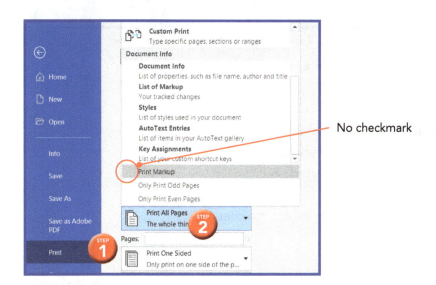

Don't send out a document with hidden or unintended comments. Let Word help you inspect the document and remove unwanted comments (refer to *7.6 Document Inspector*).

6.4 Track changes

6.4.1 What are Track Changes and why use them?

The old way of revising documents by printing them and making edits on the pages with a red pen is inefficient and impractical. Track changes is an electronic way of keeping track of all edits and changes made in a document and is one of the most useful tools for working with others on the same document, making it easier to collaborate effectively.

Track changes also provides a quick way of reviewing changes that don't need explanations, for which Comments are better suited (see *6.3 Comments*).

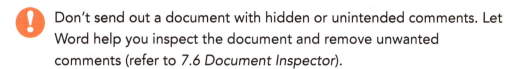

Anything to do with track changes can be found under the **Review** tab, in the **Tracking** and **Changes** groups.

- Once Track Changes are ON, Word keeps track of ALL changes.
- You can decide **what** changes you want to see and **how** you want to see them. Those you select not to see are not deleted, but hidden.
- The only way to get rid of a Track Change is to Accept or Reject the change.

Insight

6.4.2 How to turn Track Changes on and off

Track Changes ON: Click on *Review* > *Track Changes* > *Track Changes*

ON, if the button is grey

Tip **Track Changes** needs to be turned on before any changes are made. If Track Changes are only turned on afterwards, no changes will be indicated.

Track changes OFF: Click on *Review* > *Track Changes* > *Track Changes*

OFF, if the button is NOT grey

 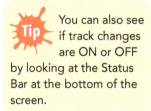

Tip You can also see if track changes are ON or OFF by looking at the Status Bar at the bottom of the screen.

Track Changes: On = ON   Track Changes: Off = OFF

Frustration

I can't see Track Changes on my status bar!

 Right-click on the Status Bar and click ***Track Changes*** to insert a ☑ next to it.

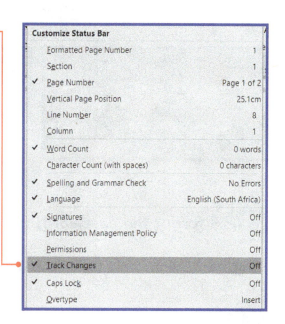

6.4.3 How are changes marked-up?

When Track Changes is ON, all changes are instantly marked-up as they happen. By default, Word indicates changes in the text as follows:

- Vertical track lines in the left margin indicate a change in the adjacent line
- Deleted words have a strike through
- Inserted words are underlined
- Format changes are shown in balloons next to the text.

Once the changes are marked-up, you can decide how much or how little of the changes you want to review.

6.4.4 Locking and unlocking of Track Changes

Locking Track Changes prevents others from turning off the Track Changes function. It will also not be possible for them to accept or reject changes in the locked document.

Locking track changes:
- Click on ***Review*** > ***Track Changes*** > ***Lock Tracking***.
- Type in a password twice and click ***OK***.

Tip When **Lock Tracking** is activated, it is highlighted in grey and shows a small closed lock. Click on it again to deactivate it. You will be prompted for your password.

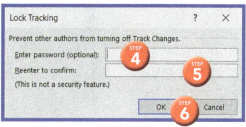

Unlocking track changes:
- Click on *Review* > *Track Changes* > *Lock Tracking*.
- Type in the password and click *OK*.

 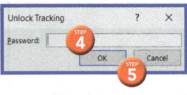

 I forgot the password!

Frustration

Sorry, Word can't retrieve the password.

6.4.5 How to view Track Changes

 I am overwhelmed by all the colours, lines, balloons, and strikes!

Frustration

> **Tip** All changes do not have to be viewed at once. Choose between four viewing options to control what you will and won't see. If you choose to hide them, don't worry, they will not be deleted; they will remain in the document until they have been accepted or rejected.

Find the four viewing options here:

Simple Markup

Only **red vertical lines** in the margin next to the text indicate where changes were made. Click on the red vertical lines to see the Track Changes.

The text shows the changes as if they have already been accepted.

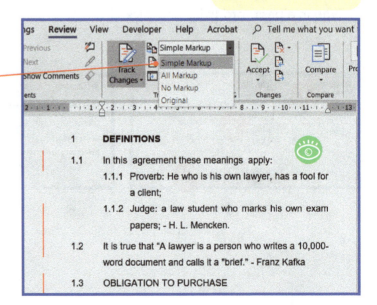

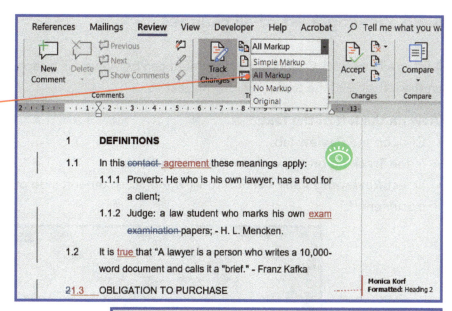

All Markup

All changes are shown.

Grey vertical lines in the margin next to the text indicate where changes were made.

No Markup

No changes are shown. The text shows the changes as if they have already been accepted.

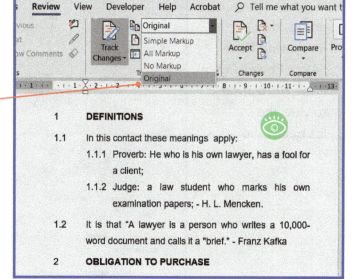

Original

No changes are shown.

The original text is shown as if all changes have been rejected.

6.4.6 Viewing a list of all changes

A list of all the Track Changes in a document can be viewed in a separate panel on the left side of the text or below the text.

View on the left of the text:
- Click on the *Review* tab.
- In the **Tracking** group, click on *Reviewing Pane*.
- Select *Reviewing Pane Vertical* to view the list at the left side of the document.

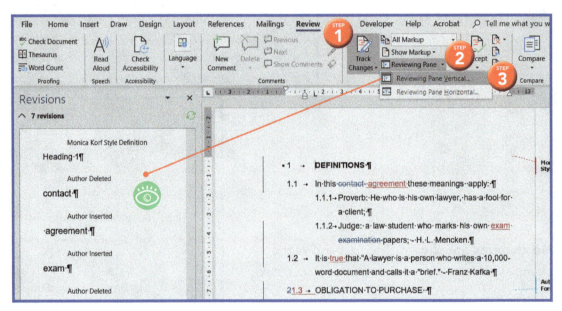

View below the text:
- Click on the *Review* tab.
- In the **Tracking** group, click on *Reviewing Pane*.
- Select *Reviewing Pane Horizontal* to view the list below the document.

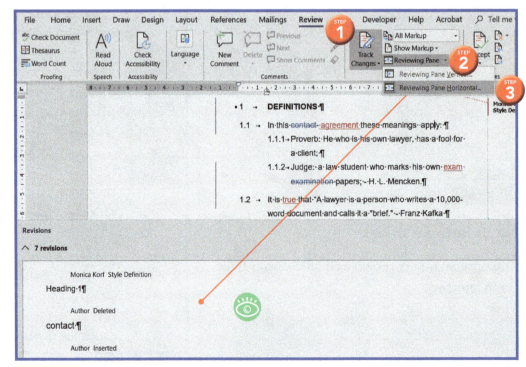

6.4.7 Viewing selected types of changes

You can choose which types of changes you'd like to see at a time.

How to select your viewing options:

Click on **Review** > **Show Markup**. Now click on an option to insert a check mark next to the type of changes you want to see. More than one option can be selected at a time.

To see changes **inline** or in **balloons**, click on **Balloons** and then click on the arrow for further options.

Should you only want to see insertions and deletions, click on ✓ Insertions and Deletions .

6.4.8 Accepting and rejecting Track Changes

The only way to remove Track Changes in a document is to accept or reject the changes. The view options discussed above hide the Track Changes temporarily, but they do not delete them.

ACCEPT OR REJECT ONE CHANGE AT A TIME

If you are still deciding between Accept or Reject, **right-click** on the change. From the drop-down menu click on either **Accept Insertion** or **Reject Insertion**.

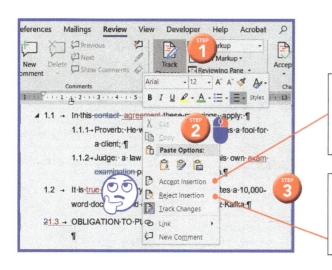

Accept Insertion: The Track Change will be deleted, and the accepted insertion will become part of the text.

Reject Insertion: The Track Change will be deleted, and the rejected insertion will no longer appear in the text.

If you are sure you want to Accept the change:

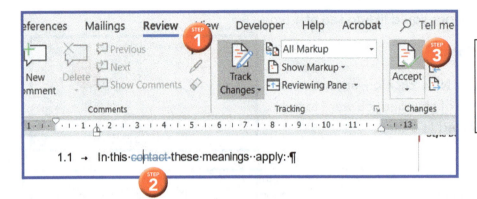

Click on the change and then click **Accept**. (Only click on the green correct mark part.)

If you are sure you want to Reject the change:

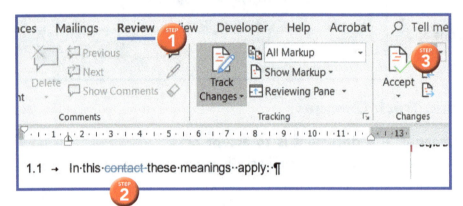

Click on the change and then click **Reject**. (Only click on the red cross mark part.)

Accept multiple changes at once

- Click **Review**, then click on the drop-down arrow under **Accept**.
- Click one of the options in the drop-down menu.

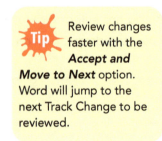

Tip Review changes faster with the **Accept and Move to Next** option. Word will jump to the next Track Change to be reviewed.

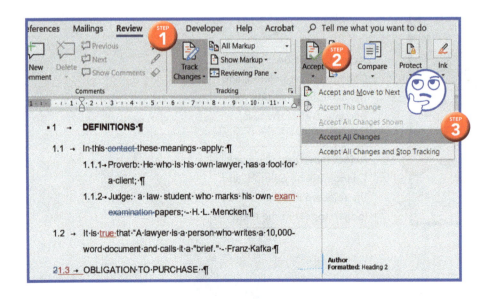

Reject multiple changes at once

- Click **Review**, then click on the drop-down arrow under **Reject**.
- Select one of the options in the drop-down menu.

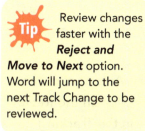

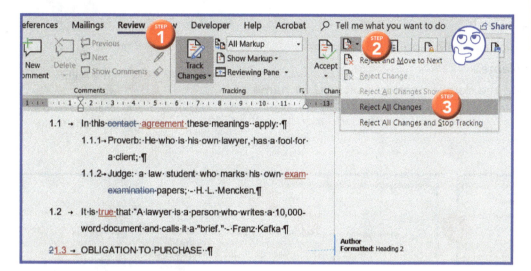

Move to the previous tracked change

Move to the next tracked change

6.4.9 Track changes headaches

My Track Changes did not print!

Frustration

Print with Track Changes visible
- Click on the File tab.
- Click on **Print** and then next to **Print All Pages**, tick **Print Markup.**

Print with Track Changes hidden
- Click on the **File** tab.
- Click on **Print** and then next to **Print All Pages**, **untick** Print Markup (No checkmark)

Frustration

I don't want everyone to know that my junior made the changes!

 Benefit

The Author of changes can be changed or left blank.

- Click on the **Review** tab.
- In the **Tracking** group, click on the dialogue box launcher.
- Click on **Change User Name**.
- In the next screen, delete the details inserted next to **User name** and **Initials**.
- Click **OK**.

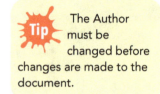 **Tip** The Author must be changed before changes are made to the document.

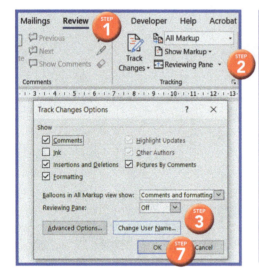

 Frustration

I don't want to see and review all the format changes!

Make sure that **Formatting** is **unticked**.

- Click on **Review** > **Show Markup** > untick **Formatting**.

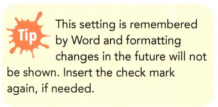 **Tip** This setting is remembered by Word and formatting changes in the future will not be shown. Insert the check mark again, if needed.

Benefit

Remove all formatting changes without affecting the other tracked changes.

First, make sure that ONLY *Formatting* is ticked under *Show Markup*.

• Click on *Review* > *Show Markup* > then tick *Formatting*.

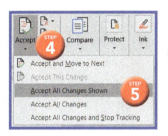 OR

Only when the Formatting changes are shown can they all be Accepted or Rejected.

Frustration

I e-mailed my document with track changes I didn't want my client to see!

Benefit

Refer to *7.6 Document inspector* in Chapter 7 to inspect the document and remove Track Changes before sending it off.

You can also set up **Document-specific settings** in the Word backstage to warn you. Because this is an advanced topic outside the scope of this book, only the path to this function is given:

Click on *File* > *Info* > *Trust Center* > *Trust Center Settings* > *Warn before printing, saving or sending a file that contains tracked changes or comments*

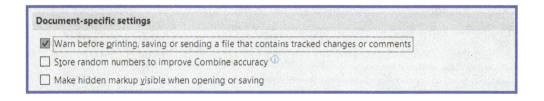

Frustration

I don't like the way Word marks the Track Changes!

Benefit

You can change the way Track Changes are indicated by using the **Advanced Options** in **Track Changes.** Because this is an advanced topic outside the scope if this book, only the path to this function is given:

- Click on the **Review** tab.
- Click on **Tracking** and select **Advanced Options**.
- Now change the colours, margins, balloons or almost anything.
- Click **OK**.

6.5 Compare and combine documents

There's no need to waste any time reading through two versions of the same document word for word to find differences between them. Word offers two special functions with which to search quickly through different documents to either compare them or combine them.

Both functions can be found under **Review** in the **Compare** group.

6.5.1 What happens when documents are compared?

Different versions of the same document are electronically compared to see what the differences are between them.

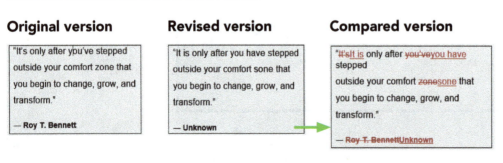

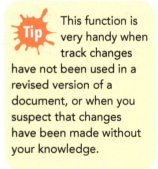

Tip This function is very handy when track changes have not been used in a revised version of a document, or when you suspect that changes have been made without your knowledge.

6.5.2 What happens when documents are combined?

Different versions of the same document are electronically combined in a single, comprehensive document.

Version 1

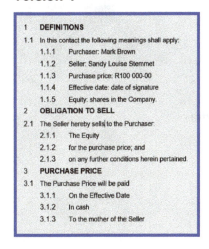

Version 2

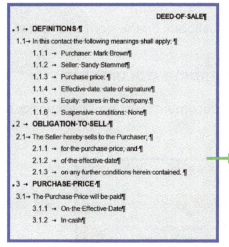

Combined version

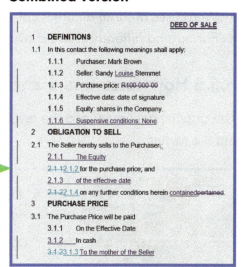

6.5.3 Compare or combine?

The results from the Compare and Combine functions are similar. The option you choose will depend on the purpose of the exercise.

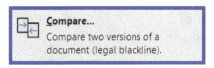

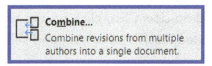

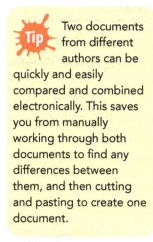

Tip — Two documents from different authors can be quickly and easily compared and combined electronically. This saves you from manually working through both documents to find any differences between them, and then cutting and pasting to create one document.

In both instances, a new document is created in which the differences are shown. Save this document under a different name.

Documents can be compared and combined in the **Review** section using the functions in the **Compare** group. The differences are accepted or rejected using the functions in the **Changes** group.

6.5.4 How are the differences indicated?

By default, Word indicates the differences in the two documents as follows:

- Vertical track lines in the left margin indicate a change in the adjacent line
- Deletions are struck through deleted words
- Insertions are underlined: Insertions words
- Word uses random different colours
- Formatting differences are shown in balloons on the right of the text.

6.5.5 How to compare and combine documents

The original document and the revised document must be saved under different file names.

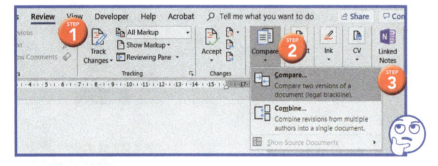

Click on **Review**, then click on the drop-down arrow under **Compare**, and then on **Compare** or **Combine** in the drop-down menu.

A new screen will appear. Under **Original document**, click on the drop-down arrow. If the document is listed in the drop-down list, click on the name of the document. If the document is not listed, click on **Browse**, and select the document as saved on your computer.

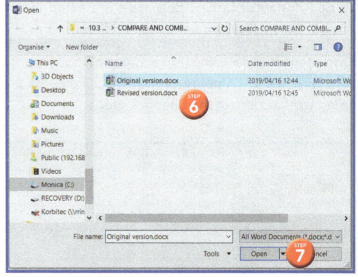

Under **Revised document**, click on the drop-down arrow and follow the same process as above to select the other version of the document.

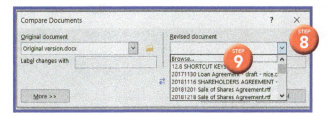

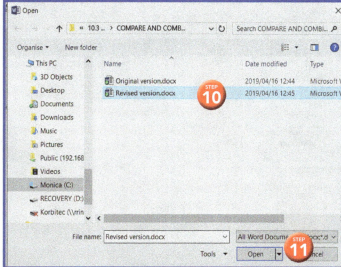

By clicking on the documents can be swapped around.

Click on **OK** for Word to do the comparing.

Word will create a new document indicating all the differences. Remember to save the document under a different name.

6.5.6 How to view compare and combine results

- Click on the **Review** tab.
- In the **Compare** group, click on the drop-down arrow under **Compare.**
- Select **Show Source documents** in the drop-down menu.

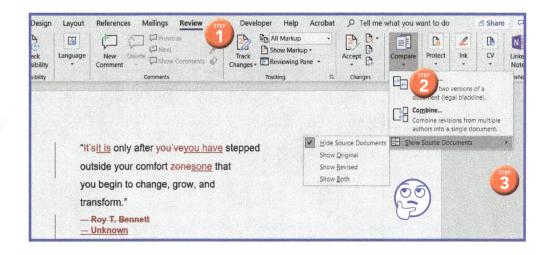

Now click on **Show Both** to see a list of the revisions and the three versions of the document on one screen.

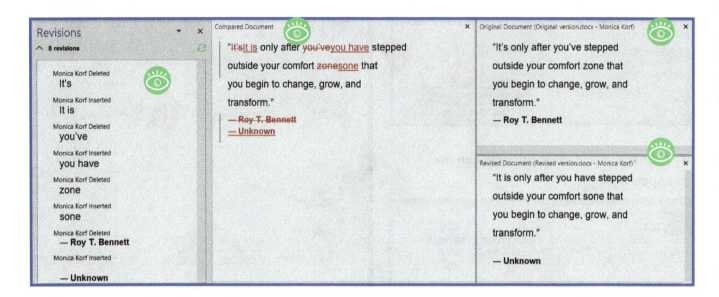

Frustration

I can't see the differences!

To see all the differences, click on **Review**, and then under the **Tracking** group, select **All Markup**.

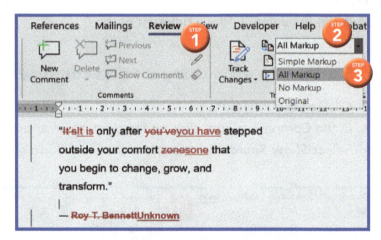

If **No Markup** is selected, no differences will be shown. The text will appear as if ALL of the differences have been accepted.

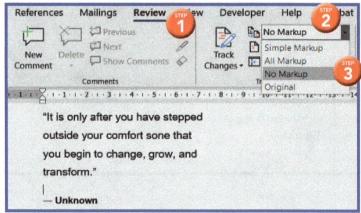

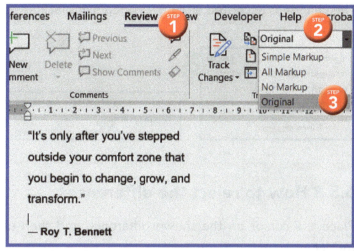

If *Original* is selected, no differences will be shown. The text will appear as if NONE of the differences have been accepted.

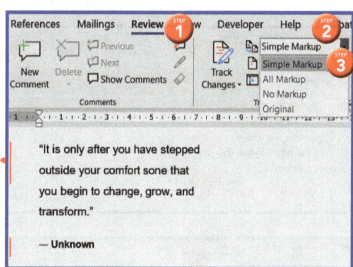

If *Simple Markup* is selected, only red vertical lines will be shown next to the text where differences are. The text will appear as if ALL of the differences have been accepted.

6.5.7 How to accept the differences

- Place the cursor on the shown difference.
- Click on the *Review* tab.
- Click on *Accept*.

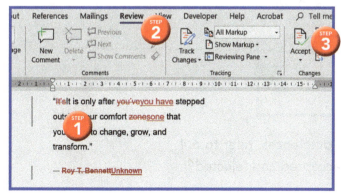

The change is accepted and now appears in black as part of the text.

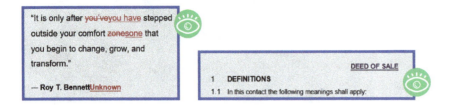

6.5.8 How to reject the differences

Place the cursor on the shown difference and then under **Review**, click on **Reject**.

A difference will only be deleted once it has been accepted or rejected. Until then it is part of the document and can be seen by others if they know how.

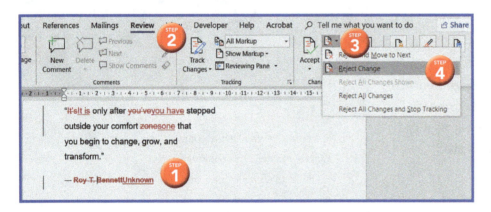

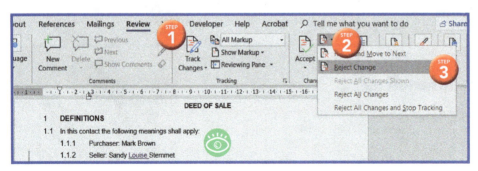

The difference has been rejected and the original text is shown.

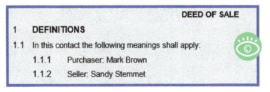

Frustration

Should you struggle to see, accept or reject differences, refer to **6.4 Track Changes**, since differences are seen, accepted and rejected in exactly the same way as Track Changes.

The importance of protecting data cannot be emphasised enough. Protecting your data can help prevent countless hours of searching for changes and unnoticed editing that may harm you or your client.

7.1 Convert to PDF

The quickest way to prevent editing of a document is to convert the document to PDF format. The *Export* or *Save As* option can be used to convert the document to PDF.

7.1.1 How to save to PDF

The final version of the Word document must be saved as a normal Word document (*.docx) and opened.

- Click on the *File* tab.
- Click on *Save As* and then click the drop-down arrow next to *Word Document (*.docx).*
- Select *PDF (*.pdf).*
- Click *Save*.

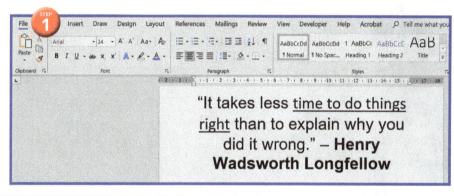

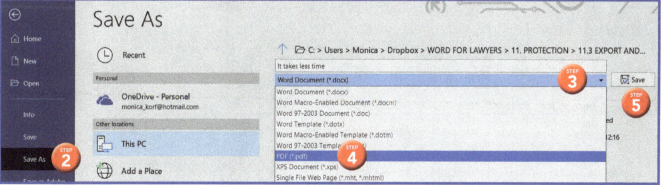

The PDF version of the document is saved in the same folder as the Word document and opens up after saving.

7.1.2 How to export to PDF

The final version of the Word document must be saved as a normal Word document (*.docx) and opened.

Click on *File* > *Export* > *Create PDF/XPS Document* > *Create PDF/XPS*

Unlike *Save As*, *Export* gives you the opportunity to choose another location in which to save the PDF document. Once done, click on *Publish*.

The PDF version of the document will open up after saving.

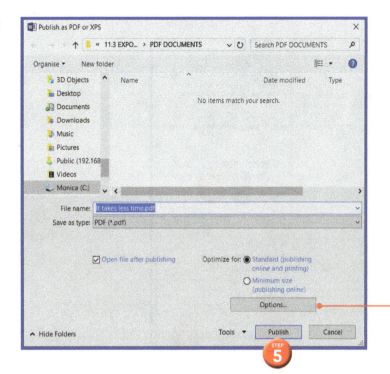

Another advantage of *Export* over *Save As* is that there are more options available, such as the option to export all pages or only the current page.

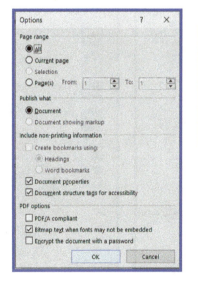

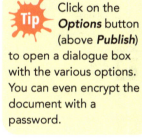

Click on the *Options* button (above *Publish*) to open a dialogue box with the various options. You can even encrypt the document with a password.

Frustration

Can the PDF be converted to Word again?

Yes, it can.

- Browse to the PDF document in the directory of files on your hard drive.
- **Right-click** on the name of the PDF document, then click on the arrow next to *Open with*.
- Click on *Choose another App*.
- Scroll to *More Apps*, then scroll to *Word*.

- Click **OK**.

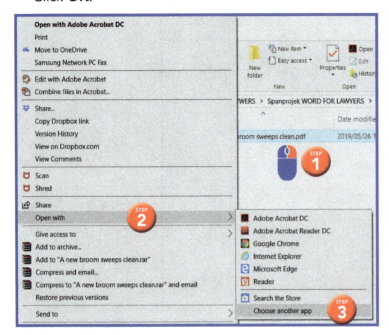

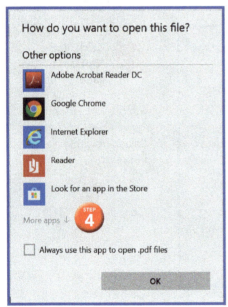

A message will pop up explaining that the Word document might not look like the PDF document, especially if it contains lots of graphics. Click **OK** to proceed.

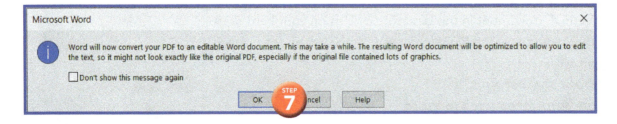

The Word document must still be saved as a normal (*.docx) file. It will automatically be saved in the same place as the PDF, unless another location is selected.

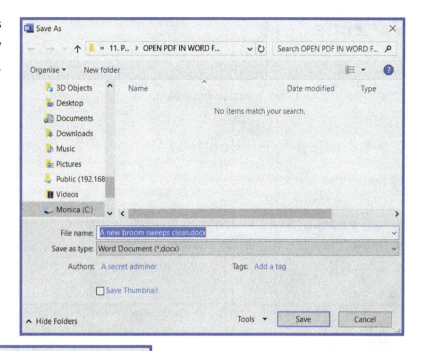

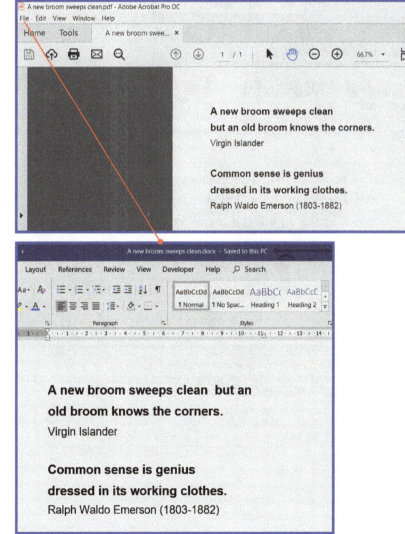

7.2 Hide text

Rather than cut text from a document, hide the text, then retrieve it again later. Word offers two ways to hide text.

7.2.1 Option 1: Hidden text

- Select the text you want to hide.
- Click on **Home.**
- In the **Font** group, click the dialogue box launcher.
- Select the tick-box next to **Hidden**.
- Click **OK**.

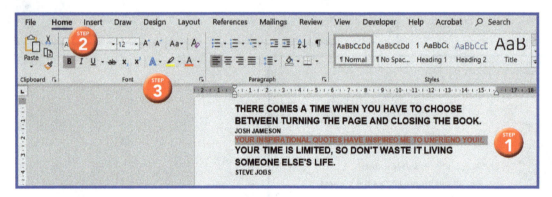

The selected text disappears as if it was never there. There is no blank space where the text was.

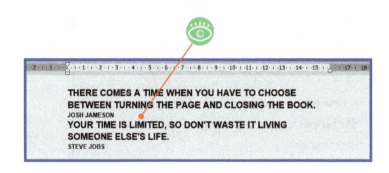

Make the text appear again:

- Click on the **File** tab.
- Click on **Options** and select **Display**.
- Under **Always show these formatting marks on the screen** tick the box next to **Hidden Text.**
- Click **OK**.

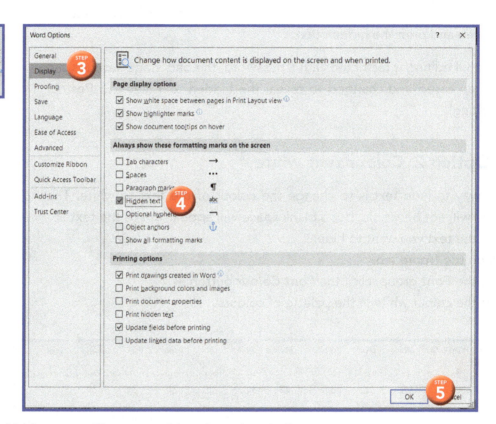

The hidden text will appear with a dotted underline.

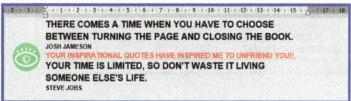

TO PRINT OR NOT TO PRINT?

Hidden text, by default, does not print. However, the backstage settings in Word can be set to print the hidden text, as shown below:

- Click on the **File** tab.
- Click on **Options** and select **Display**.
- Under **Printing options** click the checkbox next to **Print hidden text**.
- Click **OK**.

Is the hidden text secure using the hidden text function?

 Yes, if the document is printed without the hidden text showing.

 No, if the document is e-mailed or viewed in Word. Anyone who is familiar with this function will be able to change the backstage setting to see and print the hidden text.

Even if editing is restricted with a password, the backstage settings can be accessed and changed to reveal the hidden text (see *7.5 Restrict editing*).

7.2.2 Option 2: Colour text white

Another way to hide text is to change the colour of the text to white. The white text will not be visible, but a blank space will appear where the text is.

- Select the text you want to hide.
- Click on the **Home** tab.
- Under the **Font** group, click the **Font Colour** button .
- Select the colour white in the palette of colours.

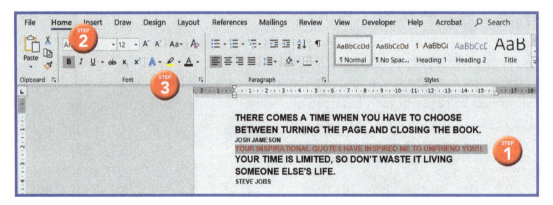

Remember where the hidden text is so that you can change the colour back again to view the text.

Is the hidden white text secure?

 Yes, if the document is printed without the hidden text showing.

 No, if the document is e-mailed or viewed in Word. Anyone who is familiar with Word and its functions might see the blank space and change the font colour to view the text.

 Yes, if editing is restricted with a password. The function to change the colour is greyed out (not available) and the hidden text cannot be seen or retrieved without the password.

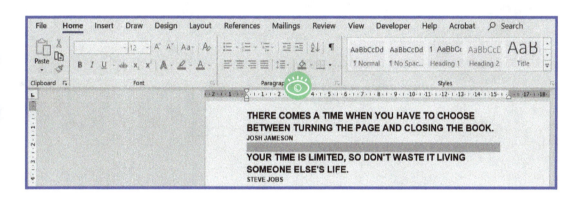

7.3 Insert a watermark

A feint design or text can be inserted behind the content of a page to show the document status (i.e. draft) or the copyright of the author, or to protect the document from unauthorised use.

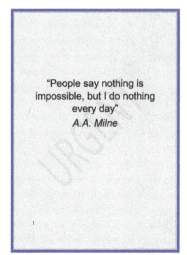

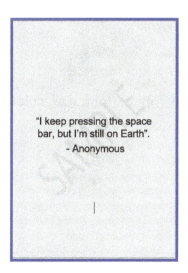

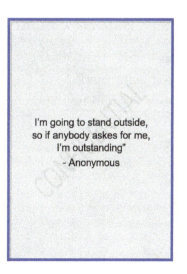

Watermarks can be inserted, customised, and saved using the **Watermark** function in the **Page Background** group under **Design**.

If the **Design** tab is not in the Ribbon, see *1.2 Tabs* on how to customise the Ribbon to include the **Design** tab.

- Click on the **Design** tab.
- Then click on **Watermark**.
- Scroll down in the Watermark Gallery and click on a watermark of your choice.

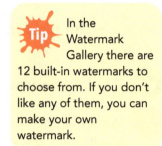

Tip In the Watermark Gallery there are 12 built-in watermarks to choose from. If you don't like any of them, you can make your own watermark.

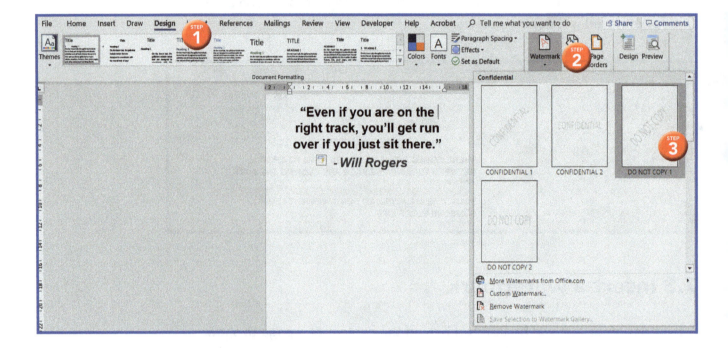

7.3.1 How to create a custom watermark

Click on **Design** > **Watermark** > **Custom Watermark**.

To insert text:
- Click on **Text watermark**.
- Type in your preferred text and choose the format (font, size, colour, and layout).
- Click **OK**.

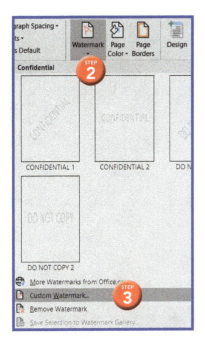

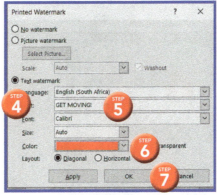

To insert a picture or logo:

- Click on *Picture watermark*.
- Click on *Select Picture*. Now browse for and select the picture or logo saved on your computer.
- Click *Insert*, then click *OK*.

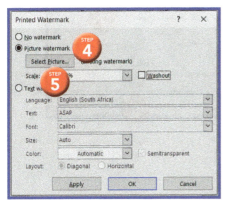

7.3.2 How to save a custom watermark

Open the document with the custom watermark. **Double-click** at the top of the page to open the header part. Click once more. The custom watermark will become highlighted and blocked.

- Click on the *Design* tab.
- In the **Page Background** group click on *Watermark*.
- Now click on *Save Selection to Watermark Gallery*.

 Tip The custom watermark is part of this document only. To use the custom watermark in other documents, it must be saved to the Watermark Gallery.

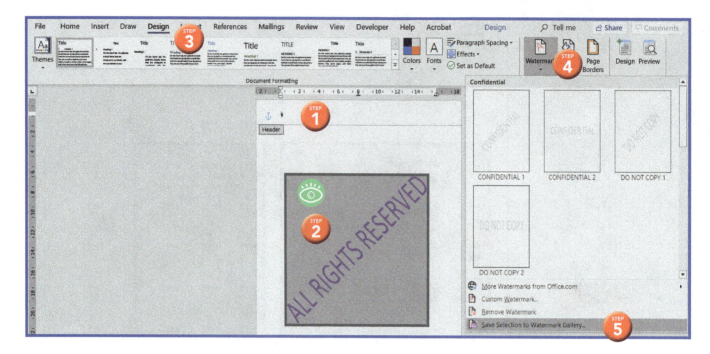

Complete the information for **Create New Building Block**:

- Name the watermark.
- The **Gallery** must be Watermarks.
- The Category can be General (unless you want to create separate categories).
- Next to **Save in**, select *Normal.dotm* (the watermark can then be used in all documents).
- Select one of the Options as may apply to the text:

- Click *OK*.

7.3.3 How to insert a custom watermark

The custom watermark is inserted in the same way as the standard built-in watermarks. The custom watermark is now part of the Watermark Gallery.

- Click on *Design*.
- Click on *Watermark*.
- Then click on the custom watermark in the Gallery.

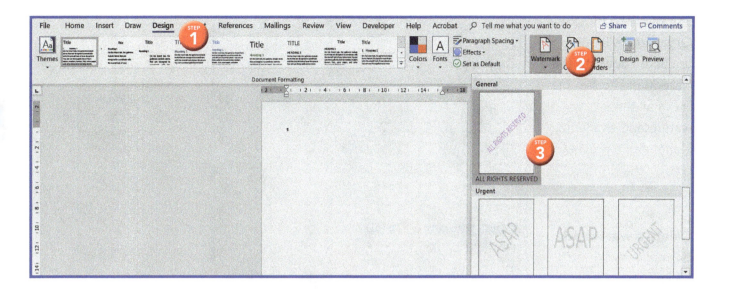

7.3.4 How to delete a watermark

Click on **Design** > **Watermark** > **Remove Watermark**.

The watermark will be removed from this document but will still be available for use in other documents because it is saved in the Watermark Gallery.

Anyone can remove a watermark from a document if they know how. To prevent unauthorised removal, the document must be protected from editing (see see *7.5 Restrict editing*).

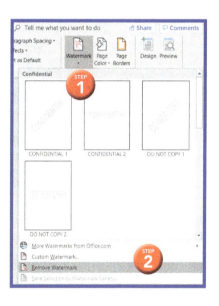

7.3.5 Adding and deleting a watermark in the Building Blocks Organiser

Word has a **Building Blocks Organiser**, which contains a list of all the watermarks available, including custom watermarks.

Click on **Insert**, and in the **Text** group, click on  and then on **Building Blocks Organiser**.

The **Building Blocks Organizer** will open up. Scroll down to the watermarks to see the list of all the watermarks available, along with a preview box on the right.

Delete a watermark permanently by clicking on its name and then on **Delete**. The watermark will no longer be available for use in any document.

Frustration

Is the watermark secure?

 Yes, if editing is restricted with a password, then the watermark function is greyed out (not available) and the watermark cannot be removed without the password (see *7.5 Restrict editing*).

Insight

Watermarks can be hidden! Make sure that you inspect a document before sharing it to prevent unintended watermarks from being distributed (see *7.6 Document inspector*)

7.4 Protect a document

Word offers several ways to protect a document if you don't want others to open, copy or edit it. The option you choose will depend on your needs. The options to protect a document range from **1** nearly no protection to **5** no access at all.

How to view the protection options:

Click on **File** > **Info** > **Protect Document** > and then from the drop-down menu select the option offering the level of control and protection your document requires.

3 **Always Open Read-Only.** The document is saved as a read-only file by default. It can be edited, but not accidently saved, whereby previous versions are overwritten.

5 **Encrypt with Password.** The document can only be opened if the correct password is supplied.

4 **Restrict Editing.** Add a password to a document to restrict or limit editing by others. The user will need the password to edit the document. If limited editing is allowed, the user will be able to add comments or Track Changes without the password, but no other editing or proofing will be allowed.

2 **Add a Digital Signature.** Verify the integrity and authenticity of the document at a particular time. It can still be edited if the signature is removed.

1 **Mark as Final.** This tells others the document is considered final. It can still be edited if **Edit Anyway** is clicked.

Although no protection is ever failproof, some talent at hand or maliciousness will nonetheless be required to access and edit the document.

7.4.1 Always Open Read-Only

It sometimes happens that a document is edited and accidentally saved without changing the file name. When this happens, the original version of  the document is overwritten and cannot be retrieved. To prevent this from happening, a document can be saved as a read-only file.

When the file is opened again, it will always open as a read-only document. The user will be able to edit the document but will not be able to save the document under the same name, unless they choose **not** to continue with the document as a read-only file.

- Select the document to be saved as a read-only file.
- Click on **File** > **Info** > **Protect Document** > **Always Open in Read-Only** > **Save**.
- Close the document.

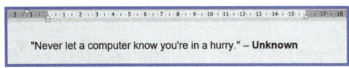

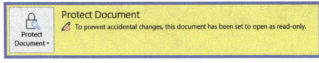

> ! Remember to SAVE and CLOSE the file to activate the protection.

- Whenever the document is reopened, a screen will appear to warn the user that this is a read-only document.

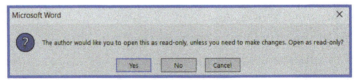

Both **Yes** and **No** will enable the user to edit the document. The difference between the two lies in the way the user saves the document when changes are made.

If **Yes** is clicked:

The document opens and is indicated as a Read-Only in the name of the document.

The document can still be edited:

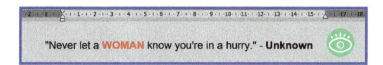

But when the user wants to save the document, it will not be possible. Word will prompt the user to save the document under a different name or in a different location.

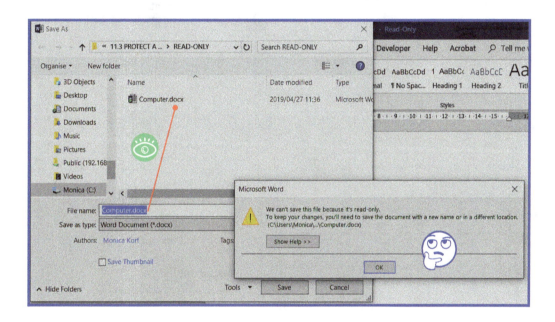

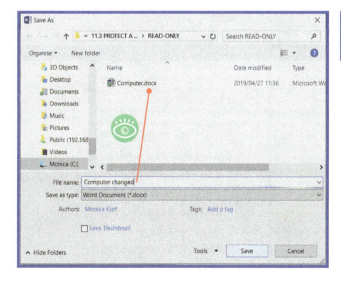

When the renamed document is opened again, the user will again be warned that the document is a read-only file because the protection remains part of the document, even when saved under another name or in another location.

If **No** is clicked:

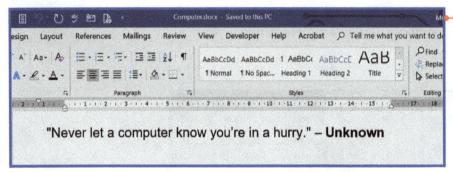

> The document is opened with no indication that it was protected as a read-only document.

"Never let a computer know you're in a hurry." – **Unknown**

The document can be edited:

"Never let a computer know *everything*." – **Unknown**

Tip Refer to *11.1 Recover an unsaved document* for the recovering of documents.

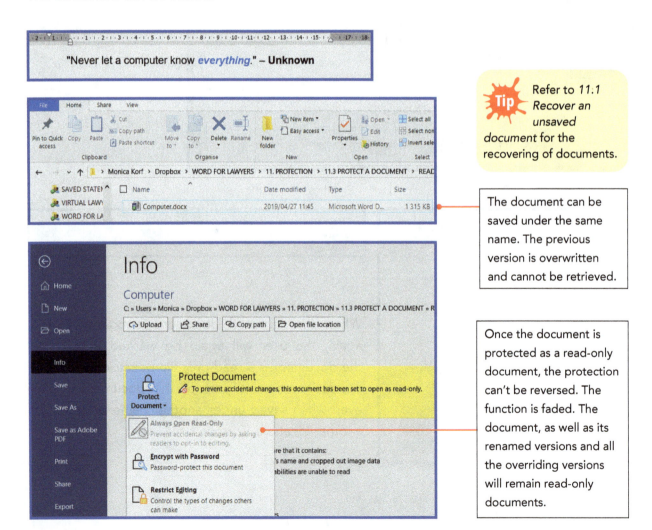

> The document can be saved under the same name. The previous version is overwritten and cannot be retrieved.

> Once the document is protected as a read-only document, the protection can't be reversed. The function is faded. The document, as well as its renamed versions and all the overriding versions will remain read-only documents.

I can't save the amended document!

Frustration

The document was most likely protected as a read-only document. If the document is opened up as a read-only document, you will have to save the document under a different name or in a different location.

7.4.2 Encrypt with a password

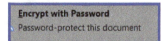

Encrypt with Password
Password-protect this document

You can encrypt your document with a password to prevent unauthorised access and data theft. A password-protected document can only be opened if the correct password is keyed in by the person opening it. If you forget or lose the password, you cannot open the document.

- Click on the *File* tab.
- Click on *Info* > *Protect Document* > *Encrypt with Password*.
- Type in a password and click *OK*.
- Type in the same password again and click *OK*.

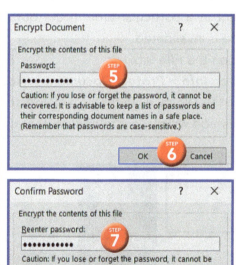

Remember to save the document to make the password take effect. Also remember to make a note of the password as you will not be able to open the document again without it!

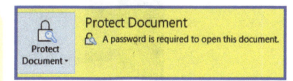

Protect Document
A password is required to open this document.

Protect Document

When you open the document again, Word will prompt you to type in the password. Enter the document password and click **OK**.

 The password can't be seen as it's being typed in, so **take care to type it correctly**. If you get an error message saying that the password is incorrect, try typing it in again slowly. Also check that CAPS LOCK is not turned on, because passwords are case-sensitive.

7.4.3 Add a digital signature

Add an invisible digital signature to verify the integrity and authenticity of the document at a particular time. If the document is subsequently edited, the signature is invalidated.

- Click on the **File** tab.
- Click on **Info** > **Protect Document** > **Add a Digital Signature**.
- Insert the Digital ID in the sign dialog and click on **Sign**.
- A message will appear to confirm that the signature has been added.

You will need to purchase a digital ID issued by an independent certification authority.

For more information on how to obtain the virtual equivalent of a wet ink signature, visit:

- www.comodogroup.com
- www.identrust.com
- www.globalsign.com

The topic is beyond the scope of this book.

If you do not have a Digital ID, **Word** will ask you if you'd like to get one from a Microsoft Partner. Click **Yes** if you do.

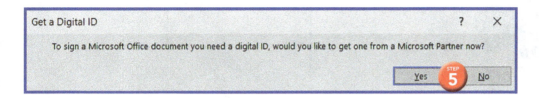

When the document is re-opened, a bar will appear at the top of the document indicating that the file is marked as final.

How to remove the digital signature

You can edit the document if you wish, but this will remove all digital signatures.
- Click **Edit Anyway** in the yellow strip at the top of the document indicating that the document is marked as final.
- Click **Yes** in the dialog box that pops up.
- You can add a digital signature again after you have finished editing.

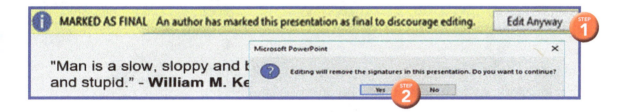

7.4.4 Mark as final

This method of document protection simply disourages but does not prevent others from editing the document. When the document is marked as final, a read-only document is created. Typing, editing, commands, and proofing marks are disabled.

To mark as final, do the following:
- Click on the **File** tab.
- Then click on **Info** > **Protect Document** > **Mark as Final** > **OK** > **OK**.

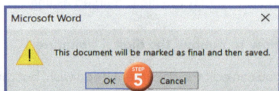

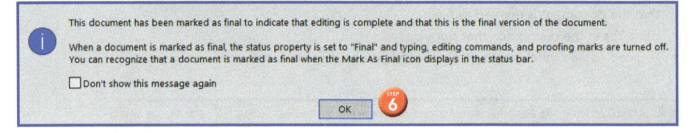

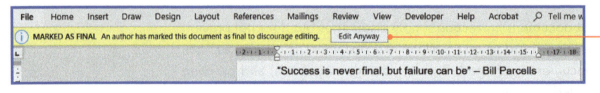

When the document is re-opened, a bar will appear at the top of the document with a message that discourages further editing, and the ribbon with the commands for editing and proofing is hidden. By clicking on **Edit Anyway**, their access to the document will no longer be restricted.

Click on **Edit Anyway** to open the ribbon and obtain unrestricted access to the document

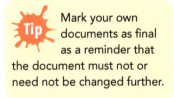

Tip Mark your own documents as final as a reminder that the document must not or need not be changed further.

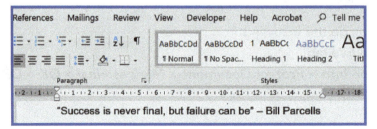

7.5 Restrict editing

All editing of a document can be restricted, or other users can be granted only limited editing functionality.

7.5.1 How to restrict editing

- Click on the **File** tab.
- Click on **Info** > **Protect Document** > **Restrict Editing** > **OK**.

A **Restrict Editing** panel opens up on the right of the screen.

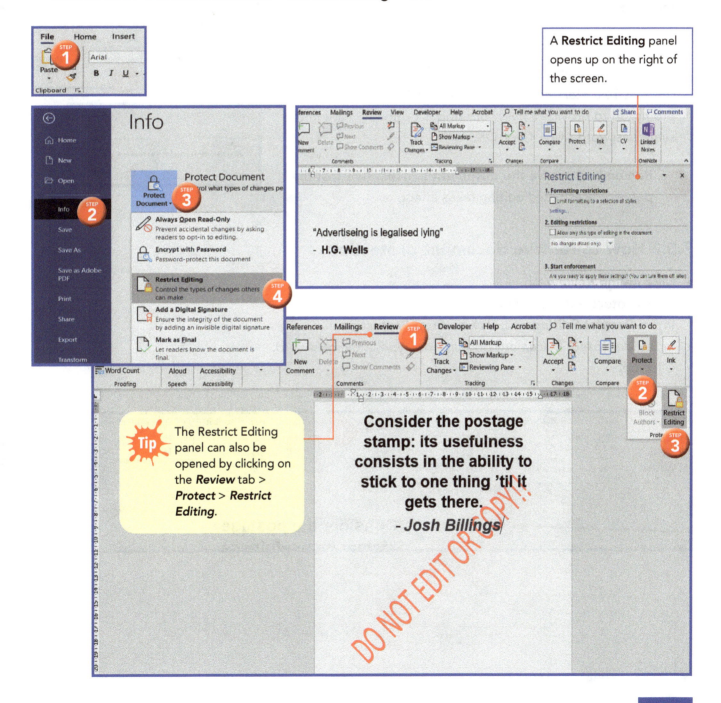

Tip

The Restrict Editing panel can also be opened by clicking on the **Review** tab > **Protect** > **Restrict Editing**.

You can now choose the restrictions you'd like to apply to your document:

1. **Formatting restrictions.**
   Click the checkbox for *Limit formatting to a selection of styles*, and click *Settings* to select the styles allowed.

2. **Editing restrictions.**
   Click the checkbox for *Allow only this type of editing in the document*, and then select the types of changes allowed from the drop-down menu.

   Exceptions are an optional setting.

3. **Start enforcement.**
   Click on *Yes, Start Enforcing Protection*. You will be prompted to provide a password (this is optional). Type in the same password twice. Click *OK*.

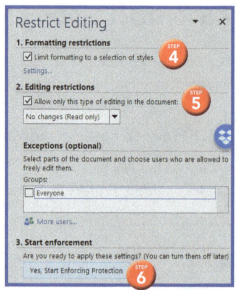

> (!) **Remember to save the document** to make sure that the password-restricted editing takes effect.

7.5.2 How to remove document protection

- Click on the *Review* tab.
- Click *Protect* > *Restrict Editing*.
- In the *Restrict Editing* box, click on *Stop Protection*.
- In the *Unprotect Document* pop-up box, type in the password.
- Click *OK*.

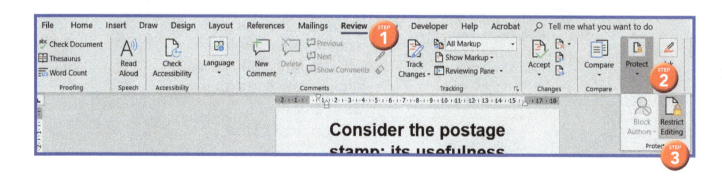

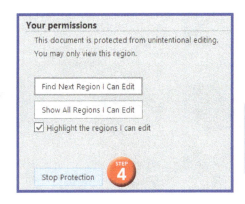

7.5.3 How to allow limited editing functions

When documents need reviewing, the ability to allow other users limited editing rather than no editing, is convenient. If you don't allow limited editing, the only alternative for the other user is to print the document and review it by hand.

You can choose the type of editing you will allow from the drop-down menu under **2. Editing restrictions**. Your limited editing options are *Tracked changes*, *Comments*, and *Filling in forms*.

> **Tip** The **Restrict Editing** functions can also be accessed from the document *File* menu.

Tracked changes

When tracked changes are allowed, the user will be able to change the text, but every change will be tracked. The user will need the document password to **Unlock Tracking** in order to disable the tracking function.

Comments

When you select *Comments*, the user will only be able to insert comments in the document and will not be able to change the text.

To add a comment:
- Place your cursor in the text where you'd like to make the comment.
- Click on *Review* > *New Comment*.
- A box will open up to the far right of the text. Insert your comment.

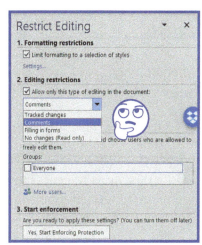

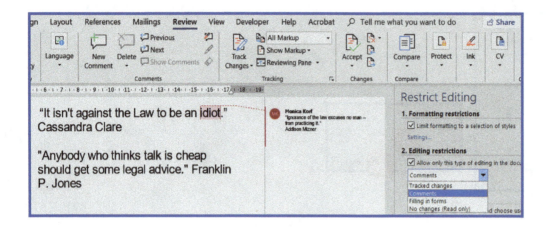

Enforce your editing restrictions

Now you will need to enforce all the protection changes you've made. Under **3. Start enforcement**, click on **Yes, Start Enforcing Protection**. Type in the same password twice. Click **OK**.

 Remember to save the document to make sure that the password-restricted editing takes effect.

 Why are the functions on the Ribbon not working!

Frustration

The document is most likely protected with a password.

When editing is restricted with a password, all the functions on the Ribbon are faded indicating that they can't be used.

To confirm this, click on **File** > **Protect Document**.

If **Restrict Editing** is highlighted, then the document is protected, and you will need a password to access the functions in the Ribbon.

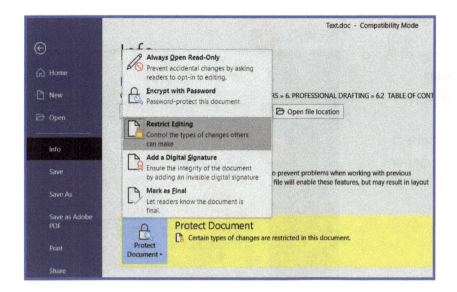

7.6 Document inspector

Word can inspect a document for any data that you don't want to share with anyone else when the document is sent out, such as hidden text, personal information, comments, tracked changes, and revision notes. It does this using an inbuilt document inspector.

The document inspector lists all potentially sensitive data it finds, which you can then choose to remove or keep.

7.6.1 Why inspect documents?

Benefit

By inspecting your documents, you will save yourself the embarrassment of sending them out with hidden text and comments, another firm's logo, or someone else's name as the Author.

Documents containing sensitive data can place you and your firm at risk of claims against you due to the leaking of confidential or private information.

> **Tip** Some of the changes made by the document inspector are permanent, so it's best to make a copy of your document before it's inspected. This is one instance where the normally helpful **Undo** button will not be helpful at all.

7.6.2 How to inspect a document

Documents are inspected in the backstage of Word.

- Click on *File* > *Info* > *Check for Issues*.
- A drop-down menu with options will appear.
- Click on *Inspect Document*.
- Word will remind you to save the document because the changes made by the document inspector are permanent.
- Click *Yes*.

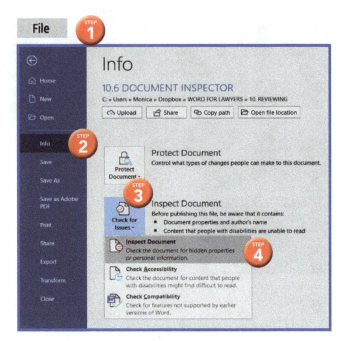

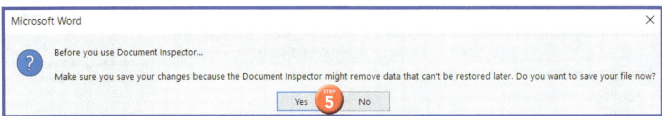

- Now select the types of sensitive information and hidden data that you want the document to be inspected for.
- Click on *Inspect* and **Word** will do the inspecting.

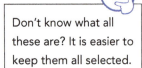

Don't know what all these are? It is easier to keep them all selected.

The results are displayed with red exclamation marks next to any potentially sensitive data and items.

- Click **Remove All** next to each item that you want to remove.
- Once done, click **Close.**
- Save the inspected and cleared document under a different name. The document is now ready to be shared.

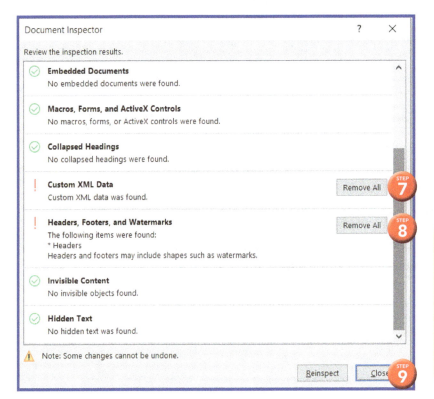

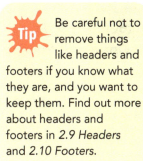

Tip Be careful not to remove things like headers and footers if you know what they are, and you want to keep them. Find out more about headers and footers in *2.9 Headers* and *2.10 Footers*.

Frustration

What is Custom XML data?

XML stands for "e**X**tensible **M**arkup **L**anguage".

It is standardised data in Word that is normally not a security risk and does not need to be removed.

Legal Practitioners tend to use Word like a typewriter – text is retyped numerous times and repetitive actions are performed manually. This not only wastes time, but it also increases the chances of introducing errors. Most of what Legal Practitioners do in Word can be performed both quickly and correctly using the various functions available in the software.

8.1 Frequently used text shortcuts – AutoCorrect code

8.1.1 Save frequently used text as an AutoCorrect code

You can save frequently used text, like "Kindly acknowledge receipt of this letter", under a special code that you create, for example, "KA?". This is done using Word's AutoCorrect function. Your line of text will then magically appear in your document wherever you type the code.

> **Tip** The AutoCorrect function is usually used to automatically and instantly correct words that have been misspelled or mistyped.

To create your AutoCorrect code, do the following:

- Click on *File* > *Options* > *Proofing* > *AutoCorrect Options*

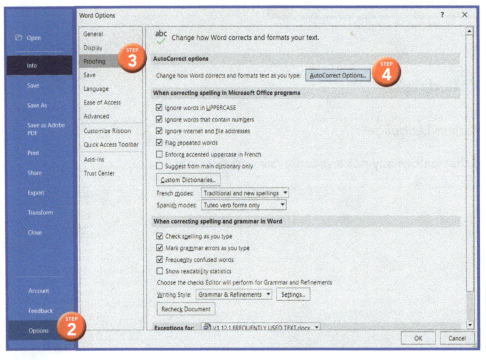

- Tick the checkbox for **Replace text as you type** by clicking on it, and in the **Replace** field type in your special code "KA?".
- In the **With** field, type your frequently used text "Kindly acknowledge receipt of this letter".
- Click **Add** and then **OK**.

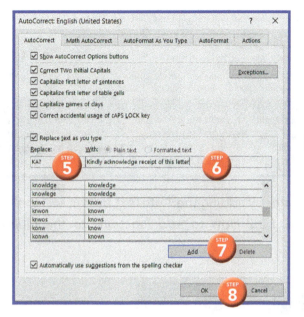

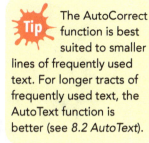

Frustration

I don't want to use the frequently used text now!

Whenever the code is typed but you don't want to use the frequently used text associated with that code, simply press **Backspace** to undo the auto correction.

8.2 Frequently used text shortcuts – AutoText

8.2.1 Save frequently used text as AutoText

The AutoText function is useful for longer sections of text, such as disclaimers. You need only type in the first few letters of the name of the AutoText and press **Function + F3** on your keyboard to insert the rest of the text automatically and instantly.

8.2.2 How to create AutoText

- Select the text that is repeatedly used in your document.
- Under the **Insert** tab click on the drop-down arrow next to **Quick Parts**.
- Click **AutoText**, and then **Save Selection to AutoText Gallery**.
- A dialogue box will appear. Type in the frequently used text name and description.

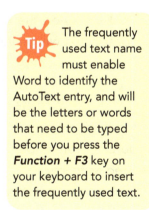

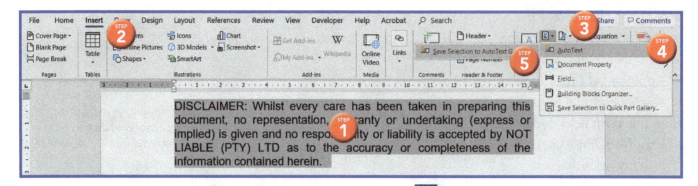

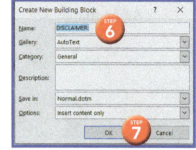

AutoText can be created faster by adding the AutoText button  to the Quick Access Toolbar (see *1.3.2 How to add functions to the Quick Access Toolbar*).

Insight

To create another AutoText entry, simply select the text you want to use again later and click on 🔲. Then as before, type in the AutoText name and description in the dialogue box that opens up. Click **OK** to save your entry.

8.2.3 How to insert the AutoText

Click your cursor in the document where you want your frequently used text to appear.

Now type in the first few letters of the name of your AutoText and press

`fn` + `F3` on the keyboard. If **Word** recognises the AutoText entry, the rest of the text will be inserted.

Frustration

I can't remember the name of the AutoText!

If you can't remember the name of the AutoText, the AutoText can also be inserted as follows:

- Click on the **Insert** tab.
- Click on the drop-down arrow next to **Quick Parts**.
- Now click on **AutoText** and select the AutoText you want to insert.

8.3 Quick Parts

Text frequently used in a document can be saved as a Quick Part and then easily inserted into any other document when needed. The formats and styles are inserted in the document along with the text.

Time saver Save and insert frequently used text that is already formatted with your preferred styles for multi-level numbered clauses (see *4.2 Multi-level numbered clauses*) to save you from having to create the styles again.

All Quick Parts are automatically saved under a separate Gallery in Word's **Building Block Organizer**. By reusing Quick Parts across multiple documents, tasks can be automated.

8.3.1 How to create a Quick Part

- Select the frequently used text.
- Click on the **Insert** tab.
- In the **Text** group, click on the drop-down arrow next to .

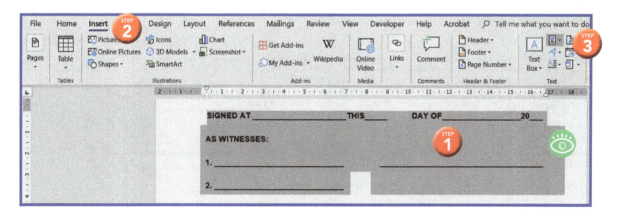

- Click on **Save Selection to Quick Part Gallery**.

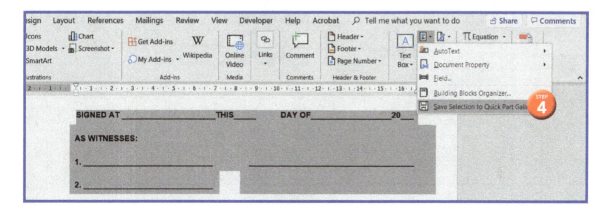

- Under **Name**, give your Quick Part a name.
- The **Gallery** must be *Quick Parts*.
- The **Category** can be *General* (unless you want to create separate categories).
- Next to **Save in** select *Normal* (the text can then be used in all documents).
- Under **Options** select the option that applies to your text:

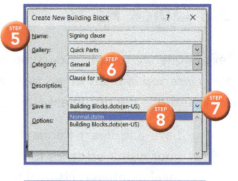

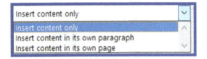

- Click *OK*.

The standard text is now saved as a Quick Part for future use.

8.3.2 How to insert a Quick Part

- Click your cursor in the document where you want the standard text inserted.
- Click on the *Insert* tab.
- In the **Text** group, click on the drop-down arrow next to [icon].

- Click on the Quick Part box that contains the standard text you want to insert.

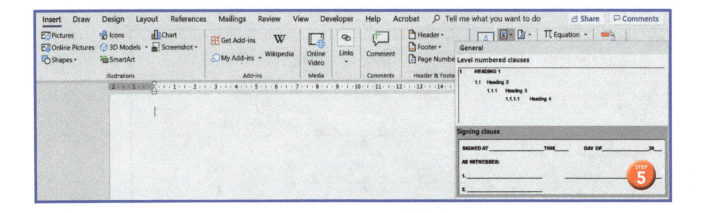

Word will insert the text at the cursor.

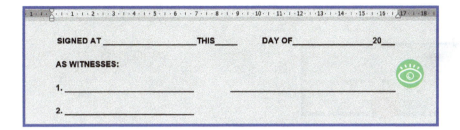

8.3.3 How to edit a Quick Part

A Quick Part can be edited by following the same steps used to create a Quick
Part. Use the same Quick Part name to overwrite the original Quick Part.

- Edit your frequently used text as needed.
- Select the edited text by highlighting all of it.
- Click on the **Insert** tab.
- In the **Text** group, click on the drop-down arrow next to [icon].
- Click on **Save Selection to Quick Parts Gallery**.

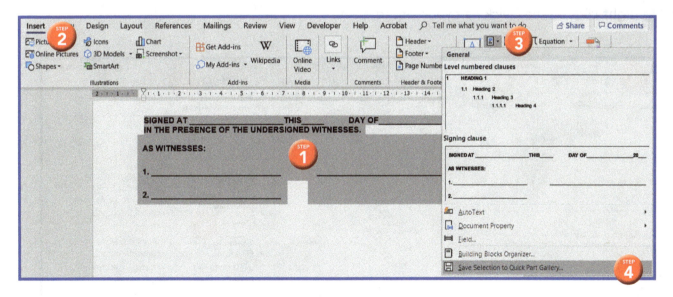

- Name the edited Quick Part the same as the Quick Part you want to replace,
  and add a different description, if needed.
- Click **OK**.
- You will be asked if you want to redefine the building block entry. Click on
  Yes.

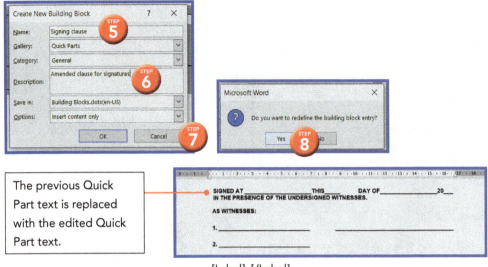

The previous Quick Part text is replaced with the edited Quick Part text.

[Label] [/Label]

8.3.4 How to delete a Quick Part

- Click on the *Insert* tab.
- In the **Text** group, click on the drop-down arrow next to .

- **Right-click** on the Quick Part you want to delete.

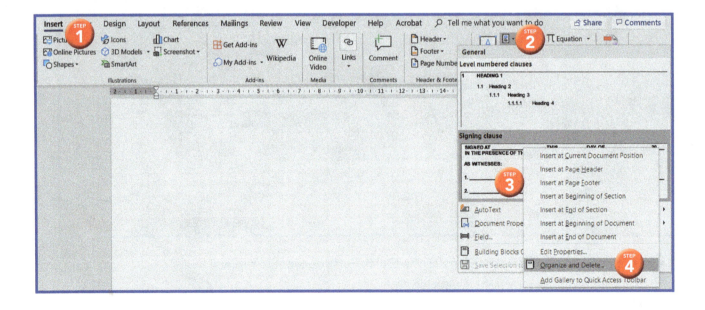

The **Building Blocks Organizer** will open up. The relevant Quick Part will be highlighted.

- Click on *Delete*.
- Click on *Yes*.

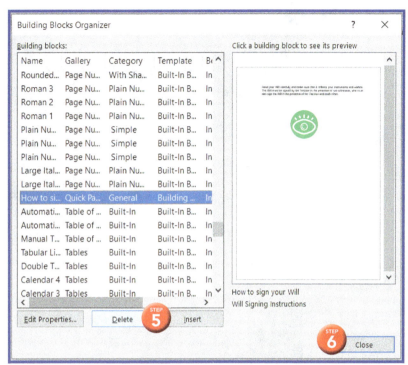

8.4 Multiple-paste clipboard

A clipboard is an area on your computer that temporarily stores text you want to copy from one place to another within the same document or to other documents. For instance, perhaps you need to move various random clauses from one section of your document to another. Instead of going backwards and forwards copying and pasting each one, you can copy them all to the clipboard and then paste them as and where needed, saving yourself lots of time.

Word has one Clipboard for all documents. When you open the Clipboard, everything that is copied thereafter – even from other documents – is saved on the clipboard and can be used again in any document you open.

The clipboard can contain a maximum of 24 copied items. When an item is copied, that item appears at the top of the Clipboard and the previously copied items move down. When a twenty-fifth item is copied, the first item (the one furthest down the list) is deleted.

Tip You can copy text from various documents to the Clipboard and then paste them all at once in a new document by selecting *Paste All*.

183

8.4.1 Add text to the Clipboard

- Click on the **Home** tab.
- Click on the dialogue box launcher next to **Clipboard**.
- Select the text you want to clip.
- **Right-click** once and then click on **Copy**.

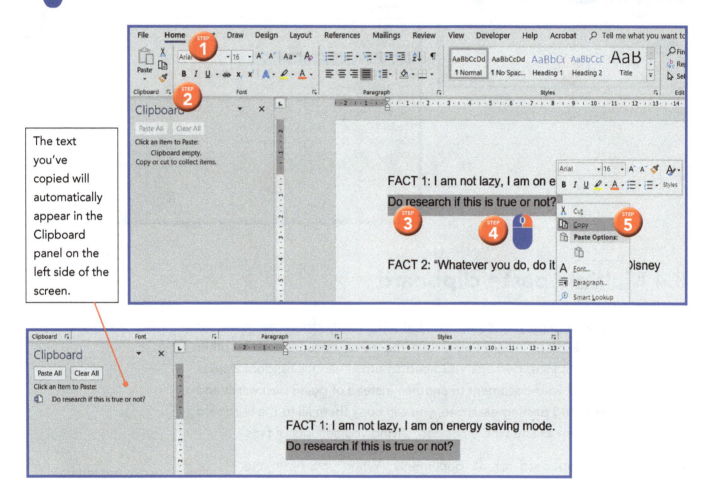

The text you've copied will automatically appear in the Clipboard panel on the left side of the screen.

8.4.2 Paste text from the Clipboard

To paste text from the Clipboard into the document, place the cursor in the document where you want the text inserted and click on the text in the clipboard.

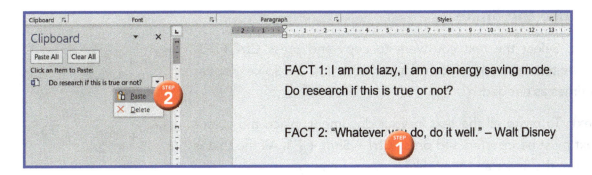

The text will appear where the cursor was placed. You can insert this text as often as you need to.

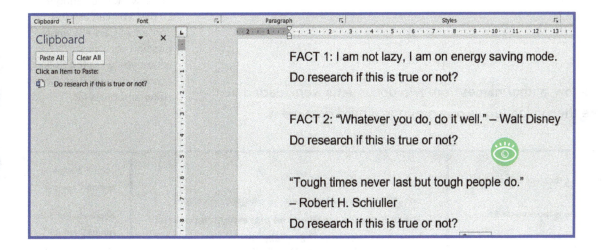

8.4.3 Delete text from the Clipboard

 Right-click on the item in the Clipboard you want to delete and then click on **Delete**.

To delete all items at once, click on **Clear All**.

8.5 The Spike

The Spike is an extended clipboard feature that enables you to move two or more items from multiple locations in your Word document and then paste them together as one group in a new location or document. It is named after the old-fashioned sharp-pronged paper holder onto which people poked things like receipts and bills to temporarily store them.

8.5.1 How to use the Spike

- **Copy the text**: Select the text you want to copy and press *Ctrl + F3*. This removes the text from your document and adds it to the Spike. Repeat this as many times as needed.

- **Paste the text**: To paste all the text in your document, place the cursor where the text must be inserted and press *Ctrl + Shift + F3*. All the text is "unloaded" from the Spike and the Spike becomes empty.

> **Tip** If you want to paste the contents of the Spike without clearing it so that you can use the contents again elsewhere, position your cursor where you want the Spike content pasted, then type **spike** and press F3.

In the example below, author names from two documents were loaded on the Spike. They were then unloaded as one group in a third document.

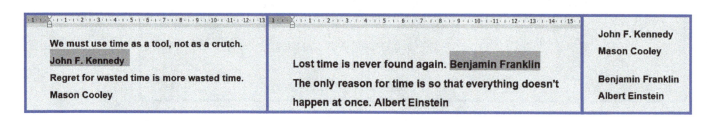

8.6 Control key shortcuts

You can type faster by using shortcut keys on your keyboard to execute common commands. When using shortcut keys, your fingers remain mostly on the keyboard and you do not have to lift your hand to move the cursor with your mouse or touch pad.

Provided below is a summary of the shortcut keys you'll find most useful when drafting legal documents. The controls on the ribbon are also shown.

> **Tip** You can still use the controls in the Ribbon on the screen if you find it easier than using shortcut keys or if you don't want to memorise the different shortcut-key combinations.

ACTION	SHORTCUT KEYS	ACTION	SHORTCUT KEYS
Move to end of document	Ctrl + End	Delete to the left	Ctrl + Backspace
Find	Ctrl + F	One word to right at a time	Ctrl + →
Find and replace	Ctrl + H	One word to left at a time	Ctrl + ←
Select all text	Ctrl + A	One paragraph up	Ctrl + ↑
New page	Ctrl + Enter	One paragraph down	Ctrl + ↓
Delete word to the right	Ctrl + Delete		

ACTION	SHORTCUT KEYS	RIBBON CONTROLS
Bold	Ctrl + B	
Italic	Ctrl + I	
<u>Underline</u>	Ctrl + U	
Copy	Ctrl + C	

Cut	Ctrl + X	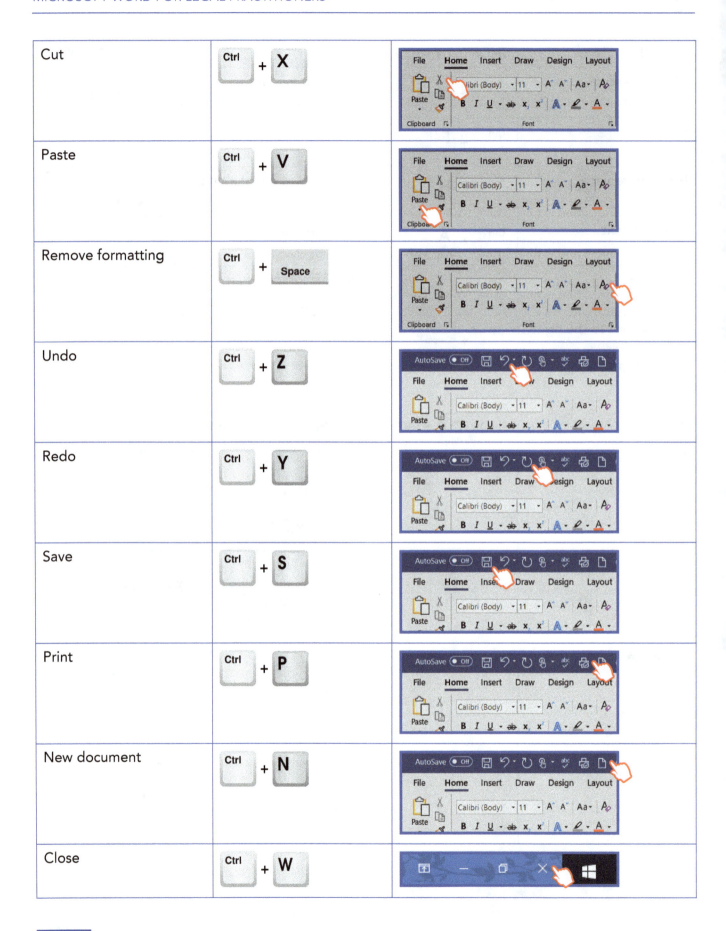
Paste	Ctrl + V	
Remove formatting	Ctrl + Space	
Undo	Ctrl + Z	
Redo	Ctrl + Y	
Save	Ctrl + S	
Print	Ctrl + P	
New document	Ctrl + N	
Close	Ctrl + W	

8.7 Format Painter

The easiest and fastest way to format text is to "paint" the text with the format copied from other text. The paint brush is dipped in the format-paint of the formatted text and then painted over the unformatted text.

8.7.1 How to format text with Format Painter

- Select the text that has the formatting you want to copy.
- Click on **Home**, and in the **Clipboard** group, click on the **Format Painter** button.

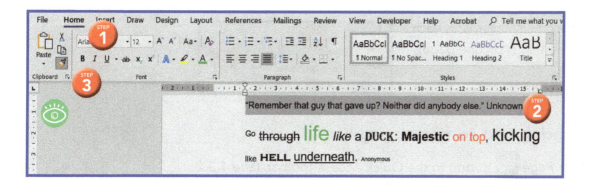

The **Format Painter** button will take on a darker shade to indicate that the format-paint has been loaded on to the "paint brush". The cursor will have a little paint brush next to it. Paint the format-paint over the unformatted text by highlighting the unformatted text.

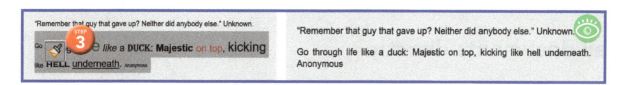

8.8 Shrink text to one page

Don't waste time adjusting margins, font sizes and spacing to make all your text fit on one page. Word offers two options to easily solve this problem. The first function (scale text) is a quick fix  option, while the second function provides a more permanent solution.

Time saver

8.8.1 Scale text to one page

- Select all the text.
- Click on the **Home** tab.
- Click on the **Decrease Font Size** button **A**.

The font size will become smaller with each click. Click until all the text is on one page.

8.8.2 How to shrink text to fit one page

Add the **Shrink One Page** button to the Quick Access Toolbar. (See *1.3.2 How to add functions to the Quick Access Toolbar*).

Select all the text. Click on and Word will fit the text to one page.

8.9 Email documents directly

Email a document in Word format, PDF or XPS directly from Word without first having to open Outlook to do so. Word will automatically convert the document, open Outlook, and attach the document to the e-mail for you.

- Open the document to be emailed and click on **File**.

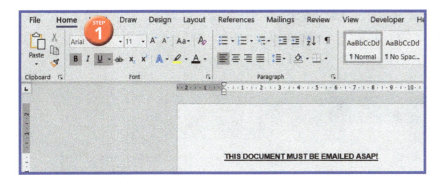

- Click on **Share** > **Email** > **Send as Attachment.**

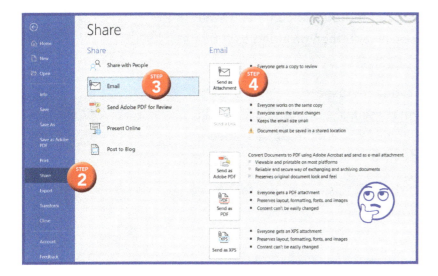

Word will automatically attach the Word document unless you select one of the other formats. You can choose Adobe PDF, PDF or XPS by clicking on your preferred option.

When Outlook opens up automatically, you need to:
- Insert your recipient's e-mail address
- Type your message
- Click **Send** .

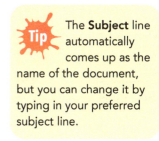

Tip The **Subject** line automatically comes up as the name of the document, but you can change it by typing in your preferred subject line.

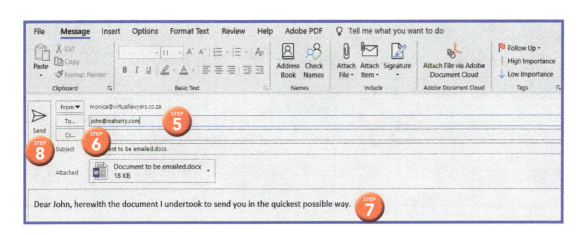

Time saver

A document can be e-mailed even faster by adding the e-mail button to the Quick Access Toolbar (see *1.3.2 How to add functions to the Quick Access Toolbar*).

8.10 Macros

A macro is a customised shortcut that consists of a group of commands that are recorded in the sequence in which they occur and then grouped together as a single command.

When using a macro, you can automate frequently used tasks and thereby save time and effort by not having to perform these tasks over and over again. Whenever you want to perform the tasks again, you simply run the macro. Word will action the sequence of commands automatically.

To create a macro, the sequence of commands used to perform the task must be recorded and saved. There are three steps involved.

8.10.1 Step 1: Establish the sequence of commands required

Make sure that you know exactly which commands are required, and the order in which they must be performed, to complete the task to be automated. Practice the steps a few times. If you make a mistake halfway through the recording, you will have to stop the recording and start over again.

8.10.2 Step 2: Name, describe and set up the macro details

- Click on the **View** tab.
- Click on **Macros** > **Record Macros**.

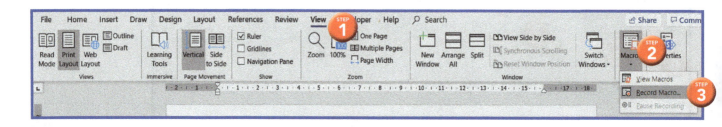

- In the **Record Macro** screen, type in a name for the macro you want to create. No spaces are allowed, so rather use underscores to separate the different words in the name.
- Select **All Documents (Normal.dotm)** under **Store macro in** to store the macro so that it can be used in all new documents.
- Add a description for the macro to remind you what the macro does or is needed for.
- The macro can be run by clicking 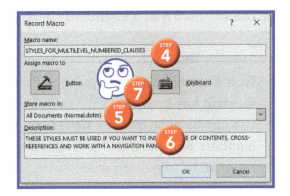 or .

To run the macro as a button

- Click on . The **Customise the Quick Access Toolbar** screen will open.
- Click on the new macro, then click **Add** and **Modify.** The **Modify Button** dialogue box will appear.
- Choose a button image and give the button a name next to **Display name**.
- Click **OK** to return to the **Customize the Quick Access Toolbar** screen.
- Click **OK** again.

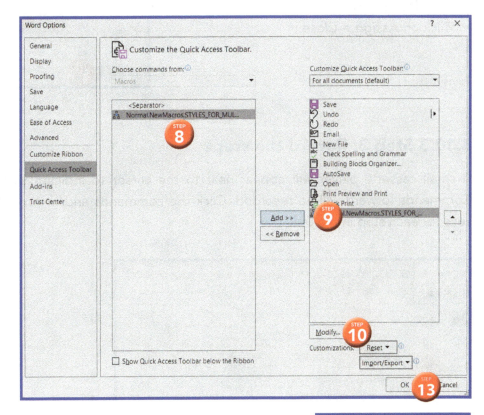

The Button for the macro will appear in the Quick Access Toolbar.

To run the macro as a keyboard shortcut

- Click on 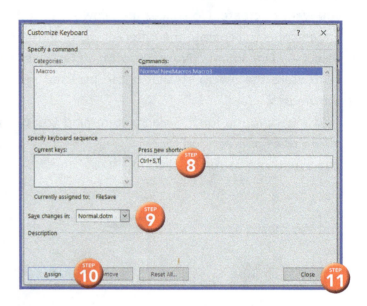.
- Type a combination of keys in the **Press new shortcut key** box.
- The combination must be *Ctrl+(any numbers or letters)* and must not already be assigned to something else!
- Next to **Save changes in** select *Normal. dotm* to use this keyboard shortcut in any new documents.
- Click on *Assign* > *Close*.

8.10.3 Step 3: Record the steps

A small cassette player will appear next to the cursor to indicate that all Commands forward will be recorded. Click the commands and/or press the keys for each step in the task.

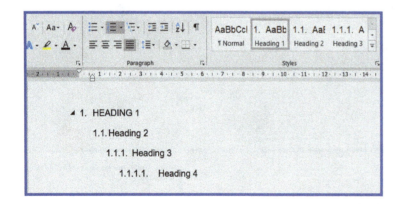

⚠ Don't use the mouse to select text while recording the macro. Macros don't record selections made with a mouse.

In this example all the steps undertaken to create multilevel numbered clauses and Heading styles were recorded.

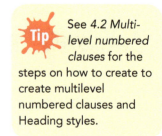
Tip See *4.2 Multi-level numbered clauses* for the steps on how to create to create multilevel numbered clauses and Heading styles.

To pause recording:

- Click **View** > **Macros** > **Pause Recording**.
- While the recording is paused, you can type what is needed without it being recorded.

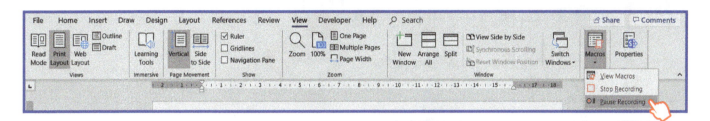

To resume recording again, click **View** > **Macros** > **Resume Recorder**. ─────────────────

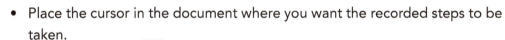

To stop recording:

- Click **View** > **Macros** > **Stop Recording**.
- The macro is automatically saved.

8.10.4 How to run a macro

- Place the cursor in the document where you want the recorded steps to be taken.
- Select the **Macro** 🔲 button you created on the Quick Access Toolbar

  OR

  Use the keyboard shortcut keys you assigned to the macro, for example:

  OR

  Run the macro from the **Macros** list.

💡 **Insight**

🔲 is the default symbol for a macro if you don't modify the button (Steps 10 to 12).

- Click on the **View** tab, and then in the **Macros** group, click on **Macros** and select **View Macros.**
- In the list under **Macro name** click on the macro you want, then click **Run**.

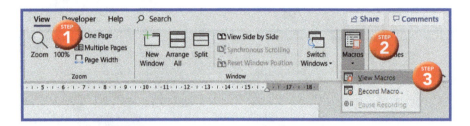

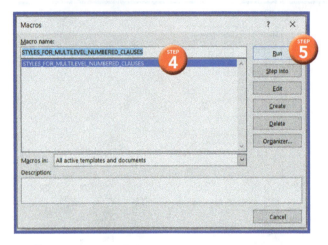

Word will automatically run all the recorded steps to achieve the task.

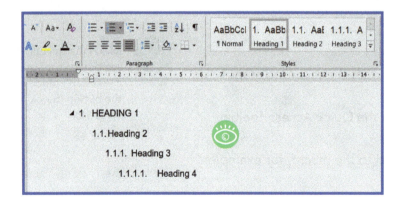

Word has many handy functions to make drafting, editing, and reviewing documents a pleasure. In this chapter we will cover some of these functions.

9.1 Insert a symbol

A symbol is a character that is not found on your keyboard keys, such as: ê, é, ï, ±, ½, and so on. Mathematical, currency and copyright symbols can be inserted in your document in the following way:

- Place the cursor where you want to insert the symbol.
- Click on the *Insert* tab, and under the **Symbols** group, click on Ω Symbol ▾.
- In the **Symbols** box, scroll down until you find the symbol you wish to insert into your text. Click on the symbol.

Tip Click on Ω More Symbols... to see the hundreds of symbol options available.

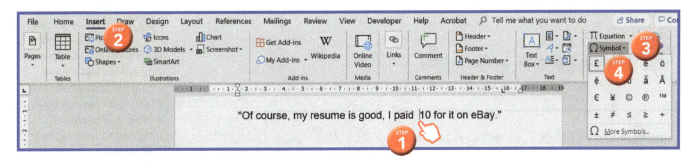

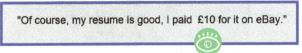

"Of course, my resume is good, I paid £10 for it on eBay."

9.2 Change letter case

Frustration

AAAAAH! I DID IT AGAIN! I TYPED EVERYTHING IN CAPITAL LETTERS!

Change Case Aa▾ is an easy-to-use function that automatically changes the letter case for you without you having to retype the whole sentence again.

- Select the text containing the letter case you want to change.
- Click on **Home**, and under the **Font** group, click on the drop-down arrow next to Aa▾.
- Select the case option you want to use.

Note You have various options available to you: Sentence case, lowercase, UPPERCASE, Capitalize Each Word, or tOGGLE cASE.

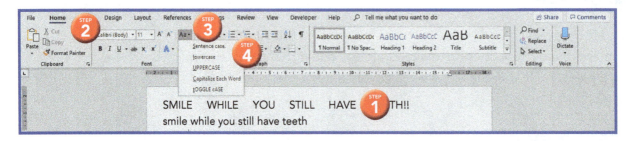

Select the text you would like to change, then press:

Do this **once** to Give Each Word A Capital Letter, **twice** to CHANGE ALL THE TEXT TO UPPERCASE, and **three times** to change everything back to lowercase.

9.3 Clear all formatting

These formats are a mess!

Frustration

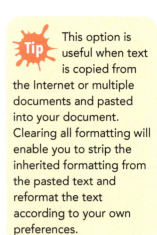

Tip This option is useful when text is copied from the Internet or multiple documents and pasted into your document. Clearing all formatting will enable you to strip the inherited formatting from the pasted text and reformat the text according to your own preferences.

The Clear All Formatting tool enables you to clear the formatting of your text and start afresh.

- Select the text containing the formatting you want to clear.
- Click on **Home**, and under the **Font** group, click on **Clear All Formatting**.

"Sometimes I wish I was an octopus, so I could SLAP eight people at once" – Anonymous"

9.4 Insert date and time

Frustration

The date is wrong!

With the function to insert a date using Word's **Date & Time** tool, this will never happen again.

- Place the cursor where you want to insert the date.
- Click on **Insert**, and under the **Text** group, click on the **Date & Time** tool.

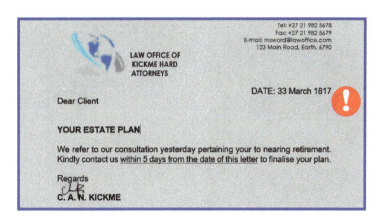

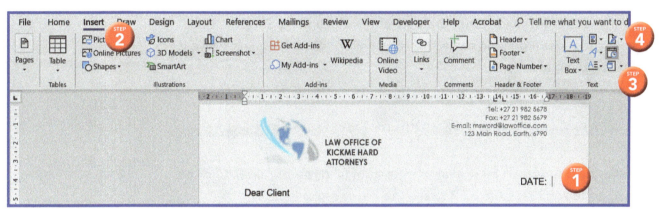

- Click on the date format you want to insert.
- Click on **Update automatically** to prevent incorrect dates in the future.
- Click on **OK**.

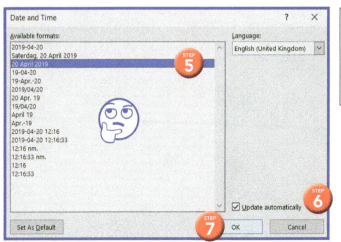

The time can be inserted on its own, or with a date.

Benefit

Tip By adding the **Date & Time** function to the header or footer of a document, the date and time will automatically appear on every page.

Today's date will be inserted. The date is highlighted to indicate that it is an active field that can be undated.

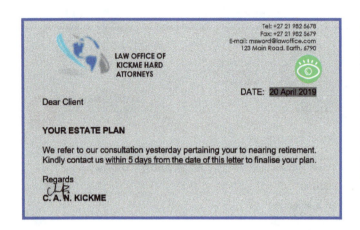

Insight The **Date & Time** settings are part of this document. Save the document under a generic name should you wish to use it again or save it as a template.

Frustration *What weird code is this?!* DATE: { TIME \@ "dd MMMM yyyy" }

Sometimes field codes will be displayed instead of field results (date). Click on the weird code and press *Alt + F9* to see the Field results (date).

OR right-click on the weird code, then click on *Toggle Field Codes* to see the date.

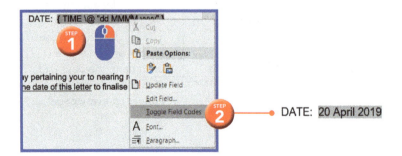

9.5 Undo and redo anything

There are two ways to undo an action in Word if you've made a mistake or change your mind about your edit. The first is to use a handy keyboard shortcut key and the second is to click **Undo** on the Quick Access Toolbar. You can undo and redo up to 20 of your last actions.

9.5.1 Undo and redo an action using a control key shortcut

Undo an action: Press: **Ctrl + Z** on your keyboard at the same time. Each time you press this shortcut, you will go back a step.

Redo an undone action: Press **Ctrl + Y** on your keyboard. Each time you press this shortcut, you will redo one of your undone actions.

 I made a mistake!

Frustration

The **Undo** button allows you to undo nearly anything you have done. Even text deleted by accident can be retrieved.

Click to instantly undo the **last** action.

Click on the arrow next to the **Undo** button to view a drop-down menu of the latest actions. A more distant action can be undone.

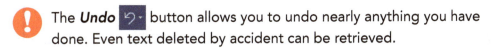
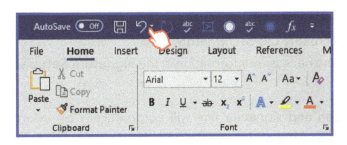

 I can't find the Undo button in the Quick Access Toolbar!

Frustration

See *1.3.2* in *Chapter 1: Overview of functions* on how to add the Undo button to the Quick Access Toolbar.

I saved but I want to go back to the text I had before I saved!

Frustration

cannot help you "unsave" a document. The version of the document before you saved cannot be retrieved. When saving your document, rather do so under a new name so that you don't overwrite the previous version.

If the **Redo** button is faded, this indicates that there isn't an action that was undone, therefore there is nothing that you can redo.

When the **Redo** button is white, you can click it to redo what you have just undone.

> **Tip** When you use the **Undo** command and afterwards decide you do not want the **Undo** action, you can simply reverse the **Undo** action by clicking the Redo button ↻! Keep in mind that you can only **Redo** something if the **Undo** command was used.

9.6 Add a signature line

Don't struggle with lines, tabs, indents and spacing when trying to include a signature line in your document. Word has a built-in function that quickly and easily inserts a signature line, along with the signatory's name and an indication of where to sign.

- Click on **Insert** and under the **Text** group, click on ▣.
- Click on **Microsoft Office Signature Line**.
- Complete the necessary information in the **Signature Setup** screen.
- Click **OK**.

The information and signature line will automatically be inserted at the end of the document.

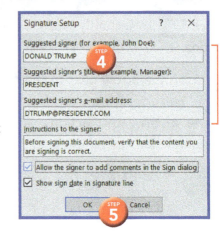

X_____

DONALD TRUMP
PRESIDENT

9.7 Sort data in alphabetical order

Word can sort a numbered or unnumbered list in alphabetical order.

- Select the entire list.
- Under the *Home* tab, look for the **Paragraph** group and click on the *Sort* button.
- The **Sort Text** dialogue window will open.
- The default settings are **Sort by Paragraphs**; **Type: Text**, and **Ascending** order. The list will be alphabetical from A to Z. (Descending order will sort the list from Z to A).
- If you are happy with these settings, click **OK**.

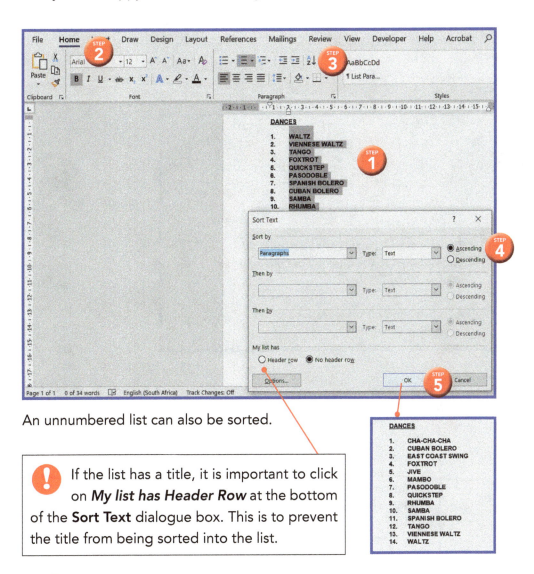

An unnumbered list can also be sorted.

> ❗ If the list has a title, it is important to click on *My list has Header Row* at the bottom of the **Sort Text** dialogue box. This is to prevent the title from being sorted into the list.

9.8 Bookmarks

A bookmark is a location in your document that you mark so that you can find it again easily. When you want to jump to that location in your document, you simply click on its bookmark. Using bookmarks is very much quicker than scrolling through a document and manually trying to locate certain sections of text. In a lengthy legal document, bookmarks are therefore extremely useful.

9.8.1 Insert a bookmark

- Place the cursor in the text where you want to place the bookmark.
- Click **Insert** > **Links** > **Bookmark**.
- Type a name for the bookmark.
- Click **Add**.

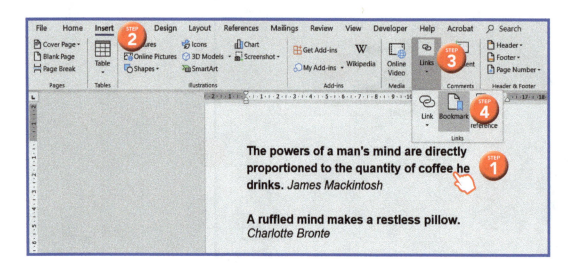

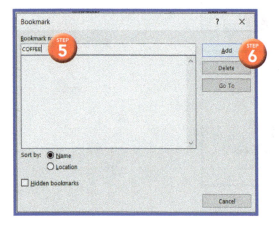

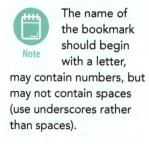

The name of the bookmark should begin with a letter, may contain numbers, but may not contain spaces (use underscores rather than spaces).

9.8.2 View the bookmarks

Frustration

I can't see the bookmarks!

The Word backstage settings must be set to show the bookmarks.

- Click on **File** > **Options** > **Advanced** > **Show document content.**
- Click on the tick box next to **Show bookmarks.**
- Click **OK**.

The bookmark can't be seen on the screen, but it is there ready for use. Click **Go To** in the **Bookmark** dialogue box to be taken to the bookmark.

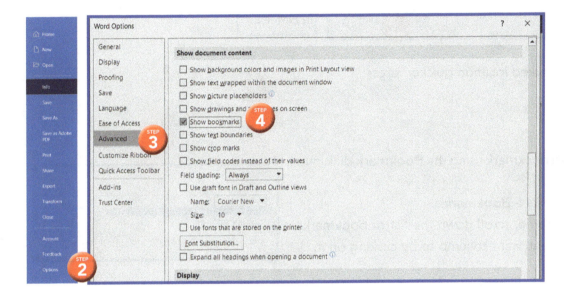

Insight

You won't know where to jump to if the bookmarks can't be seen. Bookmarks can also be accidently deleted if they aren't seen.

9.8.3 Instantly jump to the bookmarked location in the text

- Under the **Home** tab, click on the drop-down arrow next to **Find** and then click on **Go To.**
- The **Find and Replace** dialogue box will appear.
- In the **Go to what** drop-down menu, select **Bookmark**.
- Under **Enter bookmark name**, select the bookmark name from the drop-down menu.
- Click **Go To.**

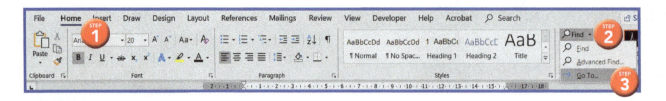

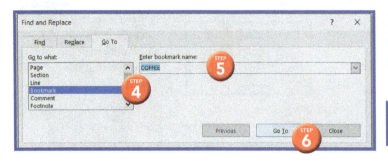

The cursor will jump to the bookmarked location in the text.

To jump to the bookmarked location quicker, press:

Ctrl + **G**

You can also jump to a bookmark using the **Bookmark** dialogue box:

- Click on *Insert* > *Links* > *Bookmark*.
- Under **Bookmark name**, scroll down the list of bookmarks and select the one you want to jump to by clicking on it.
- Click *Go To*.

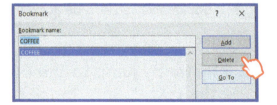

9.8.4 Delete a bookmark

- Click on *Insert* > *Links* > *Bookmark*.
- Under **Bookmark name**, scroll down the list of bookmarks and select the one you want to delete by clicking on it.
- Click *Delete*.

The bookmark will be deleted from your document and removed from the list of bookmarks.

> **Tip**
> Bookmarks are useful when automating the creation of legal documents. Bookmarks are used to insert dynamic fields, legacy forms, and content controls in a document. Important information can be inserted in one field and will automatically appear in all linked bookmarks and fields (see Chapter 10: Automation).

9.9 Footnotes

Legal Authorities, references to court cases, and other notes can be inserted as footnotes at the bottom of a page. A superscript number is inserted in the text to match up with the related footnote.

9.9.1 Create a footnote

- Place the cursor in the text where you want the footnote number inserted.
- Click on the *References* tab.
- In the **Footnotes** group, click on *ab1 Insert Footnote*.
- Type in the text for the footnote and press *Enter* on the keyboard.

> **Tip** When deleting a footnote, delete only the superscript number in the text – do not delete the actual footnote text. Word will automatically delete the footnote text when the superscript number is deleted.

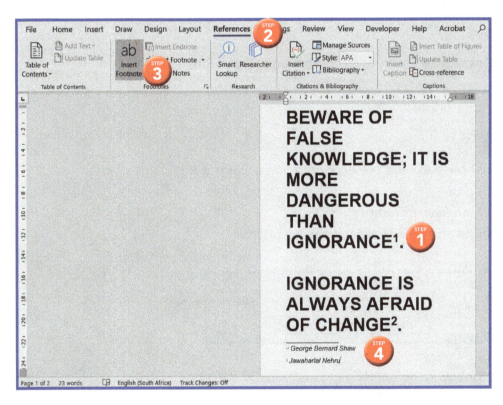

Insight Word keeps track of all footnotes and corresponding numbers in the text as the document is edited.

 Insert footnotes quicker with the shortcut keys:

Ctrl + Alt + F

9.9.2 Edit or delete a footnote

To edit a footnote, place the cursor in the footnote and make the correction.

To delete a footnote, select the superscript number in the text and press `Delete` on the keyboard. Both the superscript number and its related footnote will be deleted. Word will update all the remaining footnote numbers automatically.

9.9.3 Return to the text from the footnote

To get back to the main body of text that relates to the footnote, double-click the footnote number at the beginning of the footnote.

9.10 Endnotes

Endnotes are similar to footnotes but are positioned together on a page at the end of the document.

9.10.1 Create an endnote

- Place the cursor in the text where you want the endnote number inserted.
- Click on the **References** tab.
- In the **Footnotes** group, click on **Insert Endnote**.
- Type in the text for the endnote and press **Enter** on the keyboard.

Refer to the footnotes section for how to edit and delete endnotes (9.9.2) and return to the text from an endnote (9.9.3).

9.11 Tables

Legal documents can be drafted more neatly and professionally if tables are used to separate, list, or align items and text.

Frustration

I can't get all these dates, numbers, and amounts neatly aligned!

The easiest way to align items neatly in Word is to use tables.

Tables are made up of columns and rows. Word uses tabs 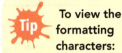 to create columns and returns ¶ to signify rows. Each new line of text becomes a row in the table you are creating. However, you will need to let Word know where to create the columns. You use tabs to do this.

> **Tip**
>
> **To view the formatting characters:**
> - Click on the *Home* tab.
> - In the **Paragraph** group, click on ¶.
> - To hide the formatting characters, click again on ¶.

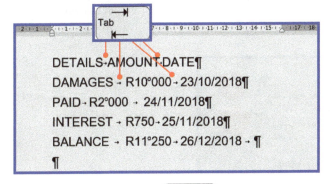

Be sure to press after each item, before you type the next item.

There are three ways you can create tables. You can 1) insert a table from selected text; 2) convert text into a table; and 3) create a new table.

9.11.1 Insert a table from selected text

- Select all the text that you want to turn into a table.
- Click on *Insert* > *Table* > *Insert Table*.

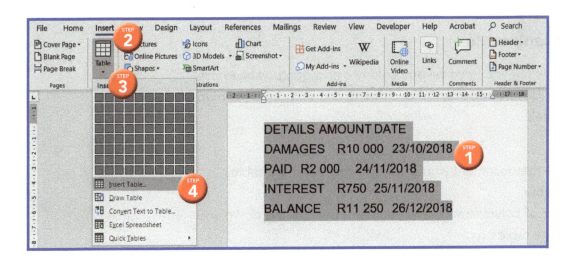

DETAILS	AMOUNT	DATE
DAMAGES	R10 000	23/10/2018
PAID	R2 000	24/11/2018
INTEREST	R750	25/11/2018
BALANCE	R11 250	26/12/2018

Word automatically inserts the correct number of rows and columns according to the tabs .

9.11.2 Convert text to a table

- Select all the text to be converted into a table.
- Click on **Insert** > **Table** > **Convert Text to Table**.
- In the **Convert Text to Table** dialogue box, select the number of columns.
- Click **OK**.

Insight This option is used for "normal" text, being without tabs in between the words.

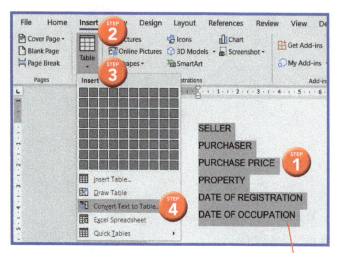

The text will be converted into a neat table.

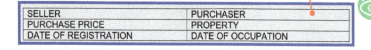

SELLER	PURCHASER
PURCHASE PRICE	PROPERTY
DATE OF REGISTRATION	DATE OF OCCUPATION

9.11.3 Insert a blank table

Blank tables are used when you have several columns and don't want to use tabs. A blank table can be inserted into the document, and text can be copied and pasted into each cell.

Method 1

- Place your cursor in the document where you want to insert the table.
- Click on **Insert** > **Table**.
- Choose the number of columns and rows you need by scrolling down and across the cells in the table box.

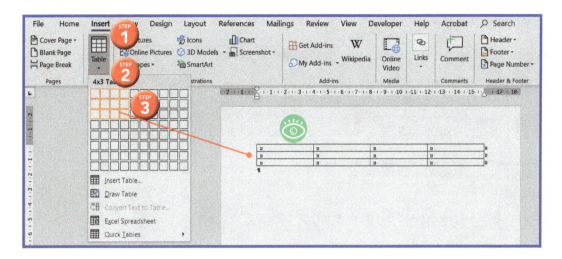

Method 2

- Place your cursor in the document where you want to insert the table.
- Click on *Insert* > *Table* > *Insert Table*.
- In the **Insert Table** box under **Table size** insert the number of columns and rows you want.
- Click *OK*.

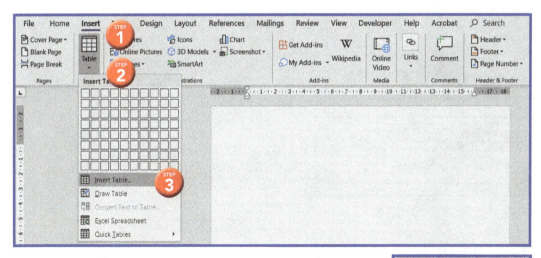

> **Tip** **Easily resize columns and rows**: Position the cursor over a line that divides two columns or rows. When the cursor changes to a cross, hold the left button down on the mouse and move the mouse to resize the column or row.

9.11.4 Insert a new row

To add a new row, place the cursor in the last cell and press Tab .

9.11.5 Insert, delete and merge columns and cells

- Select the cells you want to modify.
- Right-click and then, in the options menu, click on the action you want to perform.

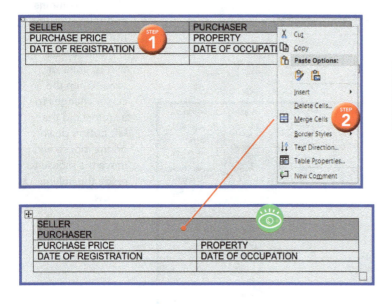

In this example, **Merge Cells** was selected.

9.11.6 Split columns and cells

- You can split a cell that has been merged back into separate columns or rows.
- Select the cell you want to split.
- **Right-click** and then, in the options menu, click on *Split Cells*.
- The columns or rows will become separate again.

Tip You can only split a cell that has already been merged. When you right-click on the cell you want to split, the **Merge Cells** option will disappear from the options menu and the **Split Cells** option will become available.

9.11.7 Change the look of the table

- Select all the table cells.
- **Right-click** to launch the options menu.
- Select the required options in the options menu to change the look of the table.

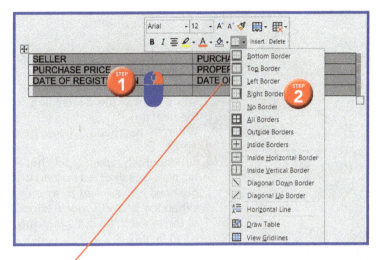

In this example, **No Border** was selected.

9.12 Columns

Two or more columns of text are sometimes required for legal documents. We will now look at how you can create columns in your document.

9.12.1 Insert columns throughout an entire document

- Click on the **Layout** tab.
- In the **Page Setup** group, click on **Columns**.
- Select the number of columns you want. For more column options, click on **More Columns**.

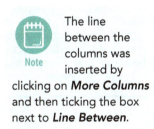

Note The line between the columns was inserted by clicking on **More Columns** and then ticking the box next to **Line Between**.

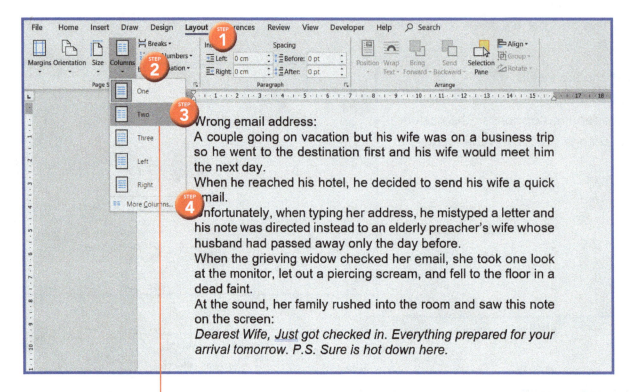

Wrong email address:
A couple going on vacation but his wife was on a business trip so he went to the destination first and his wife would meet him the next day.
When he reached his hotel, he decided to send his wife a quick email.
Unfortunately, when typing her address, he mistyped a letter and his note was directed instead to an elderly preacher's wife whose husband had passed away only the day before.
When the grieving widow checked her email, she took one look at the monitor, let out a piercing scream, and fell to the floor in a dead faint.
At the sound, her family rushed into the room and saw this note on the screen:
Dearest Wife, Just got checked in. Everything prepared for your arrival tomorrow. P.S. Sure is hot down here.

Wrong email address:
A couple going on vacation but his wife was on a business trip so he went to the destination first and his wife would meet him the next day.
When he reached his hotel, he decided to send his wife a quick email.
Unfortunately, when typing her address, he mistyped a letter and his note was directed instead to an elderly preacher's wife whose husband had passed away only the day before.

When the grieving widow checked her email, she took one look at the monitor, let out a piercing scream, and fell to the floor in a dead faint.
At the sound, her family rushed into the room and saw this note on the screen:
Dearest Wife, Just got checked in. Everything prepared for your arrival tomorrow. P.S. Sure is hot down here.

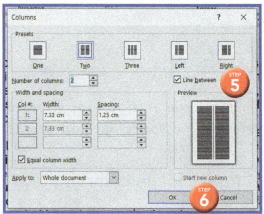

9.12.2 Insert columns in only part of a document

If you want different columns in the same document, a section break must be used (see *2.11.2 How to insert section breaks*). Insert the section break at the start of the part that must have the different columns, then insert the columns as above. Each time the columns change, a new section break is needed.

You can also format just a section of text in two or more columns. To do this, select the text that must appear in columns and insert the columns as shown in 9.12.1 above. Word will automatically insert the necessary section breaks.

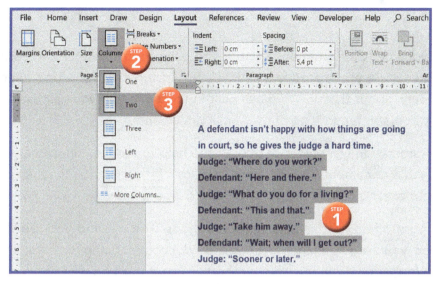

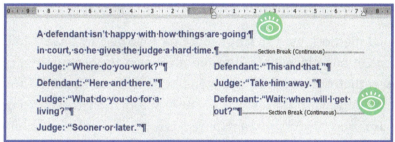

9.13 Calculate

Add the **Calculate** button to the Quick Access Toolbar (see section 1.3.2 on how to add functions to the Quick Access Toolbar).

- Highlight the amounts you would like to calculate, for example 150.00+250.00+500.00.
- Click on the **Calculate** button in the Quick Access Toolbar.
- The answer is displayed in the lower left corner of the document window.

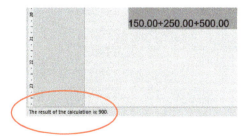

CHAPTER 10 AUTOMATION

Document automation is the new buzzword in the legal profession. Documents are automated by "robots", but fortunately you don't need to know much about that as Word has built-in functions that you can use to help you automate the drafting of your legal documents.

Automation can save a lot of time and help to reduce unnecessary interaction with a document, thus eliminating many of the mistakes that can occur when performing certain tasks or inputting data manually.

Word offers various automation methods. The method you use will depend on your requirements; the type of document being drafted; the type of information required; whether the document must be protected from editing; and whether the document must be saved as a template.

For each method, various steps must be followed to enable information to be typed in one place in the document yet also appear automatically in other places in that document. These steps must then be repeated for every new piece of information required. For the automation to work correctly, you must also map where you want certain bits of information to be inserted and repeated in the document.

Automation can only be applied effectively when a legal document is properly formatted and edited. A badly formatted template or document will produce a poor end result, even if the automation is applied perfectly.

A summary of the features of each automation method is provided at the end of this chapter.

First you will need to know about the **Developer** tab and **Reference Fields** to use some of Word's automation methods.

Developer tab

Insight

The **Developer** tab, which can be found in the Ribbon, allows you to "develop" and customise Word to suit your needs and to perform various tasks quickly and accurately.

If the Developer tab is not in the ribbon, the ribbon must be customised to include it.

Add the Developer tab to your Ribbon:

- Click on *File* > *Options* > *Customise Ribbon.*
- Select *Customise Ribbon* on the left of the **Word Options** dialogue box.
- Under **Choose commands from** select *Main Tabs.*
- Now click on *Developer* in the menu below to select it.
- Click *Add,* and then *OK.*

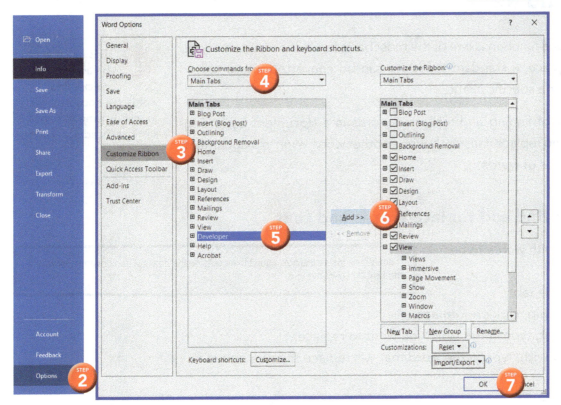

When you click on the *Developer* tab on the Ribbon, various options will become available to you. For instance, you can record macros, create drop-down menus and check boxes, as well as many other advanced options.

Reference fields

Insight

A **reference field** is a field that instructs Word to automatically insert data into a document. When you update the data in the reference field, the data in other fields connected to that reference field update automatically as well. This saves Legal Practitioners from having to type out the same data over and over again in a document.

Note

A field is simply a set of codes that allows you to input data in a specific place.

Reference fields can be inserted in various ways, so you can choose the method that is easiest for you. In this chapter, various methods have been used in each of the automation options that require reference fields. Each Automation Option and the Reference Field used are discussed in detail below.

Automation option	Type of reference field used
Dynamic fields	= (Formula) function in Fields screen
Fillable forms	Ref function in Fields screen
Content controls	Cross-reference

10.1 Find and Replace

The Find and Replace function is one of the most basic functions of automation. With Find and Replace, a standard template can be converted into a tailor-made document for a specific client.

Automate the task of finding and replacing words in a document by letting Word find a word and replace it instantly with another word, even in a document containing thousands of words.

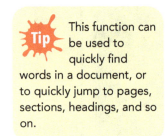

Tip This function can be used to quickly find words in a document, or to quickly jump to pages, sections, headings, and so on.

10.1.1 How to find and replace words and text

Open a document with words to be replaced.

> "I don't think inside the box, I don't think outside the box .....I don't even know where the box is." – Anonymous

- Click on the **Home** tab.
- In the **Editing** group, click on **Replace**.
- Next to **Find what**, type in the word you want to replace.
- Next to **Replace with,** type in the word that will replace the one above.

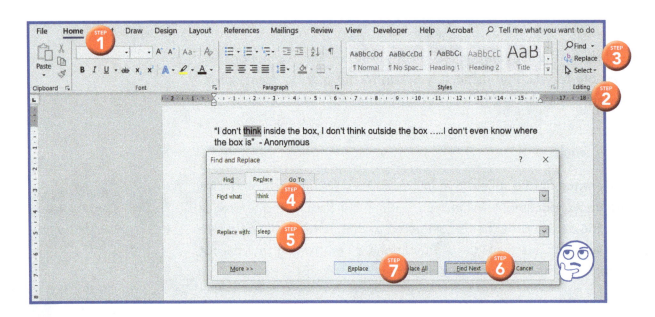

- If you click on *Find Next*, Word will highlight each instance of the word, one after the other. You can either click *Replace* (the highlighted word will be replaced) or *Find Next* (the highlighted word will not be replaced).
- Alternatively, you can click on *Replace All*. Word will automatically replace all the instances of the word and confirm the number of replacements that were made.
- Click *OK*.
- Repeat this process as needed.

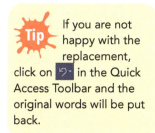

If you are not happy with the replacement, click on in the Quick Access Toolbar and the original words will be put back.

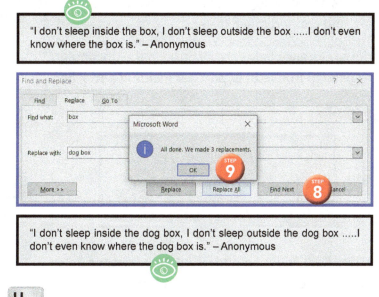

"I don't sleep inside the box, I don't sleep outside the box .....I don't even know where the box is." – Anonymous

"I don't sleep inside the dog box, I don't sleep outside the dog box .....I don't even know where the dog box is." – Anonymous

 Press **Ctrl** + **H** to quickly open up the Find and Replace screen.

10.1.2 Using the Find and Replace function in legal documents

This handy function can be used in a lengthy legal document where the same piece of information, such as the client's name and surname, appears numerous times.

In your document template, type in **XXX** wherever the **client's name and surname** must appear, and then save the template. Then, when you next draft a document for a client using that template, replace all the occurrences of **XXX** with the client's name and surname using the Search and Replace function.

The same can be done with other recurring information, such as the **client's identity number** (use **YYY**, for instance) or his **marital status** (use **ZZZ**, for instance).

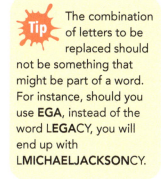

The combination of letters to be replaced should not be something that might be part of a word. For instance, should you use **EGA**, instead of the word **LEGA**CY, you will end up with **LMICHAELJACKSON**CY.

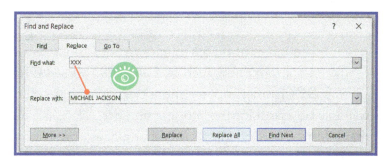

10.2 Dynamic fields

Fields are areas in a document in which information can be inserted. Dynamic fields are fields that update automatically when the information changes, so dynamic fields enable you to build a document automatically based on information provided by the user. The drafting of legal documents can therefore be automated, simplified, and created much faster.

> **Tip** A **Bookmark** is a specific location in your document that you identify and name.

To create dynamic fields, various reference fields are inserted in the document. The reference fields are then linked to Bookmarks, and Ask Fields are attached to each Bookmark.

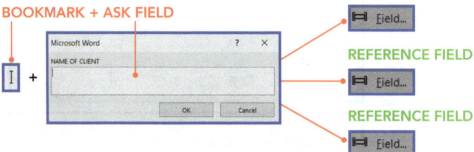

Whenever the information in the Ask Field is amended, all the reference fields in the document can be updated to contain the same amended information.

Five steps are required to create a dynamic field for each piece of information needed in the document.

10.2.1 How to create dynamic fields

Step 1: Template document

A correctly formatted and edited template document must be available. It must be clear which pieces of information will be required, and where in the document these pieces of information are to be inserted (see *Chapter 3*, sections *3.2–3.4* to find out more about templates).

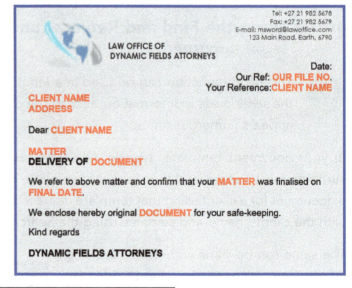

>
> **Insight** The different pieces of information are indicated in red. Some of the information, such as CLIENT NAME, MATTER and DOCUMENT appear more than once in the document. The user will only be asked for the information once. Word will automatically pull that information through to the other places in which it appears.

Step 2: Create a bookmark

For each piece of information required in the document, a Bookmark must be created. In the example above, six Bookmarks must be created, namely: CLIENT NAME, ADDRESS, MATTER, DOCUMENT, FINAL DATE and OUR FILE NO.

To create a Bookmark for CLIENT NAME:

- Place the cursor in the text at the first instance in the document where the information is required (the words CLIENT NAME must be deleted).
- Under the **Insert** tab, click on **Links** > **Bookmark**.

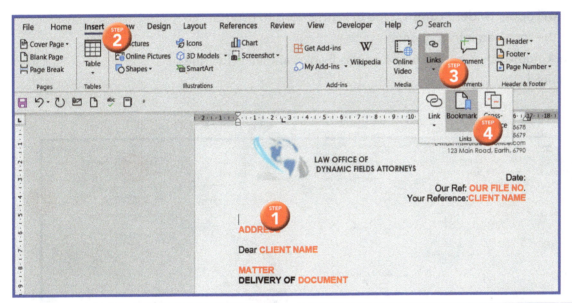

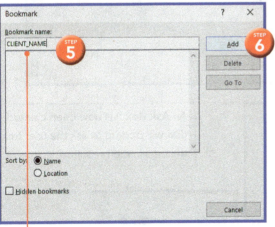

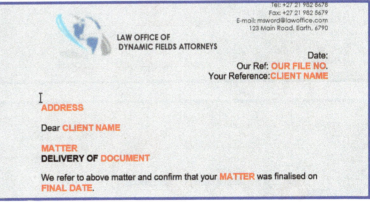

- Type in a name for the Bookmark (the name should begin with a letter, may contain numbers, but may not contain spaces – use underscores instead of spaces).
- Click on **Add**.

The Bookmark will be indicated with a ⌶ sign. If you can't see the Bookmark refer to section *9.8 Bookmarks.*

Step 3: Attach an Ask Field to create an Ask Box

Attach an Ask Field to the Bookmark to prompt the user to provide the information that will be linked to that Bookmark.

• Place the cursor on the Bookmark.

• Click on the *Insert* tab.

• In the **Text** group, click on the drop-down arrow next to the *Quick Parts* tool.

• Select *Field*.

• In the *Field* screen, under **Categories**, scroll down the list of Fields on the left and click on *Ask*.

• Another screen will open. Under **Prompt**, type in instructions to prompt the user to provide the required information.

• Under **Bookmark name**, click on the name of the Bookmark linked to the information required.

• Click *OK*.

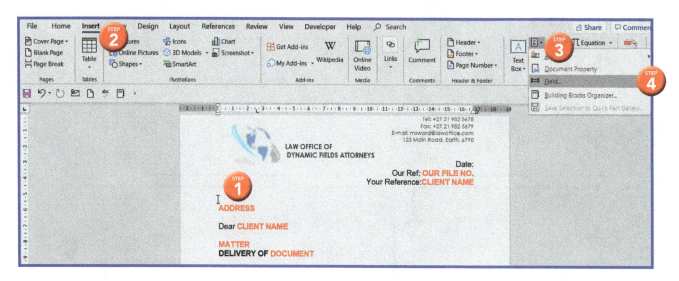

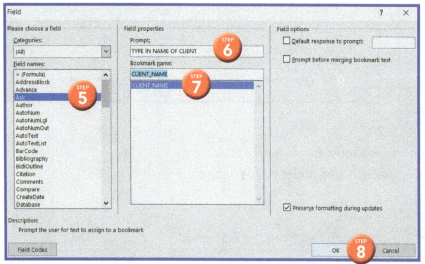

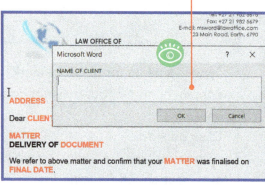

An **Ask Box** has now been created that will pop-up to ask the user for the information required.

Step 4: Insert a Reference Field

Insert a Reference Field to indicate to Word that the information in the Ask Box (Step 3) must be inserted when a specific Bookmark (Step 2) is referred to.

Since the first instance in the document where the information in the Ask Field (Step 3) is required is at the position of the Bookmark, the Reference Field is also inserted there.

- Place the cursor on the Bookmark.
- Click on the **Insert** tab.
- In the **Text** group, click on the drop-down arrow next to the **Quick Parts** button.
- Click on **Field**.

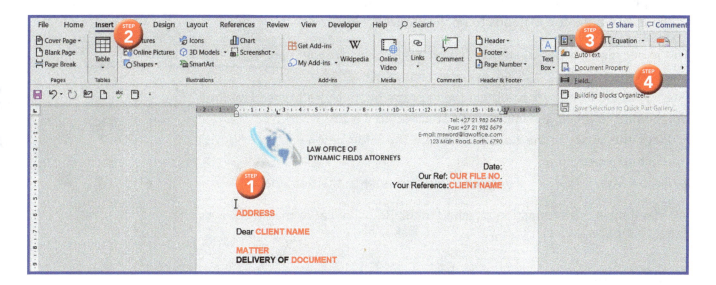

- In the **Field** dialogue box, under **Categories**, click on **= (Formula)**
- Click on **Formula**.
- A new screen will open up. Delete the = in the box under Formula.

- Type in REF and press the spacebar on the keyboard once to insert one space after REF.
- Click on the drop-down arrow under **Paste bookmark**.
- Select the name of the Bookmark created in Step 2.
- The name of the Bookmark will appear after REF under **Formula**.
- Click **OK**.
- Word will now know that the information the user typed in the Ask Box (Step 3) must show where the Reference Field has been inserted, which refers to the Bookmark (Step 2).

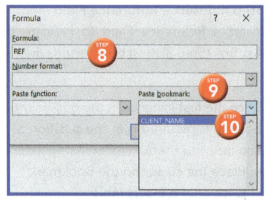

Step 5: Repeat the Reference Field

At all places in the document where the information (CLIENT NAME) is repeated, only a Reference Field (Step 4) referring to the Bookmark (Step 2) needs to be inserted.

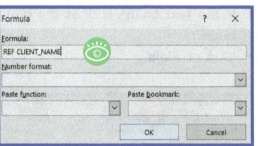

This is because the Bookmark for CLIENT NAME has already been created (Step 2) and an Ask Field has been attached (Step 3) to the Bookmark to obtain the information. Each Reference Field will be updated to reflect the information attached to the Bookmark.

- Place the cursor in the document where the information (CLIENT NAME) must be repeated.
- Follow Step 4 to insert a Reference Field to refer to the Bookmark.

Word will show the information attached to the Bookmark at each of the places where the Reference Field is inserted.

10.2.2 View dynamic fields in action

- Select all the text in the document
- Right-click, and then click on **Update Field** in the pop-up menu.

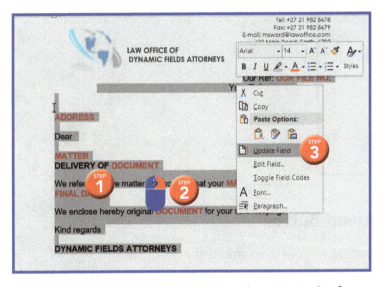

- The Ask Box will pop-up; type in the required information.
- Click **OK.**

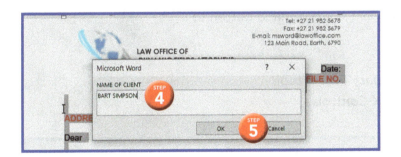

See 10.2.3 for how to insert an **Update Fields Command Button**

Time saver

Follow Steps 2 to 5 to turn all the different pieces of information required in the document (ADDRESS, MATTER, DOCUMENT, FINAL DATE and OUR FILE NO.) into Dynamic Fields.

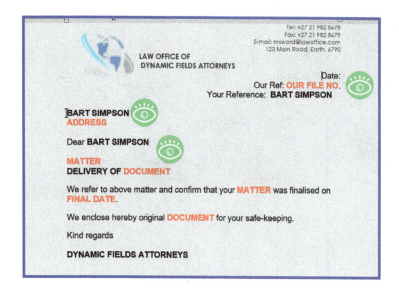

10.2.3 Insert an Update Fields Command Button

Insight

To insert an **Update Fields Command Button** in your document, the **Developer** tab must be added to the Ribbon (see the introduction to this chapter on how to insert the **Developer** tab).

Insert an Update Fields Command Button

- Place the cursor in the document where you want the command button to be inserted.
- Click on the **Developer** tab.
- Click on the drop-down arrow next to the **Legacy Forms** tool.
- Click on the **Command Button** under **ActiveX Controls**.

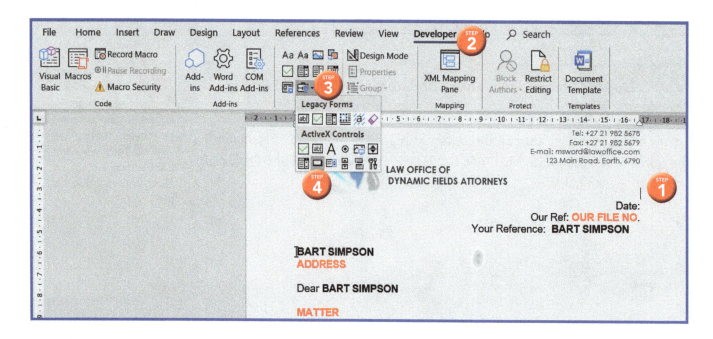

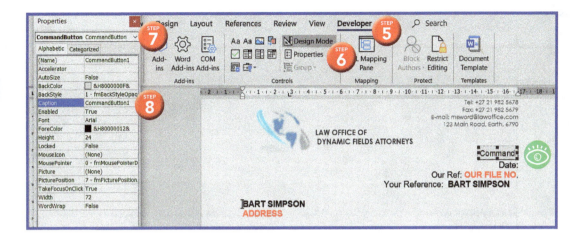

Change the wording on the Update Fields Command Button:

- Click on the *Developer* tab.
- In the **Controls** group, click on *Design Mode*.
- Click on *Properties*. A **Properties** dialogue box will appear on the left-hand side of the screen.
- Next to *Caption*, type in the amended wording for your Command Button.

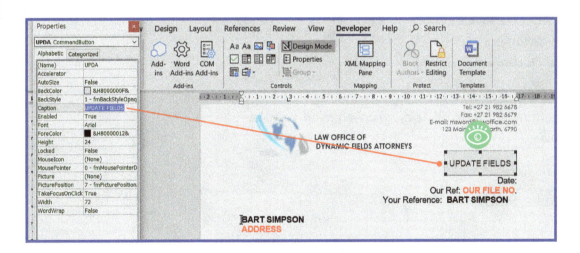

- Right-click on the *Update Fields* button.
- In the drop-down menu click on *View Code*.
- Type in the words **Fields.Update** as indicated below.
- Close the screen.

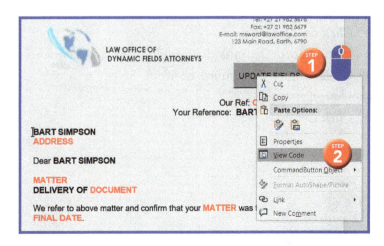

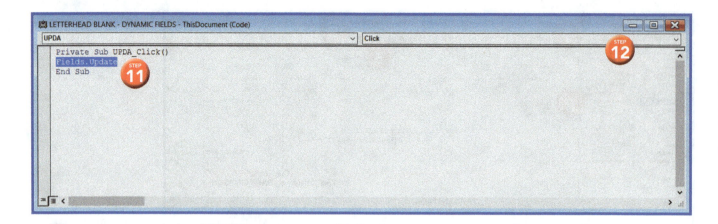

View the Update Fields Command Button in action:

Insight

Click on the *Update Fields Command Button* in your document. The **Ask Box** will open to prompt you to type in the required information. Enter the name of your client. Click **OK**.

The document must be saved as a macro-enabled document:
Word Macro-Enabled Document (*.docm)

If you want to save the document as a template, the document must be saved as a macro-enabled template: *Word Macro-Enabled Template (*.dotm)*

Frustration

I can't see the fields!

The Word backstage settings must be set to see the fields.
* Click on the *File* tab.
* Click on *Options*.
* In the **Word Options** dialogue box, click *Advanced* on the left.
* Under **Show document content**, select one of the options next to *Field shading*.
* Click **OK**.

Note

If more than one Bookmark and Ask Field were created, an Ask Box for each of them will open up one after the other. Once all the required information has been inserted into the Ask Boxes, all the Reference Fields in the document will update accordingly.

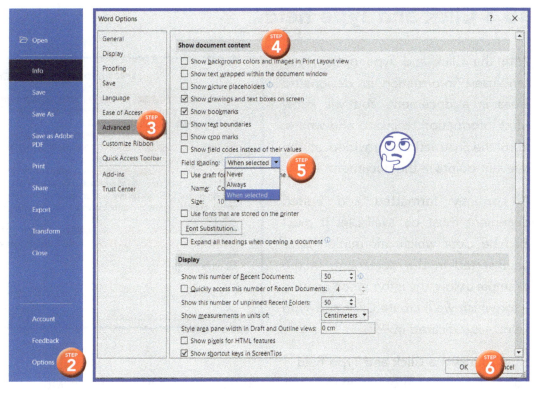

10.2.4 Restrict editing of Dynamic Fields

When editing of the document is restricted, the Dynamic Fields can't be used or updated!

The Dynamic Fields are not active, even if *Filling in forms* is allowed in the **Restrict Editing** settings in the **Protect** group under the *Review* tab (see *7.5 Restrict Editing*).

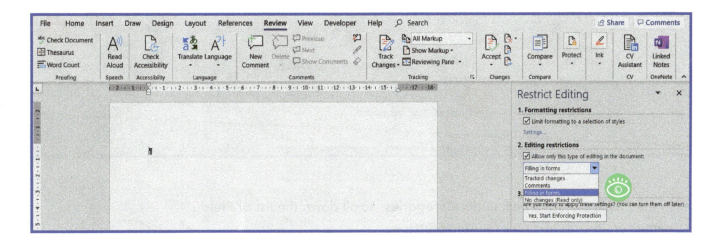

10.3 Click and Type fields

With the Click and Type option, you can insert information in designated areas in a document. You will know what information to insert, and where, from the instructions provided at the relevant points in the document.

A correctly formatted and edited document must be available. It must also be clear which information is to be inserted in the document. In the example below, the information needed – for which we'll create Click and Type fields – is indicated in RED.

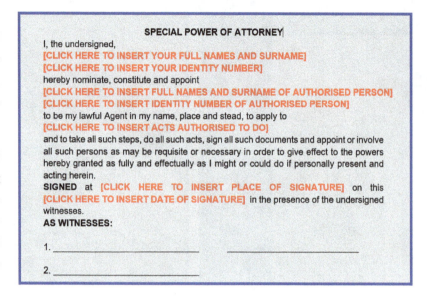

How to insert a Click and Type field

For each piece of information required in the document, a MacroButton with field codes must be created.

- Place the cursor in the text where the information is required (any text at that place in the document must be deleted).
- Click on the **Insert** tab.
- In the **Text** group, click on the drop-down arrow next to the **Quick Parts** button and select **Field**.

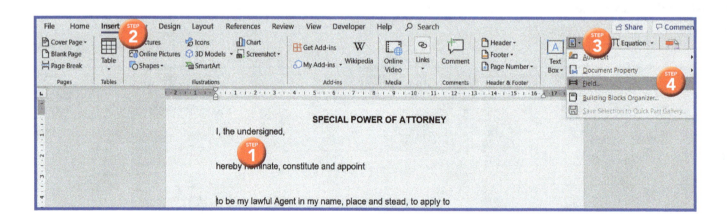

- In the **Fields** dialogue box, under **Categories**, scroll down the list of **Field names** on the left and click on **MacroButton**.
- A **Field properties** menu will open (but can be ignored for now).

- Click on the *Field Codes* button in the bottom left corner of the **Fields** screen.
- An **Advanced field properties** section will appear.
- Under **Field codes**, change the text: MACROBUTTON AcceptAllChangesInDoc,to: MACROBUTTON noname.
- Add block brackets and type in the instruction that must appear in the document so that the user will know what to type in.
- Click *OK*.
- The instructions will appear in the document. The area will be shaded to indicate that it is a field.

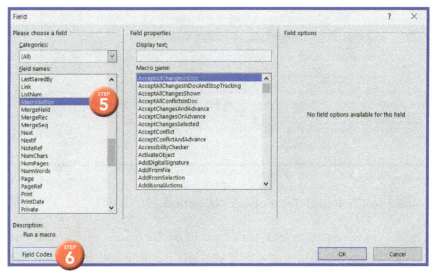

Note

The same steps must be followed for each piece of information required in the document. You will also insert a different instruction in the block brackets after MACROBUTTON noname telling the user what information must to be inserted. For example:

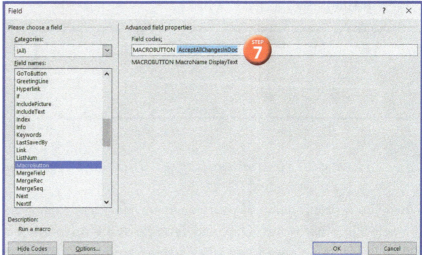

Tip When all the Click and Type fields have been added, the document can be saved as a Template. This will save you from having to repeat the process the next time you use the document (see 3.2 and 3.3 for how to create and save templates).

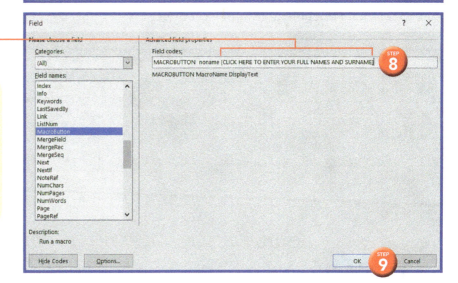

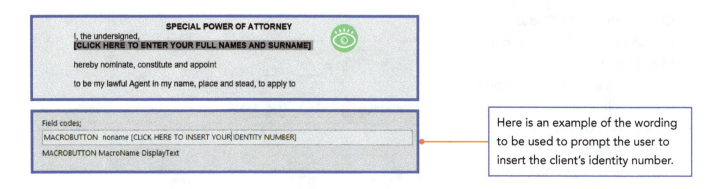

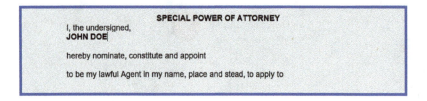

Here is an example of the wording to be used to prompt the user to insert the client's identity number.

View the Click and Type option in action

Insight

In your document, click on one of the instruction fields. The instruction text will disappear, and you will be able to type in the required information.

Frustration

How do I restrict editing of Click and Type fields?

When you restrict editing of your document, new text cannot be inserted in the fields. In other words, **Click and Type** fields are no longer active, even if **Filling in forms** is allowed (see *10.4 Fillable Forms* and *7.5 Restrict Editing* on how to restrict a document from being edited.).

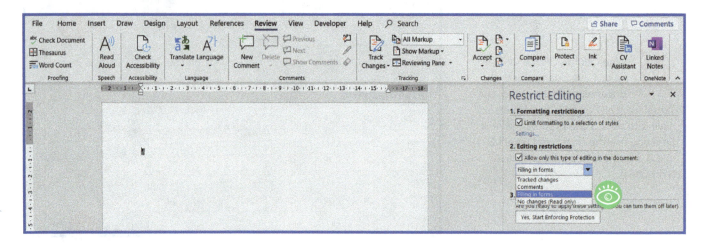

If the same information is required in different places in the document, the information will not update automatically in all the relevant fields.

10.4 Fillable Forms

Fillable forms are forms that enable easy editing and data input without messing up the structure and layout of the form. Information in the fillable form – such as a questionnaire or information sheet – can be automatically pulled through to its designated fields throughout the rest of the document.

Fillable forms are created using some of the functions under the **Developer** tab.

Four steps are needed to create a fillable form.

Step 1: Structured template

A correctly formatted and edited document must be available. It must be clear which pieces of information will be required, and where in the document these pieces of information must be inserted. The different pieces of information are indicated in red in the example below.

Step 2: Insert a text form field (with linked Bookmark)

For each piece of information required in the document, a text form field must be created.

- Place the cursor in the area where the information must be typed in by the user (any text at that place in the document must be deleted).
- Click on the **Developer** tab.
- In the **Controls** group, click on the drop-down arrow next to the **Legacy Forms** button.
- Click on the **Text Form Field** button.

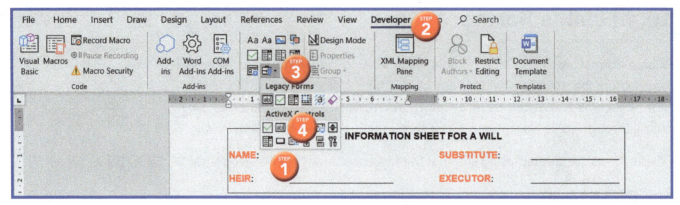

- Double-click on the field that was inserted.
- The **Text Form Field Options** dialogue box will open.
- Under **Default Text**, type in an instruction telling the user what information to insert.
- Under **Field settings**, insert a name under **Bookmark** (no spaces are allowed in the name).
- Select the boxes next to *Fill-in enabled* and *Calculate on exit.*
- Click *OK*.
- The instructions inserted as the default text will appear in the field.

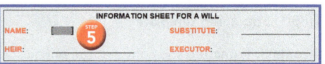

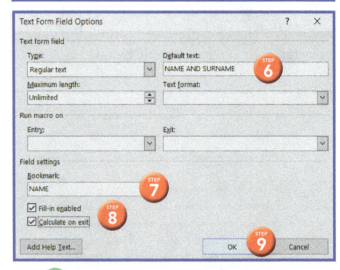

Step 3: Insert a reference field

Wherever the information (**NAME**) must be shown in the document, a reference field referring to the Bookmark must be inserted.

- Place the cursor in the document where the information (**NAME**) must be shown.
- Click on the *Insert* tab.
- In the **Text** group, click on the drop-down arrow next to the *Quick Parts* tool.
- Select *Field*.

- In the **Field** dialogue box, go to **Categories** and scroll down the list of **Field names** on the left.
- Click on *Ref*.
- Under **Bookmark name**, click on the name of the Bookmark created in

> **Note** Steps 2 to 3 must be followed for each of the different pieces of information required in the document. In our example, this would be: **HEIR**, **SUBSTITUTE** and **EXECUTOR**.

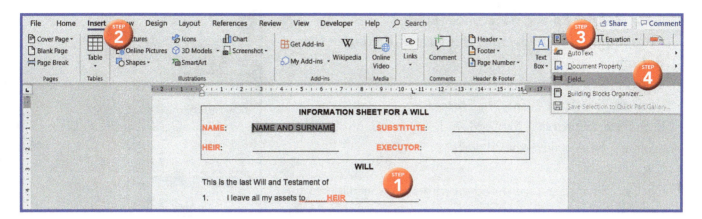

Step 2 for the relevant piece of information.

- Click **OK**.
- The instructions typed under **Default Text** in Step 2 will now also appear in the document where the cursor was placed.

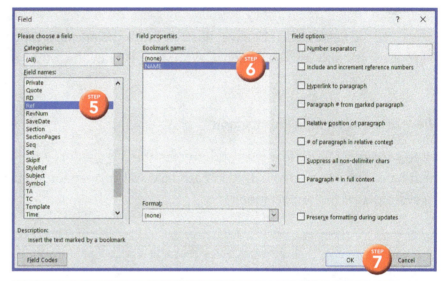

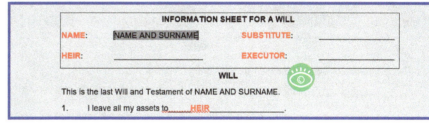

Step 4: Restrict editing

- Click on **Review** > **Protect** > **Restrict Editing**.

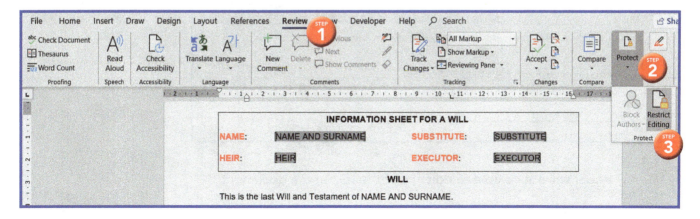

- In the **Restrict Editing** panel under **Editing restrictions** select *Allow only this type of editing in the document*.
- Select *Filling in forms*.
- Click on *Yes, Start Enforcing Protection*.
- In the **Start Enforcing Protection** dialogue box that appears, type in a password twice.
- Click *OK*.
- Click on *Save* to ensure that the protection is applied to the document.

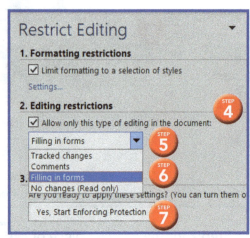

For the fields to be effective, **Restrict Editing** is an important step in the process and not an optional extra as it is with the other automation options covered.

View the text form fields in action

The user simply types in a field and presses the [Tab] key to jump to the next field. The information typed in each field will appear automatically in the relevant places in the document.

Tip When all the text form fields have been added and Restrict Editing has been applied, the document can be saved as a template (see 3.2 and 3.3 to find out how to work with templates).

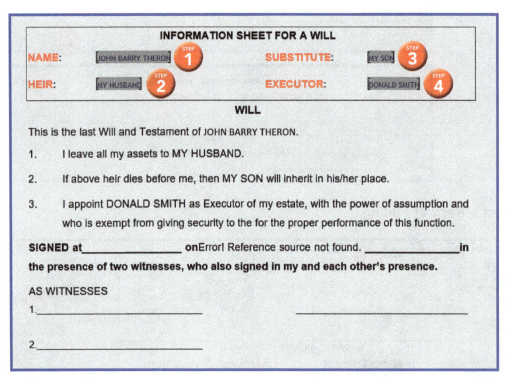

INFORMATION SHEET FOR A WILL

NAME: JOHN BARRY THERON **1**   SUBSTITUTE: MY SON **3**

HEIR: MY HUSBAND **2**   EXECUTOR: DONALD SMITH **4**

WILL

This is the last Will and Testament of JOHN BARRY THERON.

1.   I leave all my assets to MY HUSBAND.

2.   If above heir dies before me, then MY SON will inherit in his/her place.

3.   I appoint DONALD SMITH as Executor of my estate, with the power of assumption and who is exempt from giving security to the for the proper performance of this function.

SIGNED at_____ onError! Reference source not found. _____in the presence of two witnesses, who also signed in my and each other's presence.

AS WITNESSES

1._____   _____

2._____

The user will not be able to edit any of the text in the document.

Insight

10.5 Document Properties

Word tracks different pieces of information in a document, known as "properties", that can be viewed and edited using the **Document Properties** option. When using Document Properties, you can type information in one part of a document that will automatically appear in other places in the document.

Document Properties are **built-in mapped content controls**, described below.

BUILT-IN?	MAPPED?	CONTENT CONTROLS?
Word contains 15 default Document Properties that are also already named.	Document Properties with the same name are connected, so information that is inserted in the one will also appear in the other one that has the same name.	The text in certain parts of the document can be changed and controlled without affecting the text in the rest of the document.

Additional content controls can be created using the tools found under the *Developer* tab (see 10.6). Custom-creating content controls offers an unlimited number of options and greater flexibility than is available in Word's default Document Properties.

Insight Document Properties are not fields, which must be updated to show amended text throughout the rest of the document. The text in Document Properties appears automatically in the document without you needing to update it.

10.5.1 Inserting a Document Property

Each piece of information needed in the document must have its own Document Property. Inserting a Document Property involves **three steps**.

Step 1: Template document

A correctly formatted and edited document must be available. It should also be made clear where the required information is to appear throughout the document.

In our example below, the information labelled A and B must be shown in various parts of the document.

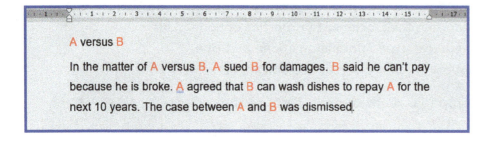

Step 2: Insert a document property

For each piece of information required in the document, a different document property must be inserted. In our example, a document property will be inserted wherever information A is required, and another document property will be inserted wherever information B is required. Each document property will have a unique name.

Insert a document property for "A":

- Place the cursor in the text at the first instance in the document where the information is required (the letter "A" must be deleted).
- Click on the *Insert* tab.
- In the **Text** group, click on the drop-down arrow next to the *Quick Parts* button.
- Select *Document Property*.
- Select a document property in the drop-down menu (other than *Author* and *Publish Date*, as these two options already have specific settings).
- In our example, *Abstract* is selected.

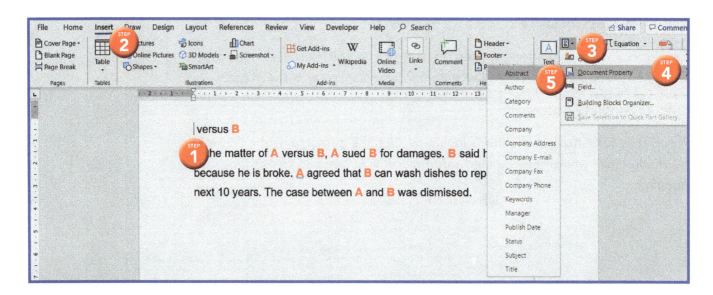

- An area is inserted in the document into which the text for "A" can be typed.

- When the area is **selected**, it looks like this: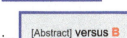

- When the area is **deselected**, it looks like this: [Abstract] **versus B**

Insert a document property for "B":

The same process used to create a document property for "A" must be repeated to create one for "B", except now you must select another Document Property, not **Abstract**. In our example, **Category** is selected.

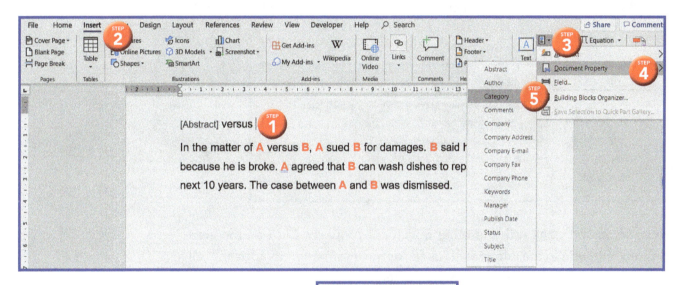

When the area is **deselected**, it looks like this: [Abstract] **versus** [Category]

Step 3: Repeat the chosen document properties

- **A:** Place the cursor at every other place in the document where the information for "A" must appear and insert the same document property, **Abstract**, as in Step 2.

[Abstract] **versus B**

In the matter of [Abstract] **versus B**, [Abstract] **sued B** for damages. **B** said he can't pay because he is broke. [Abstract] **agreed that B** can wash dishes to repay for the next 10 years. The case between [Abstract] **and B** was dismissed.

- **B:** Place the cursor at every other place in the document where the information for "B" must appear and insert the same document property, **Category**, as in Step 2.

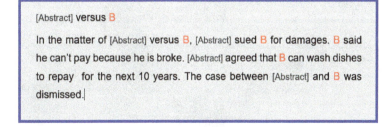

[Abstract] **versus** [Category]

In the matter of [Abstract] **versus** [Category], [Abstract] **sued** [Category] for damages. [Category] **said he can't pay because he is broke.** [Abstract] **agreed that** [Category] **can wash dishes to repay for the next 10 years. The case between** [Abstract] **and** [Category] **was dismissed.**

10.5.2 View the document properties in action

 Insight

The user only needs to click on the area indicated and type in the information **once**.

The information will automatically appear in all the other places in the document with the same document property name, without further input needed from you.

SUE DONALDS versus [Category]

In the matter of SUE DONALDS versus [Category], SUE DONALDS sued [Category] for damages. [Category] said he can't pay because he is broke. SUE DONALDS agreed that [Category] can wash dishes to repay for the next 10 years. The case between SUE DONALDS and [Category] was dismissed.

The same can be done with the other document property. Click on the area indicated and type in the information **once** for the information to appear in all the other document properties of the same name.

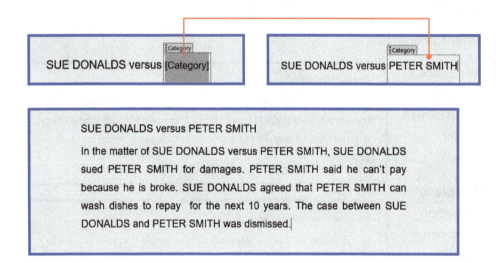

SUE DONALDS versus PETER SMITH

In the matter of SUE DONALDS versus PETER SMITH, SUE DONALDS sued PETER SMITH for damages. PETER SMITH said he can't pay because he is broke. SUE DONALDS agreed that PETER SMITH can wash dishes to repay for the next 10 years. The case between SUE DONALDS and PETER SMITH was dismissed.

10.5.3 Change the name of a document property

You may prefer to change a document property name so that it's easier to recognise or makes more sense. For instance, [Abstract] does not tell you very much, but [Plaintiff] tells you exactly what type of information is required. It also makes it easier for other users of the template document to know what information to insert.

- Click on the **Developer** tab.
- Click on **Design Mode** to activate it (the tool will become greyed out).
- Double-click on the document property in the document.
- Click on **Properties.**

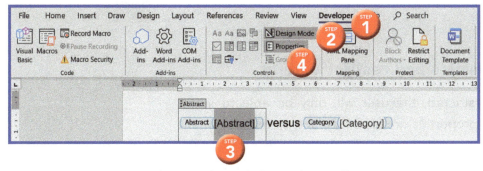

- A **Document Control Properties** dialogue box will appear.
- Next to **Title**, type in a new name for the document property.
- Next to **Tag**, type in a tag for the document property.
- Click **OK**.
- While the document property is still selected, replace [Abstract] with any other text or name. In this example, we're replacing it with PLAINTIFF.

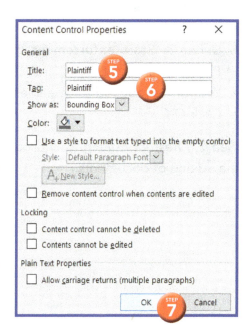

The block brackets before and after [Abstract], must be deleted when the new text is typed in.

- Click on **Design Mode** again to deactivate it. You will now be able to see the document as normal.

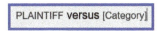

- Repeat this process for the other document property names you want to change.

10.5.4 Copy and paste the document properties

Instead of repeating the process of inserting and renaming document properties in the rest of the document, you can copy and then paste the amended document property into the other places in the document where the information must appear.

- Select the entire amended document property.

- Press 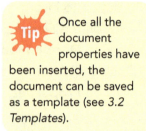 to copy it.

- Place the cursor in another place in the document where the same information must appear.

- Press to paste it.

> **Tip** Once all the document properties have been inserted, the document can be saved as a template (see *3.2 Templates*).

10.5.5 Document properties and restrict editing

When document editing is restricted, the user will only be able to insert information in the document properties areas. Other text in the document cannot be changed.

To restrict editing of the document, do the following:
- Click on the **Review** tab.
- Click on the **Protect** tool, then click on **Restrict Editing**.
- In the **Restrict Editing** pane, under **1. Formatting restrictions** select *Limit formatting to a selection only*.
- Under **2. Editing restrictions** select the box for ***Allow only this type of editing in the document***.
- In the drop-down menu underneath, select ***Filling in forms***.
- Under **3. Start enforcement** click on ***Yes, Start Enforcing Protection***.
- You will be required to type in a password twice.
- Click **OK**.

> **Tip** Make a note of the password. Word cannot retrieve it!

(See *7.5 Restrict Editing* to find out more about how to restrict the editing of documents.)

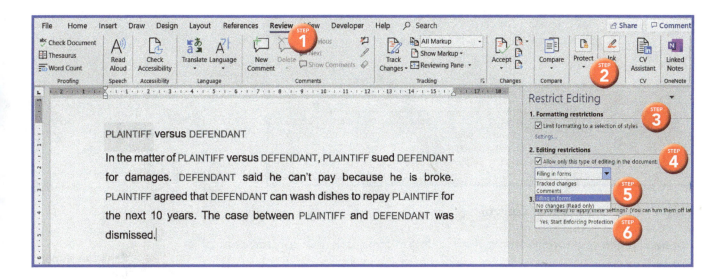

10.6 Content controls (using the Developer tab)

Should the 15 built-in document properties (see *10.5)* in Word not be suitable for your needs, you can use content controls instead. Content controls act as containers for specific content such as dates, lists, or paragraphs of formatted text in a document and are highly customisable. You can also have as many content controls as you like, and there is no limit to how long your document can be.

Content controls can also be mapped, which enables the user to type information in one location in a document, and it will automatically appear in other places in the document.

 Content controls are fields that must be updated to show the inserted content.

10.6.1 Automate a document using content controls

Five steps are needed to automate a document using content controls.

Step 1: Template document

A properly formatted and structured document must be available. It must be clear where the required information should appear in the body of the document. In our example, the required information is listed in a Questionnaire and the relevant places in the document are indicated in red. The content controls must be mapped accordingly.

COMPLETE DETAILS TO BE INSERTED IN DEED OF SALE	
SELLER	
PURCHASER	
PROPERTY	
PURCHASE PRICE	

DEED OF SALE

Hereby, SELLER sells PROPERTY to PURCHASER for PURCHASE PRICE

Step 2: Create a content control

For each piece of information required in the document, a new content control must be created.

- To create a content control for the information required at SELLER in the Questionnaire, place the cursor in the column next to SELLER.
- Click on the **Developer** tab
- Click on one of the **Aa** tools. The **Rich Text Aa** tool allows the formatting of the text to be changed, whereas the **Plain Text Aa** tool does not.

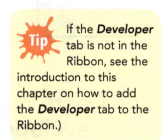

(**Tip** If the **Developer** tab is not in the Ribbon, see the introduction to this chapter on how to add the **Developer** tab to the Ribbon.)

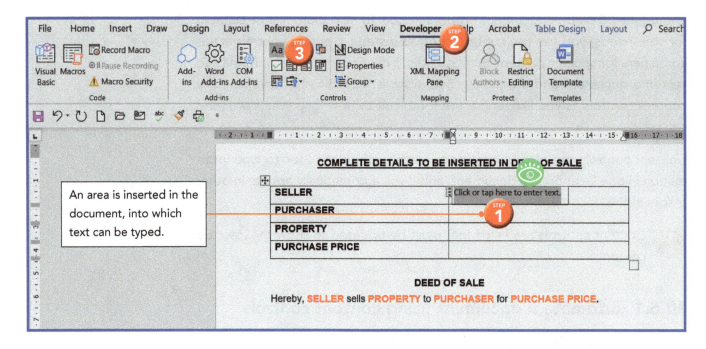

An area is inserted in the document, into which text can be typed.

Step 3: Attach a bookmark to the content control

Double-click on the content control. It is important that the content control is not merely selected – it must be shaded dark, which requires a double-click.

- Click on the **Insert** tab.
- Click on **Links** > **Bookmark**.

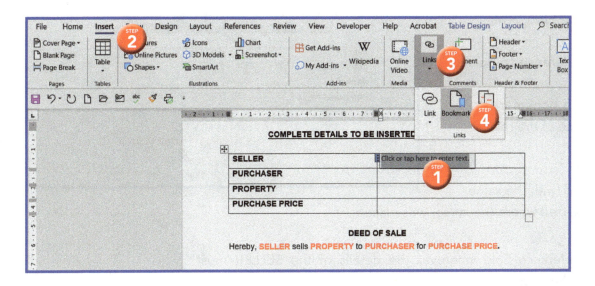

- A **Bookmark** dialogue box will appear. Type in a name for the bookmark.
- Click **Add**.

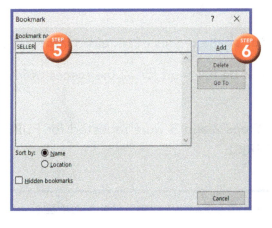

Tip The name must remind you of the type of information required.

Step 4: Insert reference fields in the body of the document

- Place the cursor in the document where the relevant information must be shown (in our example, this would be the details of the SELLER).
- Click on the **References** tab.
- In the **Captions** group, click on **Cross-reference**. A **Cross-reference** dialogue box will open.

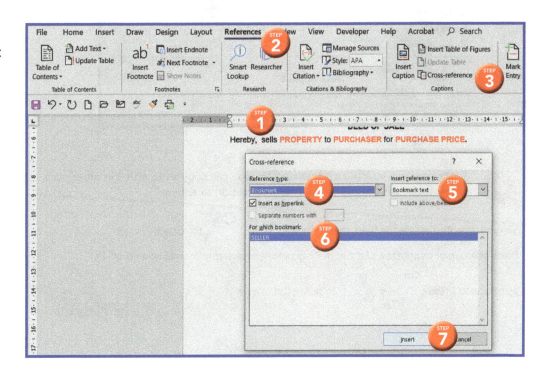

- Under **Reference type**, select *Bookmark*.
- Under **Insert Reference to**, select *Bookmark*.
- Under **For which bookmark**, click on the name of the relevant Bookmark.
- Click on *Insert*.
- A reference field (with the same text) will be inserted where the cursor was placed.

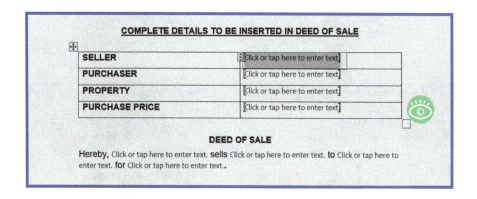

Insert a reference field wherever the details of the SELLER must appear in the document.

Insight

Step 5: Repeat for all the pieces of required information

Steps 2 and 3 must be followed for all the pieces of information required in the document.

In the example, Steps 2 and 3 were repeated for PURCHASER, PROPERTY and PURCHASE PRICE.

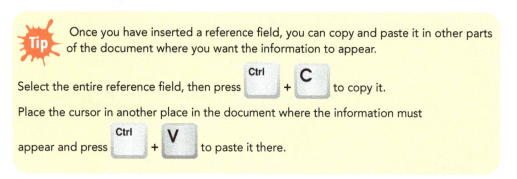

Tip Once you have inserted a reference field, you can copy and paste it in other parts of the document where you want the information to appear.

Select the entire reference field, then press Ctrl + C to copy it.

Place the cursor in another place in the document where the information must appear and press Ctrl + V to paste it there.

10.6.2 View the content controls in action

 The content controls are fields that must be updated for the information to appear elsewhere in the document.

Step 1: Type in your information

First, you must type your information in the areas indicated.

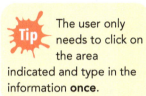 **Tip** The user only needs to click on the area indicated and type in the information **once**.

Step 2: Update the content control

Now, you must update the content control for the new information to appear throughout your document:

- Select all the text in the document by pressing **Ctrl + A**.
- **Right-click** anywhere in the document.
- In the drop-down menu that appears, select **Update Field**. The information will automatically appear throughout the rest of the document.

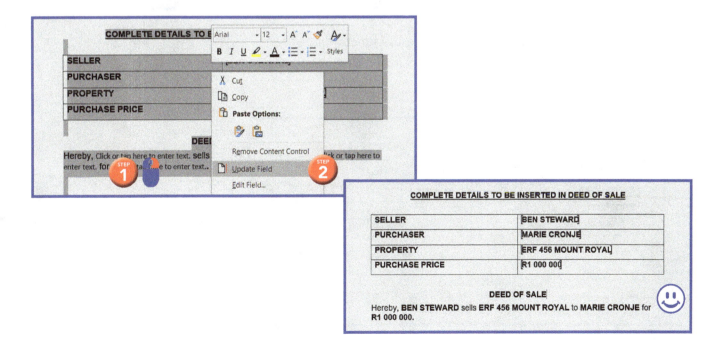

10.6.3 Change the details of a content control

- Click on the content control item in your document that you want to change.
- Click on the **Developer** tab
- Click on the **Design Mode** button to activate the function (it will become greyed out).
- Click on **Properties**. A **Content Control Properties** dialogue box will appear.
- Type in a new Title and Tag for your Content Control.
- Click **OK**.

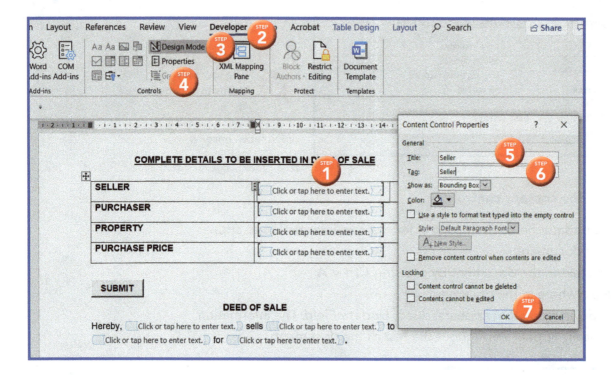

- Click on **Design Mode** again to deactivate the function.
- When the content control area is selected in the document, the new Title will show above it.

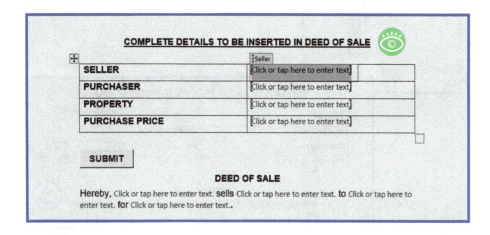

10.6.4 Insert an Update All Fields command button

- Place the cursor in the document where you want the command button to be inserted.
- Click on the **Developer** tab.
- In the **Controls** group, click on the drop-down arrow next to the **Legacy Forms** button.
- Under **ActiveX Controls**, click on the **Command** button.

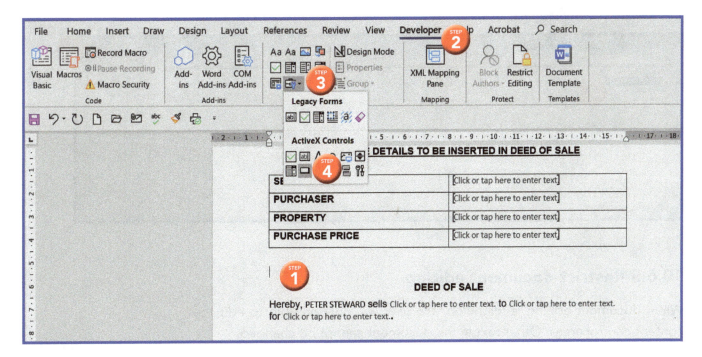

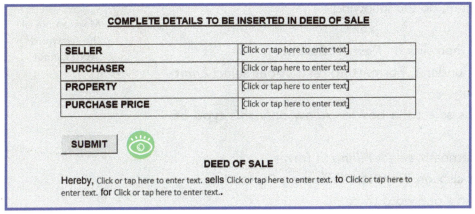

To change the wording on the button:

- Click on *Design Mode* to activate it (it will become greyed out).
- Click on *Properties*. A **Properties** dialogue box will appear to the left of the screen.
- Next to **Caption**, type in your preferred wording for the button.
- Now **right-click** on the button in your document.
- In the drop-down box that appears, type in the words Fields.Update as shown below.
- Close the box.

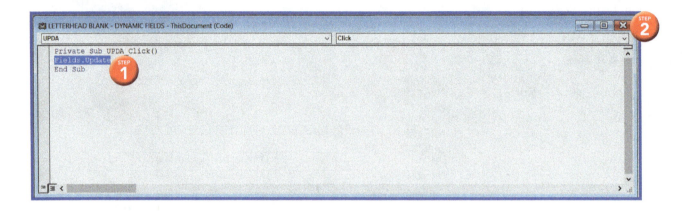

10.6.5 Restrict document editing

When document editing is restricted, the user will only be able to edit the content control areas. Other text in the document cannot be changed.

To restrict editing of the document, do the following:

- Click on the *Review* tab.
- Click on the *Protect* button, then click on *Restrict Editing*.
- In the **Restrict Editing** pane, under **1. Formatting restrictions** select *Limit formatting to a selection only*.
- Under **2. Editing restrictions** select the box for *Allow only this type of editing in the document*.
- In the drop-down menu underneath, select *Filling in forms*.
- Under **3. Start enforcement** click on *Yes, Start Enforcing Protection*.
- You will be required to type in a password twice.
- Click *OK*.

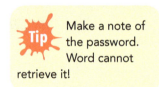
Make a note of the password. Word cannot retrieve it!

(See *7.5 Restrict Editing* to find out more about how to restrict the editing of documents.)

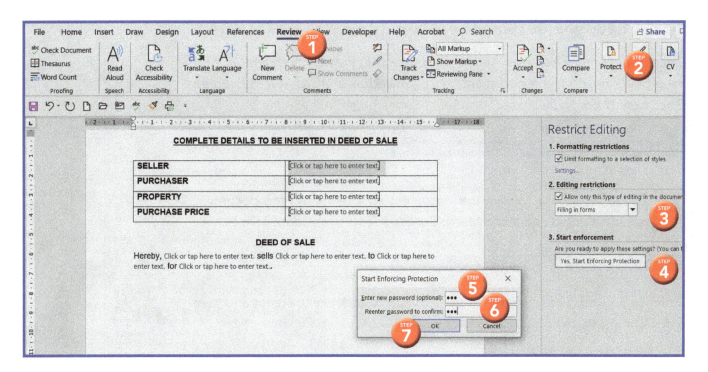

To update all the fields, **right-click** in each one and then, in the drop-down menu that appears, select *Update Field*.

However, there is a much quicker way that will save you a lot of time. You can insert an *Update All Fields* command button to update all the fields at once.

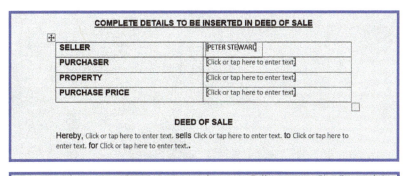

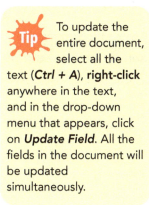

Tip — To update the entire document, select all the text (*Ctrl + A*), **right-click** anywhere in the text, and in the drop-down menu that appears, click on *Update Field*. All the fields in the document will be updated simultaneously.

10.6.6 Save the document as a template

Once the content controls and the Update All Fields command button have been inserted, the document can be saved as a *Word Macro-Enabled Document (*.docm)* file:

Word Macro-Enabled Document (*.docm)

 If you would like to save the document as a template, the document must be saved as a *Word Macro-Enabled Template (*.dotm)* file:

Word Macro-Enabled Template (*.dotm)

(Refer to 3.2 and 3.3 for the benefits of a template and how to create and save a document as a template).

10.6.7 Other uses of content controls

Content controls can also be used to created combo boxes, drop-down menus, date pickers and checkboxes. These are all powerful and excellent functions but fall beyond the scope of this manual.

10.7 Summary of features of automation methods

	Functions used	Fields Update required	Macro used	Use when editing is restricted	Use as a Template
FIND AND REPLACE	Find and replace	No	No	No	Manual template (*.dotx)
DYNAMIC FIELDS	Bookmarks, Ask Fields and Reference Fields	Yes	Only if update fields command button	No	Yes, unprotected (*.dotm)
CLICK AND TYPE	MacroButton	No	Yes	No	Manual Template (*.dotm)
FILLABLE FORMS	Legacy Forms, Bookmarks, Reference Fields	No, updates when TAB is pressed	No	Yes (part of steps to create)	Yes (*.dotx)
DOCUMENT PROPERTIES	Built-in mapped Document Properties	No	No	Yes	Yes (*.dotx)
CONTENT CONTROLS	Text Content Controls, Bookmarks, Reference Fields	Yes	Only if update fields command button	Yes	Yes (*.dotm)

If it feels like you are constantly fighting with Word, it is possible that something is happening in the backstage settings of Word that you are not aware of that simply need some tweaking or changing. This chapter covers a few common frustrations experienced by Legal Practitioners when using **Word**, and how to get around them.

11.1 Recover an unsaved document

My computer shut down unexpectedly and I hadn't saved!

Frustration

Word has an auto recovery feature that automatically saves open documents at regular intervals. If Word shuts down unexpectedly, the documents you were working on will reappear as "recovered files" when Word opens up again. All your changes up to the last AutoSave will appear in your document. The changes you'll lose are the ones that were made after the AutoSave.

You can turn AutoSave off or on. When it's set to **Off**, only the changes up to the last manual save will appear in your document when you open it again. When it's set to **On**, Word will automatically save your document at intervals determined by the default setting. You can specify how often you want Word to save your document by editing the default setting in the backstage settings of Word.

11.1.1 How to enable the AutoSave function

To activate AutoSave:
- Click on the *File* tab.
- Click on *Options* and in the menu under **Word Options**, select *Save*.
- In the Save documents group of settings, select the checkbox next to *Save AutoRecovery information* and choose how often you would like your document to be automatically saved.
- Click *OK*.

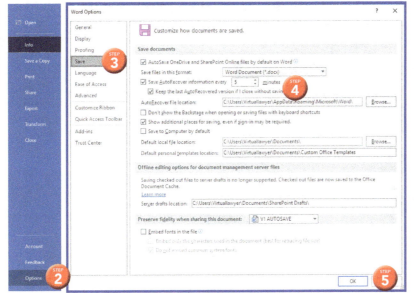

 Tip By setting AutoSave to save every 5 minutes, you will never lose more than 5 minutes of work. However, if you're working on a slow computer, saving that often may prove counter-productive, as you find yourself frequently waiting for the document to save. If that is the case, setting longer intervals may be better.

I closed a document without saving! It's gone!

Frustration

To open the unsaved document:

• Open a new document by clicking *File* > *New* > *Blank document*.

Tip The fastest way to open a new document is to click on the icon in the Quick Access Toolbar (see *1.3.2 Quick Access Toolbar*).

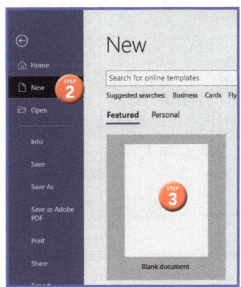

- Click on **File** > **Info** > **Manage Document** > **Recover Unsaved Documents.**
- Choose the document you closed without saving and click **Open.**

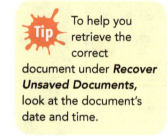

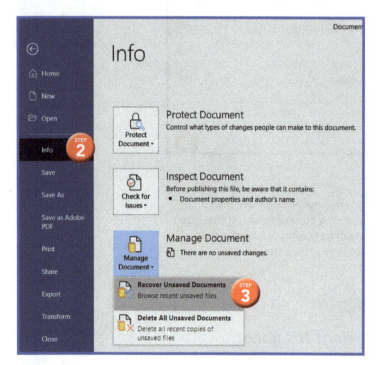

Like magic, your unsaved document is back. You can now save it in a regular folder on your computer.

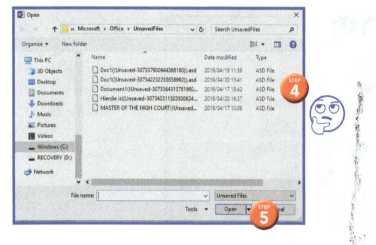

 Insight The unsaved document will open up without a name, unless you saved it previously under a name. Save the document immediately!

11.2 Missing scroll bar

Frustration

Where did the scroll bar go?!

The scroll bar is the narrow vertical bar at the side of the window that one clicks on to move the document up and down.

You cannot see the scroll bar because the screen is maximised.

- Click on ▢ to Restore Down ▢. The scroll bar should become visible again.

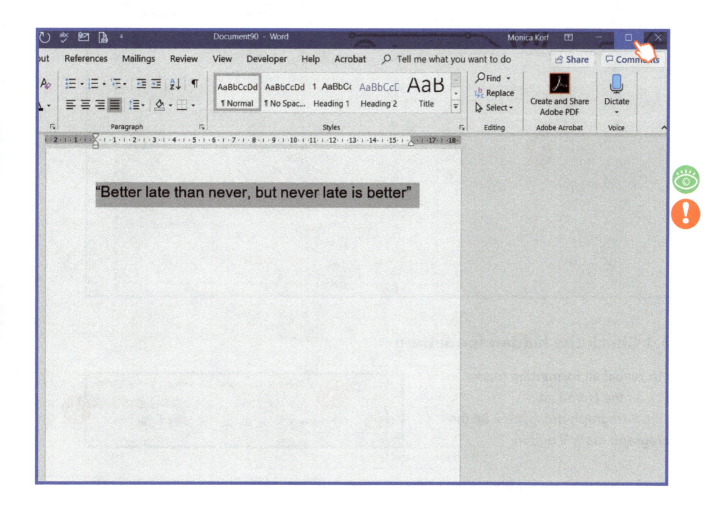

11.3 Blank spaces between paragraphs

Frustration

There are weird white spaces in my document!

The cursor jumps directly to the next page …

The first step is to **reveal all formatting marks** to see if they offer a clue.

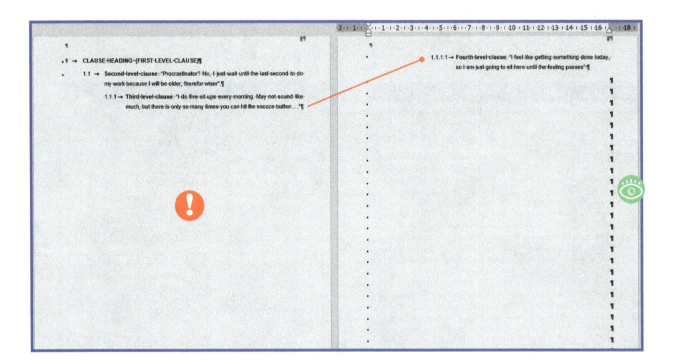

11.3.1 Check the hidden formatting

How to reveal all formatting marks:
- Click on the *Home* tab.
- In the **Paragraph** group, click on the *Paragraph mark ¶* button.

Insight

A paragraph mark is also called a pilcrow, paraph, alinea, or blind P.

It's possible that a Break (Line, Column, Page, or Section) has been inserted. If you see a Break that shouldn't be there, delete it. If a Break is not the culprit, the paragraph setting can be changed to keep paragraphs together on a page.

11.3.2 Change the paragraph settings

• Select the lines and paragraphs that must be kept together.
• Click on the *Home* tab.
• In the **Paragraphs** group, click on the dialogue box launcher. The **Paragraph** screen will open.
• Click on *Line And Page Break*.
• Select the checkbox next to *Keep with next*.
• Select the checkbox next *Keep lines together*.
• Click *OK*.

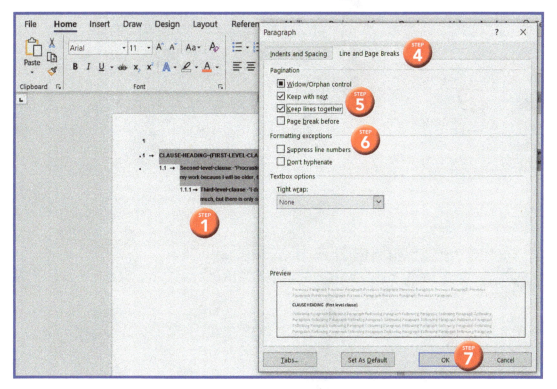

11.4 Forgotten file name and file path

Frustration

I can't remember the file name and where the document is saved!

A little trick to help you remember the file name and path is to insert them into the Footer of your document. When the document is printed or emailed, the information will be there.

11.4.1 Insert the file name and path into the Footer

- Double-click in the Footer part of the document.
- The **Design** tab will open and the text in the body of the document will become faded.
- Click on **Document Info** and select the information you want to insert.

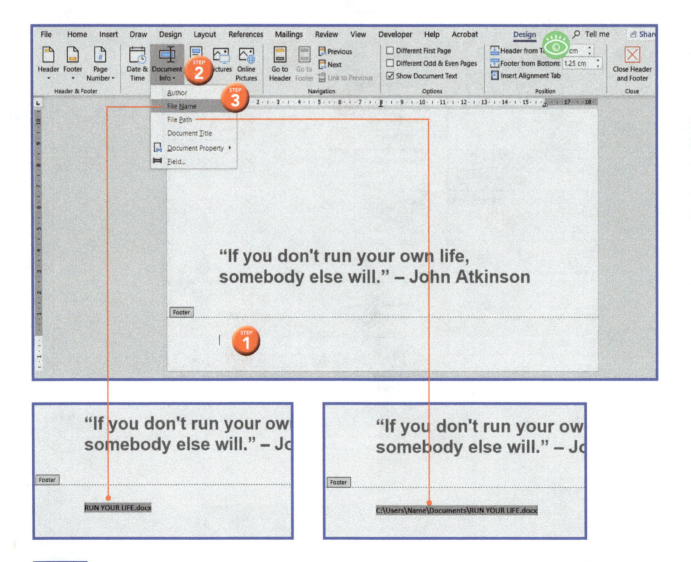

11.5 Pick up where you left off

 Frustration

I can't find the place in the document where I've just typed!

Simply press **Shift + F5**. Word will take you to the last place you edited.

 Press **Shift** + **F5** .

11.6 Change the document author

 Frustration

The document author is not me!

The author of a document is based on the User name that appears in the Word Options box in the backstage settings of Word. The name and initials that are displayed in comments and tracked changes are also based on the User name.

11.6.1 Change the author name in all new documents

- Click on the **File** tab.
- Click on **Options**. The **Word Options** box will open.
- Under **Personalize your copy of Microsoft Office**, type a new name in the **User name** field. This is the name that will now appear as the document author.

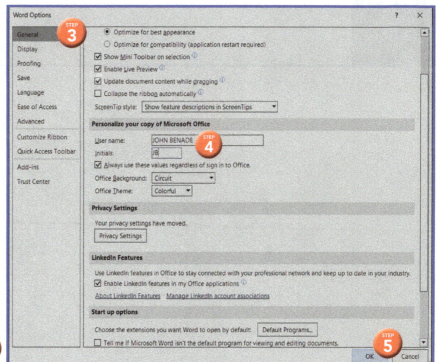

11.6.2 Change the author name in your current document only

- Click on the *File* tab.
- Under **Related People** on the far right of the box, **right-click** the author name.
- Click *Edit Property*.
- Type a new name in the **Edit person** dialog box that opens up.
- Click *OK*.

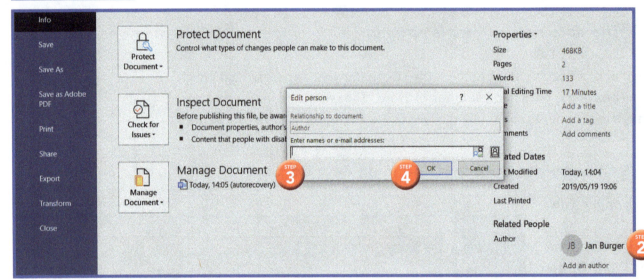

FINAL WORD

Word is a powerful word processing application that can save Legal Practitioners a lot of time and frustration. We trust that, with the use of this manual, the time that you spend using Word will be as productive as possible.

A few last tips:

 Don't use Word like you would a typewriter. It has so much more to offer.

 Word offers many ways to achieve an outcome. Find what works best for you. If you are not someone who remembers shortcut keys, rather use buttons in the Ribbon, tabs, and groups.

 Microsoft© gurus developed Word functions. Don't fight against Word or waste time reinventing the wheel. Use the Word functions that are already available and you will soon find that you can't do without them.

 Document automation is the buzz word. Word offers useful functions to generate documents and to insert specific fields automatically. These documents can be tailor-made to comply with your requirements and professional standards. Spend time learning and implementing the time-savers, templates, and automation functions to achieve the best end result in the least amount of time and with the least amount of effort.

 Keep this manual next to you when you are working. But don't forget to practise or even just play around in Word. Knowledge is power, but practice makes perfect.

Enjoy the magic that Word offers!

Quotes used with courtesy from:
www.wattpad.com
www.goodreads.com
www.short-funny.com
www.curatedquotes.com
www.brainyquotes.com
www.edlester.com
www.coolfunnyquotes.com
www.youqueen.com
www.addicted2success.com

www.ingramcontent.com/pod-product-compliance
Lightning Source LLC
Chambersburg PA
CBHW080551060326
40689CB00021B/4815